Waiting for
Kate *Bush*

Waiting for Kate *Bush*

John Mendelssohn

OMNIBUS PRESS

London / New York / Paris / Sydney / Copenhagen / Berlin / Madrid / Tokyo

Exclusive Distributors
Music Sales Limited,
8/9 Frith Street,
London W1D 3JB, UK.

Music Sales Corporation,
257 Park Avenue South,
New York, NY 10010, USA.

Macmillan Distribution Services,
53 Park West Drive,
Derrimut, Vic 3030,
Australia.

To the Music Trade only:
Music Sales Limited,
8/9 Frith Street,
London W1D 3JB, UK.

Typeset by Galleon Photosetting, Ipswich.
Printed by Creative Print & Design, Ebbw Vale, Wales.

A catalogue record for this book is available from the British Library.

Visit Omnibus Press on the web at www.omnibuspress.com

Contents

To the two I love most

Claire, by whose love I am blessed beyond my most
extravagant imaginings

and

Brigitte, whom I haven't stopped loving, not even for an
hour, in these years of excruciating silence

★ ★ ★

Moreover, I hope that Anna Chen, Mistress Antoinette,
Peter Pacey, Mark Pringle, Nancy Rumsey, and
John Rumsey all know how avidly I cherish their friendship.

Write to the author at wwwilson@londoning.com.

Prelude

Just One Thing
I Can Do About This

Something inside never failed to whisper excitedly, "Go on, jump!" at the sight of heights, and I spent my whole life shying away from them. But here I was sitting on the very ledge that sinister inner voice had always ached to coax me over, and I just couldn't pull the proverbial trigger.

Besides, I was rather enjoying winding up poor Constables Chiang and Murray, probably not yet 50 between them.

They'd been the first to arrive, presumably on the tip of someone who'd noticed me from the shorter block of flats across the road, and God knows they were doing their best, but all they had going for them was sincerity. They were genuinely frantic about the prospect of my jumping, and at first I loved them for it. But then I came to resent them. I wasn't a person to them, but an idea. It wasn't losing Leslie Herskovits that troubled them, but the notion of anybody voluntarily taking his own life. It was very much in the same vein as their calling me *sir*, pretending to respect me because I was a member of the public they were supposedly in the business of serving, rather than genuinely respecting *me*.

As though such a thing were possible, least of all by me.

Constable Chiang, a devout Presbyterian, the great or greater grandson, I supposed, of Chinese saved by Scots missionaries, was aghast that I'd be forfeiting my little corner of Heaven by jumping, whereas his mate Charlene was more concerned that I'd injure an innocent passer-by when I landed, or at the very least damage somebody's property.

They implored me to tell them what the problem was, but I thought I'd be casting pearls before swine. If I told them I was consumed by self-loathing, and had never managed to climb the metal pole in junior

1

high school, wouldn't they just look at one another in confusion and blurt something about how it made no sense for me to loathe myself when I was clearly such an altogether terrific bloke? If I related that I'd failed dismally at the one job in life at which I'd most wanted to be superb, being my daughter's dad, would they, too young to be the parents of anything but infants, have any real idea what I was on about? And if I told them how I could no longer bear my own ugliness, my own obscene obesity, wouldn't they be part of the epidemic of cruel teasing that had swept London in the past several months and pretend not to have noticed?

So I didn't tell them any of the first 29 reasons that my life hung so precariously in the balance, but gave them No. 30 instead. "If you can promise me that Kate Bush will release an album of new material in the next six months," I offered, "I'll take your hands."

They looked at each other in confusion, as I'd known they would, and it infuriated me.

"You haven't even heard of her, have you?" I said. "You haven't even bloody *heard* of her! Well, how can you imagine that I'd want to live in a world in which public servants are ignorant of the greatest British songwriter and singer in the past 25 years?" I turned back toward the abyss.

"No!" Constable Chiang blurted. " 'Withering Heights', right? Of course I've heard of her. My sister Victoria fancied her. Played her music all the time in her bedroom, didn't she?"

" 'Wuthering'," I corrected him, "for Christ's sake. Named for the Emily Brontë novel that inspired it. Also a classic film with Sir Laurence Olivier. I suppose you haven't heard of him either. Only the greatest actor of his generation." I was such a hypocrite. As though *I'd* read the Brontë novel. (As though Kate herself had!) As though I could remember having seen Sir Larry in much beside *Marathon Man* and *The Boys From Brazil*. Oh, it gets dark, just as Kate said in her breakthrough hit. But it also gets cold. If I didn't jump soon, there was a good chance I'd freeze solid there on the ledge.

"What's your music?" I asked Constable Murray, mostly to interrupt her mobile phone conversation. I assumed she was calling for reinforcements. "Me?" she said, stupidly. Then she brightened, enjoying my interest in her. "R&B and that. Craig David. The Sugarbabes. Mis-Teeq." I'd spent a lifetime making other people feel interesting.

"The real giants of the genre then, in other words," I said. "Step aside, Smokey Robinson and Aretha and Marvin Gaye and Stevie Wonder, right?" When I'd lived by sarcasm, why shouldn't I die by it as well?

2

A couple of gangly teenagers in hooded sweatshirts and enormous trousers that just barely covered their groins, probably residents of the block of flats, emerged onto the roof. They took one look at the constables and froze. But then the taller noticed me and exclaimed, "Wicked!"

"Clear off, you lot," Constable Chiang called to them.

The smaller was eager to oblige, but the taller pretended he hadn't heard. He produced a little digital video camera from one of his gigantic front pockets, almost certainly stolen, and pointed it at me. "If he goes over, dog, we'll be able to sell this to the BBC. Nuff wick-*ed*!"

"I'm not going to tell you again to leave," Constable Chiang threatened, not very convincingly.

"People's right to know, mush," the kid with the camera insisted, watching me in the little flipout monitor on the camera's side, not budging.

There were a couple of new arrivals – another, older, constable, jowly and middle-aged, with a florid complexion, and a guy in a suit. The constable put his hand over the teenager's camera and pushed it into his forehead, making the kid howl. The guy in the suit headed toward me.

I stopped him in his tracks, inching nearer the edge, calling, "Far enough." It was getting windy. We had maybe 10 minutes' daylight, or what passes for it in London in November, left.

The guy was nothing if not obliging. Indeed, he was my best mate ever. "Absolutely!" he affirmed, stopping in his tracks, holding his hands up in surrender. "Absolutely. You're the gov. See, I'm playing ball, mate. Aren't I? I'm Lt. Martyn – and that's with a y – Root, Metropolitan Police. May I know your name?"

"Del Palmer," I said, making myself smile.

He looked hard at me for a minute. "No," he said, "I suspect you're not. Del Palmer was Kate Bush's live bass player, and later her recording engineer, and Linn drum programmer, and long-time romantic partner."

I was impressed. It had taken them a remarkably short time, all things considered, to get somebody who really knew his stuff, a *bona fide* fellow Kateperson, onto the scene.

"My identity's immaterial," I said. "We're not going to be long enough in one another's company for you to care about my name."

Constable Chiang gasped audibly, but my new best mate Lt. Root, presumably bred for unflappability, seemed only to sigh. "I wish you wouldn't say that, sir. My hunch is that if we work together, we can sort everything out." He took a couple of steps toward me and then did something I thought brilliant: sat down himself.

"I understand you're upset about Kate's being 11 years between albums. Well, who among us isn't? By my reckoning, that's too long to have to wait by a factor of around five."

Oh, I felt awful now. The guy was so kind, and knew only what I'd told Chiang and Murray, and was trying so hard to work with it, even though he probably realised how foolish it made him sound. But I couldn't keep myself, by saying nothing, from making him continue.

"I phone EMI periodically, sir, maybe once every six months or so, to see if they can tell me anything. They never can. All they'll ever do is confirm she's been in the studio. As though that's news. And most of the time they just put you on hold until you get fed up and put the phone down without having heard even that much."

He was right, of course. I'd phoned them myself and been treated not as someone whose custom they valued, but as an annoyance. Arrogant record company bastards. Rotters.

"My own favourite is *Never For Ever*," he continued. "I realise that isn't a common view. At a fan convention I went to in Amsterdam around four years ago, something like 70 per cent of those attending named *Hounds* as her finest hour. What are your thoughts, sir?"

An ambulance and a couple of police squad cars arrived 12 storeys below me. A phrase from an Elvis Costello song I'd always liked, but never been sure I understood, came to mind: "Clown time is over". If I let Lt. Root seduce me with his kindness, I'd never be able to accomplish my mission. It would end, as so much of my life had, in abject embarrassment, with the locals laughing and pointing as Constables Chiang and Murray helped me with theatrical gentleness into the back of a squad car.

My getting to my feet caused a lot of commotion, both on the ground and on the roof. Lt. Root scrambled to his own. "Del," he implored me, grasping frantically at straws, desperate for us to be on a first-name basis, "*please!* Let's talk it over. There's no need to make a snap decision here. We've got all night. Are you cold?"

He turned back to Chiang and Murray and barked, "Get Mr. Palmer an overcoat," in a voice that bore almost no resemblance to that in which he'd been addressing me.

"I don't know if you love me or not," I said, quoting Kate. "But I don't think we should ever suffer. There's just one thing we can do about this." If he'd said, 'Top Of The City', I'd have surrendered there and then. But he only looked at me in confusion.

4

"It's from a song of Kate's," I said, "as you no doubt know – a song apparently about the allure of suicide. If you can't name the song, can you at least tell me which album it was on?"

There was a lot of hatred mixed in with the confusion on his face now. I could be such a sadist when I wanted to.

Oh, it gets cold. I couldn't last much longer, and I didn't believe my two original constables were going to come up with a coat. The block of flats' lift didn't work. It would take them forever to get down to the ambulance, which at best might have only blankets, and then forever to get them back up to me. And did I really want to be seen being coaxed into the back of the squad car swaddled in blankets?

"I want," I told Lt. Root, "to make a statement."

"Absolutely!" my new best mate agreed, rapturous that I wasn't holding 'Top Of The City' against him. "You make your statement, which will help me understand you better obviously, and we'll get you a lovely warm coat, and then we'll get this whole thing sorted, all right, Del?"

I motioned for the kid with the camera to come nearer. You should have seen the proud look he gave his mate. You should have seen how concerned Lt. Root was with the kid's getting the best possible camera angle. Between being absolute bastards, people can be so endearing sometimes.

My slashing wit didn't fail me, as it had never done. It occurred to me to take full advantage of my captive audience and air all my actual grievances, but in the end, I decided to confine my closing remarks to Kate, which seemed rather more droll. "From conception to release," I said, "*The Red Shoes* took around four years. Assuming it's released sometime in 2004, its follow-up will have been nearly 12 years in the making. If this pattern – of each album taking three times longer than its predecessor – holds, Kate will have her ninth album ready in 2040, assuming having turned 80 two years before hasn't slowed her down. For those of us who can thus reasonably expect to live to hear only one more Kate Bush album, this simply isn't good enough – not nearly.

"I suspect she imagines that she doesn't owe us anything. I can understand why she'd think that, but believe her to be profoundly mistaken. Were it not for our adoration, and our fiscal expression of that adoration, she would not have the luxury of taking forever and ever to make a bloody album. Had we not consumed her music in huge numbers, she might today be teaching Latin or English in some draughty convent school in Kent, hating having to get up in the frigid darkness on winter mornings, hating her meagre salary, hating most of all the insolent little bitches who are her charges.

" 'But I owe it to myself,' I can just imagine her protesting, 'to release only the best-realised version of my music I can.'

"Well, bollocks. Let us imagine that, at the time of its release, she regarded *The Sensual World*, let's say, as 90 per cent realised. Let's now imagine further that she'd quit fussing with her eighth album, still unreleased at the dawn of 2004, and released it only 40 per cent realised in 1995. Does she imagine that, rather than bringing vast joy to the countless tens of thousands of us who love her, this strategy would have resulted in the even faster proliferation of AIDS in sub-Saharan Africa, or in Margaret Thatcher making a surprise political comeback at 106, or England losing the rugby World Cup?"

Lt. Root was grinning, out of what seemed genuine amusement. My swan song: a smash!

"Let's go back – way back! – to *The Hounds Of Love*. On Side 2, the tracks 'Dream Of Sheep' and 'Under Ice' are separated by the sound of lapping waves. On hearing the lapping waves sound effect EMI had in its library, Kate decreed that it simply wouldn't suffice, that entirely new waves would have to be recorded, no doubt at substantial expense. I would guess that of the couple of million people around the world who have bought *Hounds* since it came out in 1985, not a single one would have been able to tell you sincerely that he or she enjoyed it less with the EMI sound effects library lapping waves, not bloody one!"

Now even the teenager without the digital video camera was amused.

"Or maybe she should think of the filmmaker Stanley Kubrick, that other brilliant, reclusive megalomaniac, to whom she's been compared. Is the world a better place for his having made poor Jack Nicholson play a particular scene, later cut from the final print of *The Shining*, 128 times? Better that his actors conformed with excruciating exactness to Our Stan's conception of how particular lines should be read, or one in which he'd made two or three more films?

"Oh, the colossal hubris of this woman, Kate Bush, having the ability to inspire so much joy in the world, and instead opting to deprive us, to agonise for years over preposterous trivialities!"

Nobody was grinning anymore. How very me, staying too long on stage.

"I have to take issue with you, mate," Lt. Root said, gravely. "I think one of the key reasons we love Kate's music, or Kubrick's films, for that matter, as we do is *because* they agonise over every detail. I don't think Kate's capable of releasing only partially realised work. I honestly believe she can only see the whole picture, in which the sound of the waves between tracks is no less important than the way she inflects a key lyric. She simply can't do it any way other than the way she's always done it, and I deeply resent your putting that down to hubris, especially since Kate's well known to be as far from a prima donna as it's humanly possible to be."

We could have gone on like that for hours. But I had grown far, far too cold.

1

The Most for Which
We Can Hope

WHEN I first moved into Mrs. Cavanaugh's boarding house nearly two years ago, I wasn't yet morbidly obese, and thus little trouble. I got down to the dining room without a trace of assistance. I hadn't realised definitively that there never would be a place for me out in the world, just as there never had been, not really, and I even managed the odd walk on a summer evening. But then I encountered Bharat and what he called his posse because the rap thugs he saw on MTV would have done.

There were five of them, and they were out for blood to avenge the beating of an Afghan waiter in Leeds the week before by a trio of Leeds United reserves. You might have imagined that they'd have targeted other white footballers, but they hadn't the danglies. It was junior school students and old people Bharat and his mates victimised, the lame, the halt, the blind – and people like me, people who clearly wouldn't give them much of a scrap. In this, of course, we were very much kindred spirits. It's always been my custom to antagonise only those clearly even less ferocious than myself. But our kinship was lost on Bharat's posse.

My destination was the Costcutter on the high street. I needed bickies. Over the course of a typical evening, I had by that time taken to eating a great, great many, as I had in childhood. The posse were obviously trying with all their might to look menacing, but it wasn't working very well, and when they didn't call me a disgusting fat cunt as I waddled past them, but just snickered tentatively, I presumed I was in no danger. But my ignoring the snickering apparently confirmed my passivity, and the two nearest the door stepped in front of it with their thin brown arms folded across their chests. "Where do you suppose you're going?" the one with the wispy moustache challenged me in a voice too high-pitched for effective challenging.

"Muslims only, this store," his companion asserted, lisping slightly, "or at least Asians."

If I'd told them to fuck off, they probably would have. But I did some quick computations and decided I'd be able to live with myself if I backed down on the basis of their being so numerous. I shrugged and turned to waddle back down the hill.

My shrugging emboldened them. "This," the one I would later learn was Bharat announced, "is for that waiter bloke in Leeds." He kicked me between the legs, but not very well, and I hardly felt a thing. But then one of the others hit me in the back of the neck with a brick. I dropped to my knees and the lot of them were all over me, punching and scratching and kicking, whooping excitedly. One of them got his thumb under my sunglasses and into my right eye, and it hurt terribly. A couple of them proved better kickers than Bharat himself. I pitched face forward onto the pavement. I got kicked in the right cheek, and stomped upon. They spat on me. One of them put his knee in the middle of my back and tried to pull out a handful of my hair. Another demanded, "When are you going to call somebody a Paki again?" My telling them I'd never called anyone a Paki in the first place only made them more furious.

"There's only one thing we hate more than racists," one of them revealed, "and that's white bastards that pretend they're not." And then I lost consciousness.

I'm exaggerating slightly. None of them actually touched me. But I could see in their eyes what they would have liked to have done.

After that, I stopped going out, and eventually, as I got fatter and fatter, stopped even going down to eat with the others. I had to order the gift I sent Kate Bush every week out of a catalogue, or on-line, and felt terrible about it. I felt sure Kate would begin to notice that my choices had come to lack the personal touch that had characterised my earlier ones, but she was gracious enough not to complain. Of course, I'd never heard from her about the earlier gifts either. Sometimes I wondered if I were shipping them to the right address.

Mrs. Cavanaugh came up to warn me not to bother to ask that my board be reduced because I was eating so much less, as she'd have let my quarters to someone prepared to pay full room and board if she'd known my intentions. As though she were likely to find a more fervent fellow Kate Bush fan than I! I'd intended originally to live in London, saving myself long, expensive journeys to gigs on crowded trains full of commuters who'd glance at me in a way that made me painfully self-conscious. But then I discovered in one of the nine electronic Kate Bush newsletters to which I subscribed that Mrs. Cavanaugh's boarding house, a stone's throw from Kate's native Bexley, welcomed quiet, mature, non-smoking Kate Bush fans, and I could as easily have lived elsewhere as I could have made my living as a Baby Spice lookalike.

The afternoon Mrs. Cavanaugh and I met, we chatted happily for nearly three hours about Kate and what she meant to both of us. I hadn't met anyone with more interesting insights into Kate's life and work since the last big English Katemas, in 1999. And she promised that one of her two existing boarders, Mr. Chumaraswamy, loved Kate even more than she herself did, and she'd named the two younger of her three children Gilmour (after the Pink Floyd guitarist, Kate's crucial early benefactor) and Catherine, Kate's full Christian name. She predicted that I would find Mr. Chumaraswamy's theory about why Kate spelled her name with a K rather than the C from Catherine extremely interesting. I was so keen to move in that I left the Vauxhall bed-and-breakfast for which I had paid to the end of the week three days early.

When I admitted to Mrs. Cavanaugh that I'd stopped coming down to meals not because I wasn't hungry – I was absolutely ravenous at all times – but because I could no longer get through my door, her tone changed. "I'm not sure I understand, love," she finally admitted with the utmost gentleness. "Why not?"

"Well, just look at me," I blurted. "I can just barely get out of bed to use the toilet anymore. By the time I get into the loo, I'm huffing and puffing so hard I think my lungs might explode. I've seen people like me on television. The fire brigade has to come to get them down out of their bedrooms. They have to use a special crane."

Confusion and kindness swirled in her gorgeous hazel eyes, so near, I'd always imagined, to the colour of Kate's own. She shook her head sadly. She made a soft clucking sound and wondered, in an accent very much thicker than her customary one, "Is it winding the widow Cavanaugh up you're doing, love?"

I began to cry, almost imperceptibly at first, or so I hoped. The widow Cavanaugh probably wasn't 50 yet. "If only it *were* a windup," I said. If only. The floodgates shattered. I sobbed. When she held me, I sobbed even harder. By the time I finally stopped, her jumper was drenched.

She began bringing my meals up to me. She told me she intended gradually to reduce my portion size so that I'd be able to attend a meeting of Overeaters Anonymous. Her late elder brother had been an alcoholic, and AA had saved his life (only for lung cancer to snatch it away from behind when he was 51, six years sober, and not looking). She was a great believer in 12-step programmes.

I didn't want to go. I made a joke of it. How, I wondered, do they propose to get enough of us through the door to constitute a meeting? She didn't laugh. She gave me the same gorgeous kind confused look as the night I confessed to needing the fire brigade with a crane to get downstairs. "They'll find a way," she said with the utmost gentleness. "They're experts in these matters."

The next four days when she brought my meals up, she took care to point out how small the portions were. "We want you slim enough to be able to attend the OA meeting." I implored her to be reasonable. It was inconceivable that in 96 hours I'd be able to fit through the door, or down the stairs. Her house was in jeopardy if I even tried. But she wouldn't take no for an answer.

She served me an early supper on the night of the meeting. I'd have killed for an orange-flavoured KitKat by that time. Her sons Duncan, born six years before the release of 'Wuthering Heights', and Gilmour arrived to transport me. I supposed they'd hired a lorry. I'd met Duncan, an architectural reclaimer, before. He had some of the best teeth I'd ever seen in a Briton. I found out later he'd lost the originals in a car crash, and had them replaced with his insurance settlement. He wasn't one to look you in the eye very often. His brother, 12 years his junior, made rather less than a Herculean effort to hide his annoyance at having to help get me out of the house.

Their mum had helped me get dressed. It had taken a very long time. I was sitting on the edge of my bed, worrying that at any second it might splinter beneath me, when the brothers turned up. We all shook hands. The prematurely balding Duncan didn't look me in the eye, and had a handshake better suited to a stockbroker than one who made his living removing fireplaces and cast iron bathtubs from derelict Victorian properties. Gilmour, prolifically pierced and tattooed, asked if I was all right, but generically, and made no secret of his displeasure when I wondered, "So how do you propose we do this?"

"How about if you just walk down the bloody stairs?" he said, pointedly. In the corner of my eye, Mrs. Cavanaugh shot him a look that made him sigh in resignation.

The three of them descended the stairs ahead of me backwards, their six hands at the ready. I could never have forgiven myself if I'd stumbled and crushed them all to death, and was very deliberate. My fellow boarders materialised to wonder what the fuss was all about. By the time I reached the bottom of the stairs, I was gasping for oxygen and as damp as Djakarta under my clothes, but too elated to mind.

They hadn't hired a lorry, but come in Duncan's transit van. I told them I'd never get in. Gilmour rolled his eyes and muttered something under his breath. His mum glared at him. "Suppose we just have a go," Duncan suggested gently. I wouldn't have been surprised if the van had wound up on its side. Miraculously, it remained upright. I was even able to sit in the front, beside Duncan.

I was appalled to discover that it wasn't a Kate cassette he nudged into his deck, but something by one of those comic book heavy metal bands with a name designed to appeal to 15-year-old boys homicidally furious because their hormones were simultaneously screaming at them to reproduce and making them so hideous with acne that no girl would come near them. Between songs, I learned that we were listening to The Mutilators' *Hounslow Chainsaw Massacre*. After the next song ended, I asked if we could listen instead to Kate.

"Of course we can, *me ould segotia*," Gilmour assured me from the cargo area. "Over my lifeless fucking body. Or maybe we could have a bit of Tori Amos."

I think he knew he'd said the cruellest thing one could say to a Kate Bush fan. Even John(ny Rotten) Lydon apparently agreed.

A couple of years before, Lydon, accompanied not only by his long-suffering bride, but also by a bewildered-looking old gentleman who might have been his dad, and a minder, turned up at some Q magazine awards show on a ragman's cart. He'd filled out over the years, but had retained all his original animosity for that which sprang from his own follicles. What could you say of a fellow whose hair looked more ridiculous at 46 than it had at 21? That he was trying too hard?

Well, that description wouldn't have suited Lydon, whom I'd thought one of the great wits in his Sex Pistols days, but who hadn't troubled himself to update his act in over 25 years. When it was announced that he'd won an award for inspiring others, he went up on stage to snarl and vituperate exactly as he might have in 1979. He used very naughty words as he declared himself the personification of the English working class. I felt sure that he'd expel gas loudly, orally, if not rectally, and was relieved to be mistaken. And then, after begrudgingly thanking the entourage with which he'd arrived and half-heartedly trying to give his award away (this in front of Liam Gallagher, the king of ungraciousness, a man who'd once threatened to give himself an enema with his Brit award statuette), he acknowledged Kate Bush. He called her music fucking brilliant, and was applauded for it.

Seemingly trying to recycle one of the tiredest riffs in the *Wayne's World* lexicon, seemingly referring to Kate's infamous reluctance to confer a new album on those of us who adore her, he asserted, "We *are* worthy," and the massed celebs tittered obligingly. Later the two of them were photographed together, Kate looking radiant with pleasure, Lydon as though trying with all his might to disguise his own. And what better way to keep it under wraps, when the press converged on them, than to launch into an attack on "Torrid Aimless", whom he sneeringly characterised as a brazen imitator. For those of us who adore her – and apparently Lydon is one of us – there is only The One True Kate.

Better The Mutilators than Amos, I thought as the Cavanaugh brothers and I continued on our way, and best silence. But of course we live in a world in which better is almost always the most for which we can reasonably hope.

2

The Gormless, Misshapen Few

AS we pulled into the car park of the pub in which the meeting was to be held, I began to sweat again, this time from apprehension. I told the brothers that if they didn't make me go through with it, I'd pay for them to drink all night.

"Sounds a wicked idea to me," Gilmour admitted. But Duncan said they'd promised their mum. When I pointed out that she didn't have to know, he actually made eye contact. His expression combined pity and contempt. I wanted to point out that not all of us have the great advantage of growing up in a world in which one's expected to keep his word. I wanted to burst into tears.

"Blimey," said Gilmour, astonished, for a moment, out of his sarcastic Celticness. A trio of big fellows in hospital whites were helping a gigantic pale whale of a woman out of their own van. She'd turned an alarming shade of pink from the exertion. As they unfolded a gurney and rolled her onto it, Gilmour giggled. "I'll bet she's got her own bloody postal code."

"And I," his brother snapped, "think maybe you should plug up your cakehole." I wanted to burst into tears.

The barmaid pointed out the corner of the nearly deserted pub in which the meeting would take place. It took nearly every second of the 12 minutes we were early for the brothers to get me over there and into a chair. They became ever more antagonistic. "How about we pick up the bloody pace a bit, gov?" Gilmour wondered sarcastically at one point as I stood there gasping, not wanting to fall to the ground (because it might take the rest of the day to get me back on my feet), but feeling too weak not to. I half wanted to see how he'd like my falling on him. "He's doing the best he can," said Duncan, a grown child with his mum in his eyes, his expression very much as his mum's had been the night she'd learned why I wasn't coming down for meals.

The two brothers' animosity must have gone way back, but I certainly wasn't doing much to reduce it.

People think of the fat as jolly, but this lot was anything but. And the transplanted Yorkshireman moderator, Graham, with a florid complexion and the young Bryan Ferry's suggestively lank black hair, was coy into the bargain. At first sight of me, what he said was, "This is Overeaters Anonymous, for people who have issues with food. Can I help?"

"I certainly hope so," I blurted, too nervous not to try too hard. "Nothing else has worked, none of the diets, none of the medications, not even the fasting." The four already there, including the pink whale from the car park, stopped their conversation. They stared at me in silence. I felt humid with embarrassment.

"Mr. Herskovits has a problem with his weight," the blessed kindly Duncan interjected. Gilmour snorted. One of the women harrumphed. Humider and humider. Now it was Graham's expression that was very closely akin to Mrs. Cavanaugh's on my initial mention of the fire brigade and their crane. "Well, in that case," he said, "please do have a seat."

If looks could kill, I'd have been dead before I took three steps. I felt as though back in junior high school physical education. From my first exposure to them, I adored sports, even though I was rotten at all of them. But I detested gymnastics in general and the pole climb in particular. We boys were forever being timed climbing three metal poles in a big sandpit, presumably to gauge our fitness. I was very fit, from playing baseball and football and basketball and tennis and anything else I could persuade anyone to play with me, but had no aptitude whatever for the pole. Other boys shot up it, their new adolescent biceps bulging, their feet hardly touching the bloody thing. I could climb a rope because I could hold it between my feet. But the pole just laughed at me, along with all of the other boys – save the gormless, misshapen few who shared my ineptitude.

In those days, I rode home on a school bus that let me out right in front of a liquor store whose stock of paperback novels depicting hard, bouffant-haired early-Sixties sexpots in sheath dresses slit up the sides drove me half mad with lust. "She was poured into her dress by women," proclaimed the one I seem never to have forgotten, presumably about a model with Loose Morals, ". . . and pulled out of them by men!" How I ached for those women!

Had one of them been at the top of the pole topless, I still wouldn't have been able to climb the bastard.

And the looks on the faces of The Boys Who Could as, after staring balefully at the pole until the sun-tanned sadist who was our instructor finally growled, "Either climb the son-of-a-bitch or go sit the fuck down," I slinked back among my peers.

It was those walks from the infernal metal pole back to my place that I remembered too well as I waddled ponderously from Graham.

I could hear the laboured breathing of the most attractive of my fellow overeaters before I was within 10 feet of her. She was around 25, with gorgeous white skin, huge blue eyes and extraordinary thick cornsilk hair. If this girl had been told, "You'd be so gorgeous if only you'd lose . . . (your choice of weights)," once, she'd probably been told 10,000 times. If anything, she was even huger than the pink whale. And she was unmistakably suffering, consumed by self-loathing, terrified of the others, terrified of me, terrified by the thought of living another hour in her remarkable body. She visibly trembled at my approach. Tears raced down her globular cheeks. She whimpered between gasps.

All she had in common with the behemoth beside her was immensity. The behemoth's skin and hair were those of one who eats nothing not deep-fried. She seemed to be sweating lard. She was around 40, with little piggy eyes, loose hanging blue flab, and teeth the colour of weak tea. She was as bold as Miss Cornsilk was timid. "Just what do you fucking imagine you're bloody doing here?" she demanded when I managed to smile at her. The might-have-been writer in me thought she'd have been better off changing the order of *bloody* and *fucking*, saving the best for last.

"Crinolyn," said the gigantic Afro-Caribbean woman beside her, "don't. Please."

But Crinolyn wasn't having any of it. Her little piggy eyes seared my own corneas. "Fucking chubby chaser? Is that your game, you?"

A new arrival arrived, a huge young man as pretty in his own way as Miss Cornsilk, and as bloated. I realised I'd seen him on television. He'd had a very brief career as a singer, followed by an only slightly longer one as one of the celebrities on a series called *Lose It Or Die*, about morbidly obese H-list celebrities trying to learn to enjoy exercise. Apparently the group's male sex symbol, he inspired a sharp intake of breath from one of the women behind me.

Crinolyn wasn't distracted, though. "I asked you a question, mate," she said, leaning over toward me. "What are you fucking doing here?"

"Crinolyn," the huge black woman tried again.

"If you're fine with our being infiltrated by chubby chasers,

17

Boopsie," Crinolyn snarled at her, "my hat's off to you. But I'm fucking not, am I?" She turned to me again. "I'm going to ask you one more time, mate. What's your game?"

Everyone else had fallen silent. There was nowhere for me to hide. Even Gilmour, about to go out of the door, seemed to be waiting for my answer. My shirt was pasted to my back with sweat. I cleared my throat. "My game is trying to sort out a way to stop overeating myself into a state far past mere morbid obesity. I dare say it's the same game as all of yours."

You could have heard a feather drop onto a pile of gauze. All the overeaters looked at one another. Gilmour looked at Duncan and shook his head, smirking. It was I who was sweating lard now.

"Would you permit me to ask what your present weight is?" one of those behind me finally managed. The pink whale, the one from outside. I told her the truth. I told her that I hadn't even bothered getting on a scale in months. I was blinded by my own sweat. "And you've not been to see a doctor, then?" I admitted I hadn't.

"If he's over 14 stone," Crinolyn said, "the drinks are on me. For the rest of the bloody year." No one laughed incredulously. It was my turn to wonder what their game was. Somebody cleared her throat. My mouth was the most arid place on earth.

"May I ask what you mean by chubby chaser?" I finally blurted, just to put the awful silence out of its misery.

"A normal-sized bloke who gets off on fat women," Crinolyn said. "A victimiser. An exploiter of the misery of the defenceless. First cousin to a paedophile."

Another mass sharp intake of breath. Then Boopsie: "Isn't that a little harsh, Crinolyn?"

"Fuck off," said Crinolyn. "No, I don't think it's harsh at all really. In her own way, somebody like Nicola is no more able to defend herself than a child would be."

Squirming, the young one with the cornsilk hair moaned as though in agony. And then threw up, sparingly, on her own lap. Both Graham the moderator and the late arrival, the former pop star, quickly produced handkerchiefs. Propelled back into the room by some sixth sense, Duncan hurried over with one of his own. Miss Cornsilk – Nicola – wailed as they all had at her.

"Are you pleased with yourself, Crinolyn?" Boopsie demanded angrily.

"Don't turn it on me, you, you fat black bitch," Crinolyn snarled. "Don't shoot the bloody messenger. If I'm the only one with the danglies to object to this wanker's being here, it's still him you should be angry at, innit?" Duncan and Graham each took hold of one of Nicola's wrists to keep her from trying to pull out handfuls of her own gorgeous hair. You could have heard her wailing in Finsbury Park.

Boopsie backed down. The siren that Nicola had become seemed to recede a bit. Her wailing became snivelling, and then sniffling. "What I would remind Crinolyn," Graham said, each syllable dripping accusation, "is that one person's fat isn't necessarily another's. OA doesn't say you have to weigh such-and-such to benefit from the programme. The programme is for anybody who feels they weigh too much, whatever they weigh."

"Good news for the chubby chasers," Crinolyn said under her breath, but not far enough under it to keep everyone from hearing.

"While Nicola phones her sister to dash over with another skirt," Graham said, not dignifying her with acknowledgement, "why don't we all have a nice relaxing drink."

"I don't drink with paedophiles," Crinolyn snarled, "and I don't drink with chubby chasers either." Her comment hung in the air like an awful smell. But then she smiled, exposing more of her awful teeth. "Unless they're paying."

God knows how, but she'd recognised me. "You're the bloke from the Marcel Flynn pants adverts, innit? There was a time when I couldn't turn on the bloody telly without having to look at your bloody six-pack. I reckon you must have a bob or two."

"You were the Marcel Flynn pants bloke?" Boopsie marvelled. "Fantastic. I had mates with your photo on their bedroom walls." It turned out she was a model in her own right. She'd modelled BHS's new line of active sportswear for BBWs. British-born women? I had no idea what she meant, but didn't want to appear stupid. The had-been pop star who'd arrived late helped out. "Big beautiful women," he said, offering me his hand, with its incongruously long, narrow fingers. "Jez E. Bell."

I bought a round of drinks and brought them back to where the overeaters, knowing they'd never get round a table, had made a semi-circle of their chairs. It was actually fairly jolly. Hermione, the pink whale, turned out to be a well-known former restaurant critic turned travel writer. Having got too big for all coaches and most airlines, she now confined herself to writing about cruises. She knew that, if she didn't do something about her weight, she'd be reduced to living off the royalties from her several books, as younger, hungrier, slimmer writers would supplant her. What she'd done recently about her weight was gain two stone. "I just don't seem to be able to help myself," she said. The others murmured their assent.

She told Jez that he'd been a hero to her two daughters while competing in the first edition of the notorious televised singing competition *Megastar,* in which he'd been the only non-svelte semi-finalist. Hermione's daughters weren't fat themselves, but their classmates tormented them because their mum was fat, the thought of which coaxed tears out of her eyes. Boopsie kindly touched her hand, but her kindness made matters worse.

"I wish I could have won for them," Jez said, "for them and all the other fat kids and slim kids of fat parents."

"Fat bloody chance," said Crinolyn, already glaring at the bottom of her pint glass. "As though the thin world's ever going to give any of us a fighting chance."

"It doesn't serve us to buy into the victim mentality," Graham said. It seemed very much the sort of thing one in his position would say. "I think they'd have been quite happy if Jez had won. Would have shown how broad-minded and tolerant they were. The simple fact is that he wasn't the best singer, not by miles."

"No?" said Jez, the blood rushing to his huge round face. "Maybe you'd like to tell us who was better, at least in your expert fucking opinion." He tried to get to his feet. It was easier said than done.

It was Graham's turn to redden. "The one who won, the one who turned out to be a bender. And the other one, the cute one with the cleft palate. And at least two of the girls as well."

"Bollocks," Jez snapped. If either of them had been able to get up, blows would surely have been thrown. "I could outsing the lot."

"Can we have even one meeting without the two of you having a go at each other?" Crinolyn interjected. "Just fucking one?" She handed Graham her empty glass. "Same again. And some crisps. Three bags, please. They're so small nowadays."

Graham waddled dutifully to the bar. The still-breathless Jez mopped himself with a serviette. Poor Nicola Cornsilk appeared, in a fresh skirt and an expression of profound dread, and made her way over to us. "Look at how lovely you're looking now," Boopsie exulted, and poor Nicola turned the deepest red of the day.

I tried to make small talk. I asked Graham what work he did. He worked only a month of every year, as a department store Santa Claus. But he thought the approaching Christmas might be his last. "It's a younger man's game. There are only so many greedy little brats' unreasonable demands a geezer can say *ho ho ho* to in one lifetime.

More and more, I find myself wanting to sit on one of the little buggers and feel their little femurs and what-not snapping beneath me."

That took the small smile off poor Nicola's face. Graham claimed he'd only been joking, but he was obviously lying. And such a person standing between me and almost certain death from overeating!

"Tell us a bit about yourself," Graham suddenly said to me, and I nearly choked on my sparkling mineral water. Boopsie's smacking me hard between the shoulder blades had no effect other than to make my back smart. Everyone seemed to get fed up waiting for me to stop coughing. There was much impatient tapping of huge thick fingers on tabletops.

"I come from America," I was finally able to tell them, "originally from Los Angeles, California, and later San Francisco." I wondered if I should point out that nearly all Brits mispronounce Los Angeles, which doesn't, in fact, rhyme with *ease*. I quickly abandoned the idea, as I did that of pointing out that "Californian", in correct usage, is never an adjective, but only a noun. (I was a repatriated Californian. One wouldn't speak in a Californian accent, if there were such a thing, but a California one.)

More impatient tapping.

"I love Kate Bush," I blurted. "Being nearer to her, in fact, is one of the reasons I moved to this country." Their looking at me blankly inspired more blurting. "I find much of her later music inexpressibly beautiful. In my darkest hours, in my moments of peak despair, it gives me reason to live. A world in which music of such beauty exists can't be intolerable. That's how I look at it."

"Blimey," Crinolyn said, shaking her head, smirking. I could have strangled her on the spot.

"We have a special bond, Kate and I," I said.

"A nutter," I heard Jez chuckle under his breath to Graham.

"No," I said, turning toward him. "Not a nutter at all. I'm not saying she sends me secret messages. I'm not saying I get radio transmissions from her through the fillings in my molars. Nothing of the sort, in fact. I'm saying that Kate's music communicates with those receptive to it in an exalted way I'm neither able to describe nor would want to if I could, for fear of somehow cheapening the experience."

"Don't he half talk posh?" Crinolyn quipped to Boopsie. And it had always been so. The more nervous I become, the more convoluted my syntax. And how I'd suffered for it at school!

"Very interesting," Graham, clearly keen to move on to other concerns, sighed. "Does anyone else have strong feelings about our Kate?"

"She's rather too antic for my taste, I'm afraid," Hermione admitted, "too in love with her own cleverness and audacity, wildly overblown. I can't understand why, when she has such a gorgeous lower register, she's chosen to sing so often in the voice of a nine-year-old who's just inhaled helium. In most cases, I can't see how it serves the song."

The helium line got a chuckle out of a couple of them. It was pretty clear I wouldn't be adding Hermione to my Christmas card list. She clearly hadn't heard any of Kate's albums after *The Dreaming*.

Heartened by her audience's response, she kept going. "She has a lot to answer for, hasn't she, having opened the door here and on the Continent for the extremely mannered likes of Toyah and Lene Lovich and Nina Hagen, who in turn inspired that whole American school of bleating new wave kewpie dolls. There wasn't a single one I could bear, except maybe Cyndi Lauper."

"I remember her," Graham recalled triumphantly. "Fabulous was our Cyndi. If Kate opened the door for our Cyndi, then she won't have me to apologise to."

Of the quintet of geezers who had come boisterously into the pub during Hermione's querulous soliloquy, one had a shaved head; two of the others had twisted tufts of their hair into spikes like those popularised by one of the young singers who'd beaten Jez; four had receding hairlines. One, he whose eyes were unusually close together, had only one eyebrow, extending from the outside corner of his right eye to the corresponding corner of his left. They called one another *you cunt* and *you wanker* and roared with manly laughter at their own wit. They were the sort who thought nothing of paying £50 for a replica of the football shirts worn by the team they supported, even though the shirt brazenly advertised a type of mobile phone they couldn't afford, and even though the team they supported – no, the team with which they lived and died – was made up of paid mercenaries of the sort who'd always got the sort of girl who wouldn't even have spoken to any of the five, except maybe to tell him to piss off, paid mercenaries who'd have snarled at the five's children had the children somehow got close enough to their limousines to beg for an autograph. I prayed they wouldn't notice us.

Hermione wasn't nearly finished. "In a great many cases," she said, "I feel there's a thick layer of artifice separating Bush from her listener. Marc Bolan sang in 'Spaceball Ricochet' about getting hooked by authors who spoke to him like a friend. Not only does Kate not speak to her listener as a friend, much of the time she doesn't even speak to him as Kate, but as a character Kate's playing! One can well understand why John Peel said he can't take her seriously."

"She's got *irie* chat as well, hasn't she?" Boopsie whispered to Crinolyn.

But Hermione still wasn't finished. "And what a frightful lyricist she is, if memory serves – vague, often solipsistic, nearly always abstruse . . ."

"Enough!" I could no longer keep myself from shouting. "For Christ's sake, woman!" And there went any hope of the quartet of geezers not noticing us. They grinned mischievous, laddish grins at one another and headed over to gawk at us up close while guzzling pints of the latest watery American swill to be advertised mercilessly in the UK.

"If she lost eight stone, the blonde one would give Holly Vallance a run for her money, innit?" the one with the shaved head mused. It was as though he thought us monkeys, or deaf.

"Eight? You're a cunt. I'd say at least 12," a spiky-haired one asserted. "And since when did Holly Vallance become anybody's standard of beauty? If she and the Appletons came into a pub from opposite sides, nobody would know Holly Vallance was bloody there."

"It depends which Appleton you're talking about," the one with one eyebrow said. Guys like this, with blotchy, misshapen, frizzy-haired wives waiting for them at home – but not very attentively if there were a soap opera on – always had very strong opinions about the relative attractiveness of female celebrities, just as they'd had 20 years before when they sat together gnashing their teeth while the boys who'd go on to become paid football mercenaries chatted up the school's most desirable girls.

Nicola, predictably, was absolutely trembling with shame, which didn't go unnoticed by the one who was neither bald, spiky-haired, nor monobrowed, the real catch of the five. "Talk about your jiggling," he marvelled. "There's some world-class jiggling for you."

Boopsie spoke up, but in a way guaranteed to fail, a way that presupposed there was even a trace of compassion among the five of them. "You've had your laugh. Now why don't you leave us alone?"

"Who's going to make us?" the taller of the spiky-haireds wondered, winning the admiration of the bald one. "You? Your two fat friends?" He looked pointedly first at Jez, who looked down at his own feet, and then at Graham, who shrugged and mumbled, "I have a heart condition."

I knew this was coming. "Well, how about the normal one, then?" I couldn't pretend I didn't know he wasn't referring to me. "How about you, mate? You want to stick up for your disgusting friends? Cos if you do, I'll wait for you in the car park."

You can never leave the playground. No matter how old you get, it always finds you.

Crinolyn found the bottom of her second pint, wiped her mouth with the back of her hand, belched, belched again, and addressed my antagonist. "How about if, instead of that, all five of you piss off before I bash your heads together until you won't be identifiable except by dental records?"

"I'd like to see you try it," my antagonist decreed defiantly, and very ill-advisedly.

Both the monobrow and the shaved head realised they'd just lost the moral high ground, though of course they wouldn't have put it that way, and looked embarrassed. Nicola began to sob. "Well," my antagonist challenged Crinolyn. "I'm waiting."

"Jesus," the shaved pate said, shaking his head, putting his hand over his eyes in embarrassment. "Let's leave it there, Simon."

"For fuck's sake, you wanker," the taller spiky-haired pointed out under his breath, "she's a bint."

It finally occurred to my antagonist to be embarrassed. He turned angrily back toward me. "Well, he isn't, is he?" he blurted, looking as though about to take a swing. "A cunt maybe, but not a woman." I pretended I didn't hear him, and hated myself for it. But it wasn't as though I'd arrived for the meeting exuding self-esteem.

"Let's leave them alone," the taller spiky-haired said, touching my antagonist's elbow. "Let's let them stuff their fat faces in peace."

"If you're not out of reach by the time I count 10," Crinolyn said, "it's dental records time."

My antagonist struggled to think of something face-saving to say before he took his leave. His face was that of someone straining to move his bowels after three days of no fruit and insufficient water. Finally it came to him, or at least came back to him. "I'd like to see you try it."

Crinolyn began getting to her feet, a process that threatened to last a while. His mates led my antagonist away before he could embarrass them further. I was relieved he was gone, of course, and infinitely ashamed of myself for having stood back while Crinolyn did the heavy lifting.

Our meeting proper finally got underway. It wasn't quite what I'd hoped for. As we stood up and introduced ourselves, the rest had to say, "Hello, Graham," for instance, as though we hadn't already had drinks and repelled bellicose yobbos together, which I thought quite twee. Graham spent most of his time unapologetically telling us about new recipes he'd discovered during the past week, never alluding to the effect of eating all the luscious dishes he described so lovingly. Nicola looked as though she were being tortured, which, in some key ways, she certainly was. Boopsie admitted that she needed to stay enormous to keep modelling for BHS, and everyone hated her for it. It occurred to me to ask if she thought BHS would make her redundant if she got supermodel slim, but I kept my lip buttoned. Crinolyn mentioned her weight only in relation to how difficult it made for her to catch her three defiant teenagers.

When I found out that addressing the group was strictly voluntary, I declined. Before we adjourned, I had to take everybody's phone number and give them all mine. According to Graham, mutual support was the name of the game. We were all to feel free to phone one another at any time should we be struck by the urge to overeat. "But bother me when *EastEnders* is on, or I'm having a row with one of my kids," Crinolyn said, "and you'll regret it big time."

3

My Infinite, Familiar Shame

ONCE home, I was too excited about the idea of Nicola's losing a lot of weight and becoming my girlfriend to eat. I put off calling her and put off calling her and put off phoning her. I felt 15 again. When I finally managed it, someone patently not she answered, but I nervously blurted, "Nicola?" nonetheless.

"No, her mum. Isn't it a bit late to be ringing?" It occurred to me that her mum probably wasn't much older than I, and that I ought to hang up. But I just sat there mortified into silence. "Shall I see if she's still up?" her mum wondered helpfully, her tone becoming rather gentler. I didn't say no. The next thing I knew, I was on the phone with a sleepy-sounding Nicola, marvelling at how it's possible to hear some people blushing over the phone. All that noisy blood rushing to her face!

She didn't remember me at first. "You know," I insisted, "from the Overeaters group."

"Oh," she wondered uncertainly, "the slim one who looks like that film star?" I wouldn't have guessed that she had it in her to tease so cruelly, but my exhilaration at her remembering me trumped all else. "The one Crinolyn was having a go at?"

I invited her to dinner. She actually gasped with embarrassment. I felt almost as though I had the upper hand, which I recognised as a mixed blessing. At all previous times in my life that women (or men!) had allowed me the upper hand, I almost invariably came to disdain them for it, and treated them awfully. Who but one worthy of the worst imaginable treatment would even dream of granting me the upper hand?

"I don't eat dinner," she finally managed.

"Then we'll go for a drink and a chat," I said decisively, feeling as though I was impersonating someone. She was too embarrassed to resist.

I offered Gilmour and Duncan money to drive me over to collect her. Gilmour was going with his friends to leer at pole dancers, though, and Duncan claimed his van was in the garage. I assumed it hadn't been up to the task of transporting me, and was ravaged by guilt. Gilmour wondered why I didn't take a fucking cab like anyone else. It occurred to me that he would probably always be thick. It's not something one easily gets over.

I rang for a minicab, asking that they send the biggest one available. I have no idea how I managed to get in, but I got in. I suspect, in addition to The Knowledge, drivers are required to undergo sensitivity training. The guy didn't bat an eye at the sight of me. He didn't even offer any suggestions as to how I should position myself in the passenger compartment to keep from toppling his vehicle.

Nicola lived in Coldblow, in a road lined with trees and Citroëns. I wondered if one of her neighbours was a dealer who offered everyone in the neighbourhood an irresistible discount. There were, to be honest, a couple of Fiats too.

A tiny, normally proportioned, fastidious man whose bulky blue cableknit jumper was precisely the colour of his socks answered the door. He had awful teeth and the slightly off-balance look of one trying to conceal a bald spot with hair allowed to grow long on one side of the head, and then carefully combed over to the other. "Well, you're not at all what I expected," he marvelled. He offered me his hand, giggled nervously, and wondered under his breath if I had a fag. Before I could answer, a huge voice demanded from the lounge, "Are you going to have the simple courtesy to invite him in, Cyril, or leave him out there to freeze?" It wasn't nearly as cold as all that.

He gave me a look that implored, *Isn't it something what we fellows have to put up with?* I followed him into the lounge, where a mountain of skim-milk-coloured flesh lay propped up, listening, astonishingly, to Kate's *Never For Ever*. They were Katepeople! This was going to be like taking candy from a baby. Which isn't to deny that, with the best will in the world, I'd long since given up trying to learn to enjoy most of Kate's pre-*Hounds Of Love* work. Sipping from a flute glass, overflowing the widest chaise longue in all Christendom, the mountain of flesh seemed to dislike me instantly, but nonetheless offered me her hand and pronounced herself Nicola's mum. Her teeth, while bright white in a way that those of no one over 35 are without the use of expensive bleaching agents, were rather on the small side. Nicola had inherited her wonderful skin.

She stopped the music with her remote and sighed. "Every couple of years we try again," she said, referring to the CD. "Given the extraordinarily high quality of the rest of her work – and I believe *Under The Pink* to be the greatest album of the last 35 years, we worry the failing must be ours. But every time we try, the result's the same." Being American and no good at irony, I couldn't tell if she was taking the piss. *Under The Pink* is the unspeakable Amos's.

"Nicola will be with you in a moment," my hostess yawned, still bothering neither to reveal her own name nor ask mine. "She was actually ready a quarter of an hour ago, but I said it simply isn't done not to keep a gentleman caller waiting for at least a short while. It isn't as though the poor thing has had a great many dates."

"If it's all right," Cyril said, "I'll just leave the two of you to . . ."

"It is most assuredly *not* all right," the mountain of flesh interrupted annoyingly. "For once, and let's bear firmly in mind that your second chance might be years in the future, you will do the gracious thing, and not run off to sneak a fag while I'm left to try to converse with a perfect stranger."

Cyril sighed and looked at the tops of his loafers.

"Well?" Nicola's mum demanded. "Can you think of even one thing you might want to try talking to him about? How about sport? There's a classically manly topic. Ask him if he supports anyone in the Premiership. Ask what he thinks of David Beckham. Every English male has a strong opinion about David Beckham."

He looked at me sheepishly. I envied David Beckham's golden good looks and extraordinary bankable skill, but otherwise had no opinion. "My dad used to support Chelsea," Cyril finally managed. "And I think his dad before him." The mountain of flesh snorted in exasperation.

Cyril changed the subject. "Nicola's bedroom's down here as well as Mother's. It got too hard for them going up the stairs, and they couldn't really fit anymore even if they'd had the strength. The past couple of years, I'm the only one who actually sleeps upstairs."

"Oh, that's a nice thing to be telling him," the mountain of flesh seethed. "Just the sort of thing you want to tell your stepdaughter's first gentleman caller in God knows how long!" The pair of them were coming more and more to remind me, in the one's naked contempt for and unchallenged dominance of the other, of my own parents.

Nicola, blushing luridly, stepped into the room, sideways. She was radiant. Her hair and beautiful skin glowed, and she smelled as gorgeous as she looked.

"Nicola's gained six pounds this week," the mountain of flesh informed me accusatorily. "I suppose someone like you finds that very exciting."

I didn't know what she meant. I reckoned I was very much happier not knowing. Nicola seemed to be trying to faint in mortification. "You look gorgeous," I told her, and she literally had to sit down now, as every drop of blood in her body was hurtling to her face.

"Oh, I know your type," the mountain of flesh seethed at me. "I know it only too well, in fact. You and Cyril are birds of a feather."

"You were a size 16 when I asked you to marry me," Cyril exploded. "A bloody size 16! You bought your clothing off the rack in ordinary high street stores when we started seeing each other. Let's not have another bloody syllable about me chasing chubby!"

It was all too familiar. The mountain of flesh didn't have to say a word, but only to pretend pointedly that he wasn't even in the room anymore. Cyril's fury abated as quickly as it had appeared, and was replaced by embarrassment. "Sorry, darling," he mumbled.

"You're sorry," the mountain of flesh repeated mockingly. "You cause a humiliating scene for your stepdaughter on the extremely rare occasion of her having a date, and that's all you have to say?"

"I'm *very* sorry." He looked at Nicola, who seemed to wish that a very large hole would open in the middle of the lounge floor and swallow her.

The mountain of flesh shook her head in disbelief. "You spiteful, awful little man, you."

"I said I was sorry!" Cyril blurted furiously. Oh, this was *just* like my childhood all over again – the multiple explosions, the awful recriminations, the whole grotesque dance. And then, absolutely true to form, Cyril felt even guiltier than he had on the first go-round, and burst into tears. "Nic, I can't begin to tell you how ashamed I am. I know this must be a really special moment for you, and here I've rubbished it."

I couldn't bear to see anyone suffering the agony he was in (and that Nicola was in too, for that matter, but in her case I didn't know what to do). "Not at all," I said in a hollow imitation of cheerfulness as I reached for Nicola's hand. "It's been a pleasure meeting the two of you, and I'm sure Nicola and myself will have a marvellous time."

"After this little exhibition of spitefulness on her stepfather's part you honestly believe that Nicola has any chance of enjoying her evening? I can't believe you're serious."

We got out. If we'd been with them even a moment longer, I probably would have burst into tears. Cyril followed us. I thought he was going to apologise for his wife, but it was to ask again if I had a fag. I made Nicola laugh by wondering aloud if Cyril had thought I'd taken up smoking while he and her mum were dancing their awful dance.

But when we reached the minicab, the gaping driver said, "You must be joking. You'll need a proper black cab, if not a lorry."

We decided to forego the bright lights of Dartford, and to stay local. There was a pub at the end of the road called The Goose & Syringe. Hours later, we arrived, Nicola glistening from sweat, breathless with exertion.

They did food. Their speciality, as I'd have inferred from their name if I hadn't been preoccupied thinking what I'd do if poor Nicola collapsed before we made the pub, was *foie gras*, but they did Thai as well. My intuition was that a secret law requiring 50 per cent of London pubs to do Thai food had been enacted sometime in the spring of 2000 without anyone noticing. Or maybe the media had known full well, but stood to profit somehow. I think everyone profited, in the sense that even the worst *pad thai* is more flavourful than even the most scrumptious Scotch egg, for instance.

I got Nicola a still bottled water with a lime wedge and ice and myself a sparkling one with lemon, and a couple of baskets of Thai prawn crackers. I learned that at four months old she'd won a Beautiful Baby contest. At three, she'd been in TV adverts for Cadbury's and Michelin. She was popular at school, and something of a tennis prodigy. She entered puberty early, at around 11½, and was surrounded by boys, whereupon her girlfriends, all a year or two away from full breasts of their own, abandoned her *en masse*.

Her mother, the mountain of flesh, left her biological father for having ceased to find her attractive when her weight came to exceed that which a standard bathroom scale would display, and took up with an actor whose greater interest turned out to be in Nicola. The mountain of flesh blamed Nicola, who, finding herself estranged not only from friends, but also from both her parents, found refuge in Haagen-Dazs ice cream. She knew that the brand's exotic name was fanciful, and that the company was in fact the brainchild of a cigar-smoking dese-'n'-dose Brooklynite with hairy knuckles and dark sweat stains beneath his arms, but it nonetheless tasted to her like consolation. She became nearly her mum's size. The boys lost interest, but her former girlfriends, preoccupied now with the boys, didn't return to her.

She became ever more enormous. For a while, she was able to maintain a flat of her own with her earnings from the shampoo commercials in which clever directors and editors made it appear that her gorgeous cornsilk hair, always seen from behind, belonged to girls with supermodel bodies. Then she got too big to drive, and too big even for most cabs, and moved back in with her mum and the unfortunate Cyril.

Since then, she'd actually lost close to four stone, but still weighed over 26.

As she recited this litany of horror, she maintained eye contact with me for a total of perhaps a second and a half. She'd considered suicide for a while, but then saw an edition of *Trina*, Britain's demure answer to Jerry Springer, featuring enormous fat women and the normal-sized blokes who adored them, and reckoned there might be hope for her. Here she made another couple of hundred milliseconds' eye contact. I'd have hoped she'd have asked to hear how I'd become elephantine myself, but she was either too shy or not bothered.

I needed to pee. She clearly wasn't very happy with the idea of being left alone. Praying that the gents' wouldn't have a narrow entrance, I assured her I'd be quick.

I was, but in the short time it took me, two laddish sorts with spiky hair had joined her, one on each side. I prayed they weren't ridiculing her. The look on her face suggested they weren't. Indeed, the look on her face suggested she was enjoying their company more than she had my own. I went to the bar and ordered another sparkling water even though I'd got through only half of the one on our table. I went back in the gents' and ensured there weren't unsightly deposits of masticated prawn crackers in the crevices between my teeth. Someone came in to pee and gave me an odd look, but I reckoned it was more to do with my girth than the masticated crisps between my teeth. I undid my trousers and tucked my shirt back in. I prayed the laddish sorts would be gone.

Nope. In fact, Nicola was actually laughing now, throwing back her head, the lot. One of them had his hand on her thigh. She finished her laugh and touched his reciprocally. I felt as though back in junior high school.

I waited for her to notice me. I had a long wait. I wanted it to seem that I was just getting back from the loo. I managed a smile. *Oh, you've made some new friends, darling? How lovely for you.*

The whole of a Stevie Wonder record played, and then the first 16 bars or so of one of Marvin Gaye's lesser-known duets with Tammi Terrell, before Nicola finally looked over. I'd have expected her to flush with embarrassment, in that way she did at the slightest provocation. Nope. She just smiled and turned back to the lad with his hand on her. Now it was his turn to throw back his head and laugh. How wonderfully droll she was apparently being.

All right, mate, I pictured myself marching over there and snarling decisively, *on your bike. Sorry? Who am I? I'm only Nicola's date. What am*

I going to bloody do about it? Glad you asked, actually. What I'm going to do about it is bash your heads together until you'll be identifiable only by dental records.

Hang on a second, mate. You've left your wallet behind. What do you say I take these four £20 notes out of it for you? Make it a bit lighter for you, a bit less thick. Sitting on a thick wallet can cause chiropractic problems, you know. You're going to do what? Ring a few of your mates and ask them to wait outside for me? Be my guest, mate.

I was snapped out of my reverie by the realisation that the one who didn't have his hand on Nicola was on his way over to me. *Your bird, gov? Awfully sorry. Obviously we didn't know. We'll clear right off.*

Nope. He actually said only three words, *you*, and *piss*, and *off*. And to my infinite, familiar shame, I did.

4

A Postcard From Princess Diana

THERE's something wrong with my DNA or something. Male toddlers are meant to be aggressive, but I'd be willing to bet that even as a toddler I was creative, droll, and passive, a born patsy.

Or maybe it was that there was no role model for anything other than passivity in my life. When no one ever defended himself around me, how was I supposed to have any idea how it was done? My dad happily endured all the verbal abuse my mother could dish out, and what an awful lot that was. She wasn't just aggressively nasty with him, but rapaciously so, a panzer division of contempt, an endless deluge of ridicule. Around 99 per cent of the time, he'd look sheepish and cowed, a whole mini-menagerie of quiescence. But every few weeks he'd flare up in anger for a second or two, usually out of all proportion to the situation at hand, and she'd wilt like spinach over boiling water.

And the world outside our four walls scared her to death. My second earliest memory is of her shushing me as we walked past a neighbour's window when I was around three. The thought of our being noticed terrified her.

I took my sense that looking sheepish or wilting like spinach over boiling water were what one did in the face of provocation to school, whose playground was full of boys who'd been aggressive toddlers, and whose sense was that what one did in the face of provocation was punch the *provocateur* in the nose. Naturally, I soon became known as a boy other boys could count on to capitulate.

It seemed as though I was in four fistfights a week between the ages of five and seven, and I lost every one of them. It felt like what I was meant to be doing. On one occasion, the kid who lived next door and I had an argument on the playground about chocolate milk. It was my view that chocolate milk was ordinary milk to which some sort of chocolate flavouring had been added, and his that it came from special

brown cows – and that I deserved a bloody nose for believing otherwise. I was pretty sure I was right on this one, and his stupidity made
me angry enough to put up rather more of a fight than usual. (I
couldn't suffer fools even at seven, as I would continue not to be able to
into my fifties, halfway through which it finally occurred to me that he
who prides himself on his inability to suffer fools is usually the biggest
fool of all.) I got him a good one in the neck. He couldn't breathe.
There was panic in his little piggy eyes. I could have finished him off in
a heartbeat. But wasn't it my role to lose? I let him get his breath. I
lowered my hands. He got me in the nose, and I went home crying,
preserving the natural order of things. I'd never come so close again, in
large part because I stopped even trying. Somebody wanted to intimidate me? Be my guest!

The next year, we moved out of the San Fernando Valley, and near
to what would later come to be known as LAX, Los Angeles International Airport. We boys played a game called tetherball, which
involved trying to hit a ball tethered to a metal pole harder than your
opponent was trying to hit it in the opposite direction. I have always
adored baseball, basketball, and football, and always detested tetherball,
for which I had even less aptitude than for basketball. But one day I was
on the verge of actually beating someone at it when the bell summon-
ing us back to class rang and one of my classmates, little Kirk
Something-or-Other, grabbed the ball and hollered, "Game over!" I
screamed at him. There was terror in his not-piggy eyes, but only for
the blink of one of them, as he remembered me as the boy who always
backed down and screamed back at me, louder. I walked away, cowed
and sheepish, while a little crowd of girls hooted at me for not daring to
stand up even to the smallest boy in the class. Like my mother, I'd
come to believe anyone who'd stand up for himself as someone to
whom I ought to defer.

How I loathed myself that day, and how I would continue to forever
after, as I began to reek of cowardice. Bullies could smell me from the
width of the playground away. I reckoned, in my abject stupidity, that
it was better to avoid fights than risk being made to cry in front of girls.
That I might get to an antagonist's nose first never even occurred to
me. The more I allowed myself to be bullied (I see now that even
ineffectual self-defence would have been infinitely preferable to no
defence at all, and would have made the whole question come up less
often), the more I was bullied, and the more I hated myself.

A couple of weeks after I started high school, a year or two before
the growth spurt that made no genetic sense in view of no one in my

family being much over five eight, I had the look of prey about me. My second day, in Physical Education, I caught the eye of a guy who had the look of a predator about him, a greasy-haired auto shop tough who hardly even bothered concealing the pack of cigarettes in his breast pocket, even though it was illegal to smoke at school. You wanted someone who exuded danger? This was your man! A lot someone like this guy cared about being expelled from school when there were hundreds of garages in the vicinity that would be delighted to employ a mechanic of his gifts.

He'd been looking for someone at whom to throw a handful of grass cuttings, and I seemed a prime candidate. Normally, I'd have pretended I hadn't noticed, but my brain wasn't working very well that afternoon, and I instead responded in kind. Oh, the look of delight that spread across his face as he gathered up a bigger handful of grass cuttings. I saw the writing on the wall, and retreated, but not so quickly as to preclude his catching me, as not allowing myself to be caught, even by someone who'd probably have fallen to the ground gasping for nicotine if I'd just kept running long enough, wasn't part of my job description. He tried to feed me the grass, but succeeded only in rubbing it in my face.

If I had it to do over again, I'd have taken a bite out of his hand, and then kicked him as hard as I could in the trachea while he writhed in pain. But of course, I don't have it to do over again, and am ashamed of myself for what I didn't do.

Later, there were twins, the Irvings, Robert and Richard. I hoped we could become friends, but was cheeky with them because I didn't know a better way to interact with people. I either said nothing to people at that age, or gently taunted them. One morning in Physical Education, while playing basketball, Robert suddenly decided he'd had enough of my rapier-like wit, and came at me with his fists. Even at the time I knew he was hopeless. He wasn't hurting me at all, and he was giving it everything he had. So did I wait for him to wear himself out and then throw a punch or two of my own? Of course not. What I did was appease him while the other boys, disgruntled at the realisation that there'd be no bloodshed, stood around us jeering.

In my early twenties, I became linked, to my limitless astonishment, with a blonde universal object of desire, the Cameron Diaz of one generation before the real one, Michelle Pfeiffer crossed with Catherine Deneuve. The world saw her on my arm and thought I must have something major on the ball. But my DNA hadn't changed, and neither had my upbringing.

We played a lot of pinball, mostly at the bowling alley on the corner of Santa Monica and La Cienega Boulevards that later became a famous roller disco, and later still the place where film stars bought their furniture. One night, while it was my turn, a drunk-sounding male voice asked from behind if we could spare any change for a drink. Without turning around, I said, "Shove off." The universal object of desire gave him a couple of quarters. Our supplicant, no authority on gender issues, snarled, "Lady, you're a better son-of-a-bitch than your old man." I tensed. I knew that I should wheel around and flatten him. But he sensed that I was considering it, and snarled something about how, if I turned to face him, he'd kill me. I stayed where I was. It's over 30 years later, and I'm still ashamed.

About five years after that, long after the universal object of desire had packed me in, I had a moment. I was leaving a drug store on Sunset Blvd. where Fairfax crossed it. As I pushed open the glass door to the parking lot, a voice behind me said, "Faggot." I surmised that its owner thought I should have held the door open for him. I ignored it and kept walking toward my car with him right behind, my passivity emboldening him. "Is that what you are?" he demanded, "a faggot?"

I don't know what came over me. I stopped, spun on my heel, and confronted him. He wasn't exactly Lennox Lewis, but he wasn't a pipsqueak either. "Listen," I snapped, enlightened enough even in those days to dislike the way the lexicon of homophobia felt in my mouth, but too angry to care, "maybe *you're* the faggot, expecting somebody to hold doors open for you."

His mouth dropped open. Looking chastened, he hurried past, giving me a wide berth. He looked back at me nervously as he reached his car. I wondered if there was someone standing behind me, but I was alone.

He didn't know how lucky he was. If he hadn't scarpered, all those decades' repressed rage would have come out of me. I'd almost certainly have kicked his head in.

Whatever it was that had come over me never came over me again. Five years later, I holidayed in London during a heat wave. My girlfriend and I went to Hyde Park, and sat by the Serpentine in some deck chairs that seemed to have been provided for the public's use, I in my stylish new Star of David drop earring. A swarthy little man came over and demanded money for our use of the chairs. I told him I hadn't realised they weren't free, and thus wouldn't pay him, although we would certainly quit them. He called me a fucking Jew. I, shocked, told him to fuck off. He spat on me. And I, intimidated by the wild hatred in his eyes, let him. I thought about how his family had probably been tyrannised by Zionists. It didn't make me feel better. I could hardly have felt worse.

I could go on like this all night, but I'll leave it at recounting the worst time, the time that makes me want to eat gallons of ice cream or cry or both. My daughter Babooshka wasn't cheerleader material, wasn't an effervescent, lithe little blonde with no sense of irony. When she began her own high school career, she tried out instead to be the school's mascot, which involved her dressing up as a puma, complete with a huge, hot, heavy rubber head, and dancing around on the sidelines, putting herself at risk for heat stroke, at football and basketball games. After it was determined that she was alone in applying for it, she was given the job.

I had to collect her one Saturday from a football game against her school's archrivals, played on the archrivals' ground. Passions ran high. The other school's team ate my daughter's team's lunch. Afterwards, she decided not to change out of her infernal puma outfit before we walked back to the car park. I don't know what I was thinking when I acceded. I was vaguely aware of there being three people behind us, one of them extremely tall, and of there being tension in the air. I say vaguely because the part of me that would have pretended I wasn't having grass clippings rubbed in my face my second day at Santa Monica High School was at the controls, and wanted to maintain what politicians would later call plausible deniability. (A much smaller, if absolutely genuine, part of me didn't want to take a chance of doing the wrong thing. One is on very, very thin ice when intervening on a teenager's behalf. However lovingly or reasonably one may do so, it's always with the understanding that the teenager might be mortified with embarrassment by the intervention.)

When we reached my car, my daughter said they'd been giving her little shoves from behind. I told her she should have said something. And if she had, would I have taken on all three of them, one of whom could have rested his chin atop my head? I was beside myself with self-loathing for even thinking to ask myself that question.

The next evening over dinner, I recounted the episode to my girlfriend, and suggested that my daughter would surely have been mortified with embarrassment if I'd made a scene. "No," my daughter said, without malice. "I'd have been proud." Those words rank right alongside the universal blonde object of desire's telling me, "I'm not in love with you anymore," as the most excruciating I've ever heard, or ever will hear.

★   ★   ★

All of which might seem to have little to do with the first known antecedent of the worst president in American history, Reynold Bush, having left the north-east Essex village of Messing for greener pastures across the deep blue sea in 1631. Kate Bush's first known ancestor, descended from Saxons, was first officially sighted in nearby Pebmarsh in 1769. Draw your own conclusions. Her great-great-grandfather Henry is known to have been a nasty piece of work who died of injuries sustained when he plummeted drunkenly into a ditch. When an agricultural depression closed both the silk mill and the straw plaiting plant that had been their area's most prolific employers, Henry's farm foreman son John and wife Martha moved down to South Ockenden, noted for its red brick Wesleyan chapel.

Kate's grandfather Joe, an abattoir worker, was imprisoned in Wormwood Scrubs for his conscientious objection to the Great War. He later worked as a milkman, and then as a deliveryman for a local hardware business, and came to adore the daughter of the village's most noted daredevil and amateur barber. The quiet, aloof couple's son, called Jackie, won a scholarship to a grammar school, and then went on to medical school, from which he graduated in 1943. He married Hannah Daly, three years his senior, a County Waterford Irish farmer's daughter turned Epsom nurse, became a GP in Bexley, and bought East Wickham Farm.

'Twas there that his sons Jay and Paddy and daughter Cathy enjoyed idyllic childhoods in a beautiful 350-year-old wooden farmhouse with a swimming pool where once there had been a brick pond, oak beams salvaged from scrapped man-o'-war ships consigned, in their old age, to the Woolwich dockyard, and rooms nearly beyond counting, all of them well ordered except for the two younger kids'. Cathy occasionally sneaked into Paddy's room to try her hand at the collection of accordions and concertinas he played when the family sang Irish folk songs and ribald Victorian sea shanties together. Years later he became a member of the English Folk Dance and Song Society.

Around the time Cathy heard The Rolling Stones' 'Little Red Rooster' in her parents' car on the way home from the shops, and was struck by Mick Jagger's singing somehow being more expressive for its seeming indifference to pitch, her family emigrated briefly to Australia, where Paddy is thought to have communed with an emu. But the family soon returned to what future biographer and antagonist Fred Vermorel would characterise as their "rustic sprawl in the heart of inch-pinching suburbia". In the barn loft illuminated by a small oval window, Cathy and her mates sneaked fags and listened to Dave

Edmunds, of all people. Kate's den was like a secret room, entered first through what looked like a cupboard door in the upstairs corridor and then through another door across a narrow passage. Adults could enter by invitation only. In the course of helping to clear the room for habitation, a friend had found a big glass bottle with a stopper. Cathy, sure that evil spirits would come out, implored her not to open it, as one might have expected from a girl whose idea of fun was visiting nearby Plumstead Cemetery with school friends.

The den's floors came over time to be littered with cushions, records, books, magazines, and Incredible String Band, Dylan, Beatles, and T. Rex record sleeves, the walls to be covered with her poems and drawings, several of the latter inspired by Jay's poem "The Devil's Mouth". She was fond of hamsters, cats and a rabbit called Took, named after Marc Bolan's Tyrannosaurus Rex bongo player, but less so of her purpose-built Tudor-style Wendy house at the bottom of the garden, though Took is thought to have enjoyed hiding beneath it.

One evening in the Sixties, she and a chum from school agreed it might be fun to frighten Took into the open by jumping up and down, little realising that he was not only inside with them, but under foot. The school chum, landing atop him, broke his leg, requiring an emergency visit to the vet. But if the school chum expected to be called an imbecile, she'd come to the wrong place. The Bushes were too kind for that.

In between playing Chopin, Beethoven and Schubert, the genial, balding, ginger side-whiskered Dr. Bush accompanied Kate on piano when she practised violin pieces for school, where every student was compelled to learn an instrument. After he showed her a C-major scale, she twigged that what worked in one key would work in others as well, and soon had chords sussed. She took to grinning and bearing it while practising her violin, yearning for the moment when she could consign the infernal thing to its case and improvise happily on piano. And when she tired of the piano, she retired to one of the farm's outbuildings, formerly a Victorian wash-house, where she played the ancient church harmonium that had been home to countless generations of mice, and which a new, spiteful generation of them would soon gnaw to splinters.

Paddy, later to specialise in medieval instruments at the London College of Furniture, seemed to feel compelled to learn to play every exotic stringed instrument of which he got wind – including mandolin, balalaika, sitar, koto, and violin. He played old English folk songs popularised by A.L. Lloyd, whose 'The Handsome Cabin Boy' Kate would later admit to Radio One remained one of her favourite songs.

Bigger brother Jay, who'd later read his poetry on the radio and be published in *Poetry Review*, introduced her to Greek mythology and the work of the Sufic mystic Gurdjieff.

Having passed her 11-plus, Kate was enrolled at St. Joseph's Convent Grammar School, run by enlightened nuns in modern clothing, but housed in a gloomy Victorian building in Abbey Wood. Small and skinny, younger than her classmates by virtue of having been born in late July, she would occasionally get walloped, but never fight back, not even verbally. The ability to slash her tormentors to ribbons with her tongue might have served her well, but East Wickham Farm was a sarcasm-free zone. She declined to play in the school orchestra, but sang, without particular distinction, and not very high, in the school choir. She did well at English, Latin, biology, music, and made her first contribution, the poem "The Crucifixion", to the school's end of year magazine when she was 11, at which age a school photograph shows her to have been dumpy, with no idea of what to do with her hair. (She'd seemingly tried to brush it straight, but had succeeded only in splitting a great many ends.) She would later contribute poems entitled "Blind Joe Death", "A Tear and a Raindrop Met", "Death", and "You" to the school magazine, but didn't tell boys she was making songs of them for fear of being seen as an emasculating overachiever.

She read science fiction, and was keen on John Wyndham. She shared her own stories with chums on the playground at lunchtime and in at least one instance – that of *The Haunted Mill* – was able to induce them to come over and act the story out. Isolation seemed to fascinate her. Those trusted few who heard her early songs often found them unnervingly morbid. Between her second and third years at school, she claimed to be writing a children's book. To be a bright teenage girl is to claim to be writing a children's book.

Though terribly shy elsewhere, she blossomed at the parties she hosted at East Wickham Farm, where her guests would hurl themselves into the swimming pool at evening's end to try to make themselves sober. Commonly, one presumes, they succeeded only in making themselves damp. She admired Elton John's piano playing, but reserved her biggest crush for a local boy who looked like Dave Gilmour of Pink Floyd, and regularly implored a school friend to traipse with her past their local, Fanny On The Hill, in hopes of glimpsing him. She packed in the idea of his noticing her after meeting her first boyfriend, Al Buckle, at nearby St. Laurence's Youth Club, at 16. Playing him tapes of her music, her shyness was such that she had to leave the room.

Treated with kindness at home, Cathy treated others with kindness

40

out in the world. When a classmate was hospitalised, it was she who circulated a card of condolence for everyone to sign. But most children are sadistic little monsters, and sometimes her friends sent her to Coventry purely for the pleasure of seeing the sadness and confusion in her pretty hazel eyes. She found being ignored more painful than being walloped. Still, there is no evidence of anyone having described her as unbuckled when she and Al packed it in.

Her pipe-smoking *pater*, whose accent betrayed the occasional trace of the Essex countryside, was aloof, but generous, to the tune of Cathy being free to help herself to the change he left around the house. She stashed cash in the mouth of the lion-skin rug in the front room, removing some to buy herself Simon & Garfunkel's *Bridge Over Troubled Water* LP, and a ticket to a Who gig, the first gig she ever saw. She was there at the Hammersmith Odeon the evening David Bowie, who'd grown up a short bus ride from East Wickham Farm, announced that the Spiders From Mars would be no more after that night. She wept along with much of the audience.

During her fifth year at St. Joseph's, she spent a week with a friend at Newcastle Polytechnic and thought she might become a psychiatrist. To be a bright, empathetic teenager is to consider becoming a psychiatrist. It also crossed her mind to do social work.

What she really wanted to do, though, was music. At 12, she'd begun recording her songs, some of which amazed her dad by seeming to emerge as whole verses at a time, on the family tape recorder. Within a year, she'd composed the clumsy but gorgeous 'The Man With The Child In His Eyes'. A family friend who worked in the music business encouraged her to send tapes to music publishers and record companies. No one paid the slightest attention, and not entirely because most vetters of unsolicited tapes in the music business have no business in the music business. Her voice was unusually assured, but not quite extraordinary. Her songs occasionally betrayed traces of melodic ingenuity, but squandered them by rarely condescending to provide a recurring "hook" (think of the "Ooh, he's here again" section of 'The Man With The Child In His Eyes') a listener could look forward to hearing at regular intervals. The mostly unrhymed lyrics, unmistakably the work of a precocious schoolgirl who did a lot of reading, were no help at all (as they would remain!). But the family friend's belief in her precocity was undiminished, and he was able to persuade his acquaintance Dave Gilmour, he of Pink Floyd who resembled her first crush, to come hear her.

What a perfect choice – not only a rich, famous guitar god, but also the living embodiment of male gorgeousness! Though rigid with terror, Kate impressed him a treat, and he invited her to his studio near Harlow in Essex to record better demos than she could manage on the family tape recorder. When he proposed she overdub a little electric piano part, one imagines her eyes becoming pinwheels, like Mr. Toad's on first sight of a motorcar. She'd had no idea that there *was* such a thing as overdubbing.

Out, in any event, went the better demos, with Gilmour's guitar and the bass and drums of a band he was producing, Unicorn, supporting Kate's piano and voice. In came no positive feedback. Whereupon Gilmour decided that no mere demos would do, that nothing less than master quality recordings were required. He introduced Kate to EMI record producer Andrew Powell, who chose three of the more than 60 songs she'd written at that point – 'The Child In His Eyes', 'Saxophone Song' and 'Maybe' – to record at AIR London, high above Oxford Street. Gilmour couldn't attend in person because of his Pink Floyd commitments, but might not have fitted in the studio anyway, given that Powell had hired an actual orchestra, for which Gilmour was generous enough to pick up the considerable tab. Powell had been afraid that his protégé, an unschooled teenager from the suburbs, might find it intimidating being surrounded by so many professional musos. If so, she kept it well under wraps, not missing a beat as she sang 'The Man With The Child In His Eyes' live right along with them. Powell's jaw plummeted in wonder.

The next month, in spite of her parents' apprehension, she declared that there was no point in remaining at school, and left with 10 – count 'em! – O-levels. One suspects that none was in penmanship, as her handwriting would come in years to be distinguished by enormous looped descenders (g, p, f, and y) and, because she writes them lazily, making the downward-pointing diagonal stroke of the taller main part of the letter, K's that look for all the world like W's. Wate Bush, you see.

Gilmour, meanwhile, was presenting the Powell-produced masters to EMI pop division general manager Bob Mercer when Bob popped into Abbey Road Studios to observe sessions for Pink Floyd's *Wish You Were Here*. Impressed by her voice, and not oblivious to her gamin sexuality, Mercer invited her in for a chat, to which Dr. Bush, wanting to save her from the casting couch, accompanied her. EMI were definitely interested, Mercer said, but without reaching for the corporate chequebook. Not until the following summer would EMI put its money (and not much of it – £3,500, including a £500 publishing advance) where its mouth was. Mercer described it as money to grow up with. The company wondered gently if she'd consider being . . . a little less idiosyncratic.

Understandably deflated, Kate, who'd not got on with St. Joseph's dance teacher, spent the money she'd inherited from an aunt (Dr. Bush seems to have stopped leaving change around the house by this time) for classes with Robin Kovak at the Dance Centre in Covent Garden. She received offers of work dancing in clubs in Germany, but didn't pursue them. She studied with Arlene Phillips, the creator of Hot Gossip, and morosely decided that she had a great, great deal of hard work ahead if she hoped to get really good. She went out with Steve Blacknall, an EMI promotion man earlier rescued from Decca by one Simon Drake. Remember the latter's name. She moved out of the family farmhouse, but stayed close to family, renting the top floor of a house in Lewisham that her parents owned, with Paddy and his burgeoning collection of musical exotica one floor down and Jay and his family on the ground floor.

She saw former Bowie mime mentor Lindsey Kemp's solo show *Flowers* at the Collegiate Theatre and was transformed. "I saw this funny little guy up there on this stage giving himself physically to other people's music and thought if one person could actually produce the music and give themselves physically at the same time, then you'd get double energy coming from one person. I thought, 'Golly, that's what I want to do.'" Before using one of her own songs, though, she worked up an elaborate routine for Paul McCartney's 'Eleanor Rigby' after what she described as a day of living in its world.

She fell contentedly into a daily routine. She'd get up in the morning and practise the piano until it was time to set out by train for London. Commuters were being blown to bits by IRA bombs left in unattended bags at the time, and you could cut the paranoia on London public transport with a knife, but Kate – as she'd begun calling herself, seemingly to draw a line under the first part of her life – revelled in it. Indeed, the danger somehow enhanced her feeling of being on a mission. In the evening she'd commune with her feline roommates Zoodle and Pye(wacket), and play the piano and sing until she could barely keep her eyes open.

It was a broiling summer, that during which British punk was effectively born, and she left all her windows open. Some poor bugger down the street whose shift work compelled him to rise at five in the morning sent her her first fan letter, advising that, while he enjoyed her singing, *he would bloody well prefer not to have to listen to it night after bloody night when he was trying to kip, thanks so much.*

It got cooler and she closed her windows, but she wouldn't stop composing late at night, not if everyone in Lewisham wrote her an irate letter. One midnight in the following March, while looking out at the full moon for inspiration, sniffling and dribbling with a frightful cold, she happened to remember something she'd seen as a child, a telefilm adaptation of Emily Brontë's *Wuthering Heights*. Years later she'd speculate that the memory had remained because the spirit in the story, who slashes herself with broken glass at the end, was called Cathy, just as she had been. But if that's what made her remember the story, what enabled her to put lines from the novel in her song when she'd never read the novel? In times past, a girl could have got herself drowned as a witch for less, but in the enlightened times in which we live, she would suffer nothing worse than the Brontë Society's emphatic scorn.

Actually, by that full-moonlit midnight in the early spring of 1978, it was a wonder she had any time to compose, as she was busy rehearsing with the band that Paddy, apparently thinking that she'd benefit from singing to live punters, had assembled around her. The presumably hygiene-minded Brian Bath played guitar, Charlie Morgan drums, and Del Palmer, as smitten with the songwriter as he was with her songs, was on bass. Their repertoire – 'Brown Sugar', 'I Heard It Through The Grapevine', 'Sweet Soul Music', 'Sailin' Shoes', 'Honky Tonk Women', 'Come Together', and the nearest Kate would ever come to a bog-standard rock song, 'James And Cold Gun' – wasn't much more imaginative than the name Paddy had come up with – The KT Bush Band. (One might have hoped for rather more from one who'd had an exhibition at the Whitechapel Art Gallery of weird, sometimes unplayable instruments, some of them with arms and legs, others made of unusual materials, he'd made at the London College of Furniture!) No callow amateurs, these – Bath, Morgan, and the smitten Del had all been members of Conkers, who'd had an actual recording deal (albeit a dodgy one) with Cube Records.

Their uninspiring name aside, they had in mind from the very beginning such enhancements as dry ice and a light show – not to mention the flower Kate wore behind her ear in homage to Billie Holiday. The first night, at their local, The Rose Of Lee in Lewisham, there were more of them on the tiny stage than in the audience – at least until Jay and Dr. Bush materialised just before last orders. The next week, though, the audience numbered a dozen. And after that, the place was heaving.

Having outgrown Lewisham, they headed for the bright lights of

Putney, there, injudiciously, to perform on the eve of an England-Scotland football match. It was absolute chaos, as the besotted laddies from the highlands flocked on stage in droves, great tartan armies of them, waving their flags, embracing the musicians, bellowing their allegiance to the glens.

★   ★   ★

On the way home from the Goose & Syringe, I asked the minicab driver to stop at an off-licence, and to go in and buy a case of Stella Artois and a couple of cans of Pringles, for me, and a bottle of Courvoisier, which I'd send to Kate. He studied me at some length in the rear-view mirror before asking why I didn't do it myself. Because, I explained, I'd had quite enough trouble getting into the cab in the first place. "Not that I saw, gov," he sighed. One meets a cab driver who isn't a clever dick these days about as often as one receives a postcard from Princess Diana. Mentioning that there was an extra five quid in it for him did the trick.

I should have rung one of the others from OA. I did no such thing. By the time I'd got through the Stella and Pringles, through Kate's *The Sensual World* album and half of *The Red Shoes*, I was very drunk, and no longer fit to listen to Kate's music. It was nearly half-eleven. I turned on the TV. The news had a report about a boy in Exeter who'd hanged himself rather than face another day of being bullied at school. His parents were holding onto one another for dear life, barely able to speak through their sobbing. How, I wondered, were they going to get to sleep? Indeed, how were they going to get to sleep ever again? I wept along with them for a minute, but then it was on to the introduction of Victoria Beckham's new line of hip hop–inspired fashion. I marvelled at the ugliness and stupidity of the world we live in, and phoned Nicola.

Her fastidious little stepdad Cyril answered. "No," I said because I was too pissed to care what he thought of me. "I haven't got a fag."

"Well, who is it?" I heard the mountain of flesh demand from across the room.

"Nicola's new boyfriend," he said, failing to get his hand over the receiver. I couldn't help but be flattered.

The mountain of flesh began a tirade about how poorly bred I was showing myself to be, ringing so late. But a few seconds into it, I began demanding that Cyril hand the phone over to her.

"You don't want to do that, mate," he whispered. "Believe me, you don't."

"Do what?" the mountain of flesh demanded from across the room. "Give me the phone."

"Don't tell me what I do or don't want," I shouted at Cyril. Whereupon he put the phone down on me.

It occurred to me that I'd read somewhere about La Beckham being fat and lonely as a child. It made me slightly more patient with her hip hop-influenced fashions. It occurred to me as well that I had Nicola's mobile number, that all of us overeaters had, at least in theory, given one another complete contact details, though I'd given the loathsome Hermione made-up numbers. If ever she needed me to keep her from a fatal orgy of overeating, she would be in very deep water indeed.

Nicola answered. "Are you having a good time, you slag?" I demanded.

I'd fully expected her to break the connection instantly, and to flush with blood in that way she had. I couldn't be sure about the second part, but I couldn't have been more wrong about the first. "Probably not as good as I'd be having if you hadn't buggered off." She'd obviously had a couple of her own.

"Who's that?" someone demanded yobbishly.

"What's your name again, darling?" I heard her ask the guy.

"Says his name's Tarquin," she came back on the line to inform me. "The bloke who was trying to chat me up when you disappeared. He's lied about other things, so why not about his name as well?"

"What are you on about?" Tarquin, who'd had many more than a couple, demanded. "You've heard no porkies from me, darling, not a single one."

How I wished I wasn't full of Stella, and able to make sense of what was going on. I had to leave it to her to correctly interpret my silence as the child of my confusion.

"I fancy a bloke who's willing to fight for me," she explained, "not one who turns tail and pisses off home at the first challenge. It's biological, isn't it? Something deep inside, some primal urge, wants me to mate with the male most likely to defend our young."

"I'll give you something deep inside," Tarquin snickered in the background. And then the line went dead.

I've always found being hung up on extremely sexy, and this time was no exception. I wanted her so much I could almost have pictured masturbating. I refuse to masturbate anywhere but in the toilet, though, and either Mr. Chumaraswamy or Mr. Halibut was in it.

5

An Odd Choice
For A New Vegetarian

SOME months before, a junior NHS doctor of around 22 had pre-scribed an antidepressant called Cypramil for me, probably because she hadn't been practising long enough to have heard of any others. I'd always thought of a doctor as a kindly, twinkly-eyed older man (I am the product of a sexist culture) with one of those things attached to his head to make it easier to look at patients' throats. It had been lavishly unnerving to be asked if I'd "experienced suicidal ideation" by a girl who wouldn't have looked out of place in a pop group geared to 14-year-olds.

The Cypramil she prescribed made me feel neutered. For the three weeks I forced myself to keep taking it, even though I found myself yearning for a nap around a dozen times a day, it didn't even occur to me to masturbate. It hadn't the slightest effect on my despair. I packed in taking them with nearly half left.

Still, after sleeping forever the next morning and missing breakfast, I wondered if I should seek psychopharmacological solace before decid-ing instead just to turn on the TV. Trina, all lips and smugness, was interviewing the parents of school bullies. I imagined that her produc-ers were probably elated by the coincidence of the programme being broadcast virtually simultaneously with the suicide of the boy in Exeter. I was feeling pretty cynical.

The parents, nearly all working class, were unrepentant. One of them clearly spoke for the rest, judging from the enthusiastic nodding of all their heads, when he pointed out that, insofar as his sons' behav-iour at school was concerned, he wasn't his brother's keeper. I'd have been lying if I claimed that failed to amuse me. He'd tried, this emphatic labourer, to teach Graham and Ian to be good blokes, but if they forgot what he'd taught them when they got to school, how could he or the missus be held accountable? What more could a parent do, innit?

In that skilful way of hers, Trina brought to light that this particular parent generally thought the most effective way of ensuring his sons' being good blokes was walloping them when they were otherwise. "Hear! Hear!" a couple of the other parents agreed. When a member of the studio audience asked, in a middle-class accent that made the wallop-prone labourer sneer from the first syllable, if the dad saw any connection between him walloping his smaller, weaker sons and his sons walloping their smaller, weaker classmates, one of the other working-class parents answered for him: "Bollocks!" If the occasional wallop had been good enough for them, it was good enough for their kids as well, innit? "You coddle a brat," one of the mums observed, "all you get is a bigger brat."

Were they sorry when they heard of how their kids tyrannised their classmates? Well, some were and some weren't. The weres wondered if maybe they hadn't been guilty of too much coddling of their own. The weren'ts thought it was the job of the parents of the bullied to teach their children how to stick up for themselves. "You don't get the respect in this world that you deserve," one of the working-class dads, heretofore silent, suggested. "You get the respect you bloody well demand." I, who'd never dared demand any, and received exactly as much as I'd demanded, was surprised to find myself agreeing.

A few of the working-class kids were brought out, blinking in con-fusion at the audience's applause. If anything, their accents were even rougher than their parents'. The first to whom Trina tried to speak would hardly let her begin. "Who said I done anything to anybody?" he demanded pre-emptively, smirking defiantly. "If somebody at my school has a problem with me, let 'em tell me about it to my face, innit?"

"Since when," one of the working-class dads wondered enthusiasti-cally, "does somebody what's meant to have committed a crime not get to face his what's-it, his accuser?"

Trina sighed in that world-weary way she has. "In some cases, we have CCTV footage of your kids – not yours specifically, Dave, but yours in general – taking classmates' money, or intimidating them physically."

"Bloody Big Brother we're turning into, innit?" Dave snarled. "How about a person's right to privacy?" All of his fellow parents, all of the kids, and about a third of the studio audience erupted in applause. I wanted to cry.

I went to the toilet. It was still occupied. I'd got breathless walking all the way from my room, and didn't want to have to walk all the way back. I sat down on the stairs to the third floor and tried to be as quiet as I could. I can't bear to have anyone within hearing distance when I'm using the toilet. I learned from my mother that one should be deeply ashamed of the need to eliminate. I kept as still as possible in case whoever was in there had been similarly poisoned.

When the door finally opened, I was surprised to see Cathy, the youngest of Mrs. Cavanaugh's three children, emerge. I'd met her briefly months before, when I first moved in, and found her very hard work, as who isn't at 15? She seemed to have lost a great deal of weight. She'd been slim to start with.

"All right, Cathy?"

"Yeah. OK." Had I found it that much of an imposition to make eye contact when I was her age? I could hardly believe she didn't remember me. It wasn't as though her mum was boarding others of my proportions. Get two of us on the same side of the house and it was apt to tip over! I reminded her of my name and asked what she was doing home in October. My understanding was that she was away at school.

"Having a bit of a break," she said, not quite managing a smile, clearly wishing I'd let her go. I obliged.

I returned to my room, found a couple of gifts in the Littlewood catalogue for Kate, thought about bullying, and was ashamed to remember that I hadn't always been the bullied. For a long stretch there between 11 and 13, I'd done more than my own share of bullying.

There was something just a bit off about a girl in my elementary school class called Mary Priscilla Enser. She had sharp features and frizzy hair and, at least where her classmates were concerned, a weird middle name. (Girls were meant to be called Susan or Nancy or Cathy or Patty or Bonnie or even Melody. It wasn't as though her parents hadn't had miles of leeway.) There was one and only one workable response to taunting at my school, and probably at every other school in human history – to punch the taunter in the nose hard enough to make it bleed, or, if you were a girl, to ridicule the taunter far more hurtfully than he or she had taunted you. Mary Priscilla Enser only looked sort of confused. Her eyes asked, "When I've never so much as spoken to you, why are you trying to hurt me?"

Naturally, the more she didn't fight back, the more cruelly she got taunted, to the point at which she became the class scapegoat by a wide margin. (I never had to endure half of what she had to, though of course it didn't seem so at the time.) As children of later generations would call one another dorks or nerds, we called one another priscillas. We accused her, in the time-honoured American tradition dating back to the Salem of the 1600s, of being a witch. We made her day at school a living nightmare.

And guess who was always right there in the forefront, trying to win his classmates' esteem by taunting Mary Priscilla Enser more imaginatively and implacably than all the others? I, who knew from the inside how much it hurt to be shunned and ridiculed. I, who should have been more empathic than anyone.

I have my excuses, my patently inadequate excuses. Who could blame me for trying to encourage my classmates to give someone else a hard time for a change? And who could help me for despising her, in view of how vividly her passivity reminded me of my own?

I have somewhere the little autograph book that each pupil at my elementary school was given at the end of his or her sixth grade term, just before going on to the unimaginable horror that was junior high school. Inside the first page is a group portrait of my class. In the margins, in my precociously gorgeous 12-year-old's penmanship, I have written the names of all my classmates. In one case, though, I wrote not a name, but an epithet. Witch.

I believe, at my age, that it's the exception, rather than the rule, for people to get what's coming to them. Arrogant wankers with no perceptible talent, but fantastic luck, make fortunes early in their thirties, and then spend the rest of their lives imagining themselves clever and talented, being deferred to as though they are indeed clever and talented by people who want some of their money. Conversely, noble, kind, hardworking, genuinely gifted people live lives of almost unendurable frustration, or even lose their children in freakish accidents.

But in the case of Mary Priscilla Enser, I got exactly what was coming to me, in the second semester of my fifth-grade year. There was an unexpected epidemic of decency, gentleness, and sense of fair play in my class just before we were to elect a new president and vice president, and both Mary Priscilla and I were nominated. I was beside myself with joy. How, in her wildest dreams, could Witch get even a single vote?

I came in a distant second.

★ ★ ★

When at last EMI deemed Kate ready to record, Andrew Powell, apparently believing The KT Bush Band fine for pub gigs, but not up to the task of recording (save for Paddy's appearance on one track), introduced her to the musicians he'd recruited to be her backing band – drummer Stuart Elliot and keyboardist Duncan MacKay from Cockney Rebel, and guitarist Ian Bairnson and bassist David Paton from Pilot. They were embarrassed by the subject matter of some of the songs she played for them – by the incest in 'The Kick Inside', for instance, and by the unusually candid expression of female lust that was 'L'Amour Looks Something Like You' – but far less embarrassed than gob-smacked by how good both she and her songs were. If they'd had any thoughts of patronising her, of playing the seasoned studio hotshots to her 19-year-old naïf, there was no trace of them left by the end of the first session. And it turned out that she wasn't only a terrific songwriter and singer, but also quite happy to make everyone else tea, or dash out for sarnies.

Seven weeks later, the album was finished. EMI scheduled its release for November and sent out advance copies to DJs. Listeners to Tony Myatt's Capital Radio *Late Show* thought Kate's music really . . . weird, and God knows it was. However weird, though, no one seemed content to hear it only once.

Kate posed for Gered Mankowitz, best known for his mid-Sixties photos of The Rolling Stones. Such was her energy that he described himself as feeling, at shoot's end, "as limp as a rag". Few heterosexual males would feel similarly when they saw the work they'd done together.

But stop the presses! Kate decided she had a better idea for a cover than EMI's art department, that she wanted a rendering illustrating the song 'Kite' on the cover instead of Mankowitz's extremely soft porn, and the album's release had to be postponed until after Christmas. Then she was further mortified to learn that EMI intended to release 'James And The Cold Gun' as the first single. Bob Mercer, who wasn't at all sure there were *any* hit singles on the album (on first exposure to which other EMI employees had been observed looking queasy with appre-hension), told her pointedly that he knew how to do his job, and she burst into tears of frustration. Whereupon, depending on which legend you choose to subscribe to, one of two things happened. Either Mercer told her he'd make her own choice, 'Wuthering', the first single, even though the bloody cleaners who hoovered his office floor at night could have told you it hadn't a prayer, and she'd see what a foolish, wilful girl she was being. Or his colleague Terry Walker happened to be sauntering past, ducked in to say hello, and said something about 'Wuthering' being the obvious first single.

He and Kate were right, Mercer and the bloody office cleaner dead wrong. In terms of songwriting craft, it was rather a mess, with lyrics and melody so badly mismatched that poor Kate had here to accent the wrong syllables of words ("Cathy", most notably), there to add multiple syllables (to "cold" and "window"), and Bairnson's guitar solo during the coda, unable to decide where it wanted to go, wound up not going much of anywhere. *But who cared?* The audacity of Kate's vocal was simply breathtaking. Had anyone ever sung so high, or so zanily? And the arrangement! When Andrew Powell hits that note on his bass guitar in the bar before the chorus kicked in, you feel as though your lungs might burst. Countless great records have done that, created unendurable tension at the end of verses, and then relieved it with the refrain, but few had done it better.

All in all, the record was thrilling, hilarious, irresistible, inevitable, glorious, a breath of exhilaratingly fresh air! Twenty-five years after the fact, listening to it still gives one chills. To compare The Beatles' first single, 'Love Me Do', to it, or The Rolling Stones' 'Come On', for that matter, is to make yourself snicker.

Some sussless cow condemned it in *Record Mirror*, but two weeks later it was in the charts at number 42, and on top of them by the end of the first week in March. Thanks in part to the poster EMI had caused to be displayed on the front of London buses (Kate's right nipple suggested it might have been a bit nippy in Mankowitz's studio), the album was flying out of the shops.

And Kate's life would never be the same. "I didn't think it would be like this," she would admit years later. "All I wanted was to make an album. I'd been writing songs since I was little, and just wanted to see them on an album. That was my purpose in life – to just look at the grooves and think, 'I did that.'" Suddenly, she had absolutely no time for herself, not to commune with friends, not to read or watch TV, not even to have her bath when she was accustomed to having it. She was talking non-stop to the press now, appearing on television – on ITV's *Magpie* children's show, on the current affairs programme *Today*, on BBC's *Saturday Night At The Mill*, feeling eaten alive by the ravenous beast that is instant celebrity. When she appeared at the HMV shop in London's Oxford Street, she had to stand on a table to address the unexpectedly (terrifyingly!) huge crowd that had turned out to gawk at her.

The Brits imagine themselves to love their irony, and here was some Grade A. In being compelled to submit to endless interviews, she was being taken away from exactly that which had made her potentially interesting to interviewers in the first place. But she came from a loving home, and was a trouper, and dutifully came up with tasty morsels aplenty for her interrogators from the press, pointing out that, while Emily Brontë was racked with consumption during the seven years she worked on *Wuthering Heights* – The Novel, she, Kate, had had a frightful cold while composing 'Wuthering Heights' – The Pop Song.

They loved it. They loved too to hear that she'd not actually read *Wuthering Heights*, and had only ever seen the last few minutes of the 1938 film with Merle Oberon playing Cathy to Sir Larry's Heathcliff because it had looked . . . corny! Scrumptious sacrilege: good for circulation! She'd smirk conspiratorially, lower her voice, and admit she was grateful that the tabloids didn't seem to read lyric sheets. If Mrs. Whitehouse were to get wind of what her album's title track was about (incest and suicide), wouldn't there be hell to pay?

The 'Wuthering' video clip, in which Kate, clearly someone who'd just taken a lot of dance classes, unabashedly under the influence of Lindsey Kemp, looked defiantly ridiculous, inspired naff comedians and impressionists like Bobby Davro and Faith Brown to swoon with delight. Grist for their mills! (Kate, a jolly good sport, was nonetheless said to have written Brown a long letter of commendation.) Had any new artist ever had One Hit Wonder branded more distinctly on her forehead?

6

The Worst Sorbet
You've Ever Tasted

I FOUND myself aching to talk to Nicola, aching for her reassurance that she hadn't gone home with Tarquin from the pub, and aching only slightly less, or maybe a little more, to hear that she had indeed gone home with him. The more unattainable she seemed, the more I would want to attain her.

I thought for a moment that someone had tapped on my door, but that wasn't possible, as no one ever tapped on my door. When she came in twice a week to hoover, Mrs. Cavanaugh knocked quite forthrightly. I didn't get up. And then I did. It had been Cathy, now three-quarters of the way back down the hall. I called after her twice. She heard me the second time. It took her a moment to decide it was worth the trouble coming back down the hall.

She needed to talk to someone. I was the only person in the house. The other boarders had apparently gone out, and her mum was on the first of her thrice-weekly grocery-buying expeditions.

She sat down tentatively and said, "I've got an eating disorder, you know. Got diagnosed a couple of months ago, didn't I?"

It was awful, shocking news, of course. I didn't know what to say.

"The doctor gave me this nutrient mush I'm meant to eat. It couldn't be more revolting. The only way I can get it down – and I eat maybe a fifth of what I'm meant to – is to freeze it. It's like the worst sorbet you've ever tasted, but not as bad as at room temperature."

"Oh, Cathy," I finally managed, "it makes me so sad to hear that."

"There was a stretch a couple of weeks ago where I was actually blind for about a day and a half. Really terrifying, that." I was horrified to realise that she was actually proud of it. "I reckon my being fat is why it's OK for me to be in your room like this. I'd never have to worry about your trying to touch me inappropriately."

I felt as though I'd fallen through the looking glass. It was I who was fat, she who was alarmingly skeletal. It hadn't occurred to me that anyone in his wildest dreams could have imagined either of us having the faintest erotic attraction to the other. The thought made me shudder.

"You're as far from fat as it's possible to be, Cathy."

"Well, that's what the disease is all about. When I look in the mirror, I see something even more obscenely obese than your new girlfriend." I gaped at her in confusion. "My mate Jennifer's sister works at the pub where you went last night," she explained. "Word gets round."

I couldn't decide whether I was more irate about my privacy being invaded or flattered that someone had bothered to invade it. I decided on the latter, but had to pay lip service to the former. "Spying on me, were you, Cathy?"

She shrugged. I realised it was her breath I'd been smelling, from half the width of the room away. "I know it's pathetic, but I've fancied you from the day Mum took you in. I know nothing could ever come of it."

"Cathy, Jesus. I'm old enough to be your granddad, if I'd started really young and had a kid who started really young as well."

"You're old enough to be Fatso's granddad too, at least biologically." She smoothed the duvet beneath her. She was hardly heavy enough to wrinkle it. "But I reckon you fancy her because she's not as fat as me."

"What on earth would a pretty young thing like you want with someone like me?" I finally managed, mortified even to be posing the question.

"I've seen your Marcel Flynn adverts. You were well fit in those days. You must know you were."

Well, I did and I didn't. My great gorgeousness seemed to come over me very quickly. One day I was Leslie Herskovits, childhood bully magnet, wallflower, non-climber of The Pole. The next I was someone else entirely, judging from the way women responded to me. I'd get in a lift with three women, and they'd all go silent. They'd gape at me. They'd giggle. Invariably, one of the three would play the predator, would show off for her mates by asking if I'd fancy a drink some time. I'd walk into stylish singles bars (my loneliness engendered desperation) and women would lose their places in their conversations with the poor devils they'd been letting chat them up, suck in their tummies, stick out their chests, and pout at me. It was exhilarating, and deeply embarrassing.

Kate would have understood. One week she's an unknown little doctor's daughter from the suburbs with an absurd collection of O-levels, the next a fabulous superstar whom everyone's putting on the covers of magazines and Bobby Davro and Faith Brown are imitating on the telly and people are gaping at unashamedly in the street, and buses are being delayed because lads are standing in front of them gawking lasciviously at the outline of her erect nipple.

"But that was longer ago than you've been alive," I said. "Lots longer."

"In a weird way, it doesn't matter, though. I look at you now and I see you in your Marcel Flynn pants, looking fitter than any other bloke I've ever laid eyes on. Here. Suppose I survive my anorexia. What are the chances of my meeting a bloke who's ever been or ever will be as fit as you were? Almost nil, I'd reckon." She sighed deeply. It didn't smell very nice.

"It's like muscle memory or something. You'll always have that inside you, the memory of what it was like to be that incredible-looking. And that gives you something that no bloke I'd ever go out with will ever have. It's just like what happens with women. You see these old film stars, these has-been sexpots, with fantastic younger blokes. It isn't just their money that attracts the blokes. In a lot of cases, I'd bet the women aren't even that rich anymore. I mean, it isn't as though there are lots of roles for faded female sexpots, are there? Their famous big tits would probably be down to their waists if they weren't full of silicone. And most of them have that unnerving permanently startled look people get after their second facelift. What attracts the blokes is the knowledge that there was a time when millions of other blokes had their girlfriends' photos on their bedroom walls."

I was mortified to realise I was indeed coming to find her attractive – for her precocious intelligence, for the confidence with which she expressed it. I was beginning to sweat.

"Honestly, Cathy, what interest could someone like you have in a big tub of lard like me?"

What a very odd look she gave me. I had to look away. When I looked back, I was aghast to see tears welled in the corners of her eyes.

"You're taking the piss, aren't you?" she accused, getting to her feet. "Well, why shouldn't you? Everybody at my school did. I used to think it was only the fatties who got picked on. I found out otherwise the hard way, didn't I?"

For a moment, it appeared as though she might collapse where she stood. I wanted to hold her to me, but I didn't think I ought to after what she'd revealed. I thought for a fraction of a second of Michael

Jackson, and how cruelly he's been vilified for inviting teenage boys to share his bed, and about how, if his feelings for those boys were like mine for Cathy, the world's outrage really would be quite incomprehensible to him. For which, of course, he'd be vilified all the more.

There's nowhere to hide in this world, is there, even if you're fabulously rich.

She sat down again, standing apparently having required too much effort. She stared at a spot on the duvet. "Maybe they think their jokes about being slim didn't hurt as much as the jokes they made about the fat girls. Who can understand their logic?

" 'Don't turn sideways, Cathy. No one'll be able to see you.'

" 'Would somebody please chuck that used toothpick in the rubbish bin?'

" 'Don't swallow a meatball, Cathy. Everybody'll think you're in the family way.'

"Fucking hilarious, all of them, except if you're on the receiving end. And especially if you look at yourself in the mirror and can't imagine what they're on about."

I was horrified to realise how well I'd come to know that very feeling lately. And more horrified by the suddenness with which her mood changed. "Don't flatter yourself, mate," she said, seeming on the verge of trying once more to rise. "I was only interested in your dosh. I reckoned if I got over my disease, I had two choices. I could go on to university, even though I can't bear school, and get some sort of qualification to help me get some sort of job I wake up every morning dreading going to, or I could marry an older bloke with money I'll inherit when he dies. That way I'd probably only have to suffer a few years. With the job, I might have to suffer the rest of my bloody life."

Kilogram for kilogram, it occurred to me, she must be the most cynical girl on the face of the planet. Or maybe she was trying to hurt me for having hurt her, even though hurting her had been the farthest thing from my mind. "Just out of interest," I wondered, "what leads you to imagine I've got dosh?"

"There was an article in *Marie Claire* about the top supermodels getting royalties. It said it was actually blokes who started getting them first. Big surprise. As though, in this culture, anyone would have thought to have cut a woman in first."

I couldn't help but laugh, albeit without mirth. "And when do you suppose this began, Cathy?"

"I don't think it said."

"Probably within the past ten years, I would think, and more likely within the past five. In any event, I can assure you I've never got royalties, not for anything, including the Marcel Flynn campaigns."

She glowered at me. "Then what are you living on? You don't seem to have a job."

"As though that's any of your business? Well, I'll tell you anyway. My mum died." I waited for her to tell me she was sorry to hear that. She was content to keep glowering. "She had Alzheimer's Disease the last nine years of her life, and it was expensive to keep her, but there was still a bit left when she finally died. My sister and I each took half."

"Blimey. Don't you feel sort of . . . ashamed about that?"

"Ashamed? Why?"

"To be living off money your mum left. Instead of working."

"What sort of job do you suppose someone my size could get?" I asked, not even trying to keep the irritation out of my voice. I didn't feel obligated to mention that, until recently, I'd also made a few hundred quid a month as a George Clooney lookalike, turning up at Leicester Square premieres and launch parties in formal wear or Italian sportswear the agency provided and letting people infer what they chose to infer. If the agency that kept hiring me hadn't noticed that I probably outweighed George by something like 4-1, it hadn't been my responsibility to point it out to them.

For a split second, as she abandoned any thought of my taking the mickey, Cathy, the child with her mum in her eyes, couldn't have looked more exactly like her mum. You'd have sworn she'd spent endless hours in front of a mirror watching a videotape of Mrs. Cavanaugh the day before when I spoke of needing the fire brigade and a crane to leave the house. Her voice became very gentle. "Yes, I suppose that bears thinking about."

In fact, I'd originally intended to tell my sister to take both halves. In view of how much I'd grown to hate her, it hardly seemed fitting that I should take any of my mother's money. Or if I did take it, I could put it into a trust fund for my daughter Babooshka. But then – and this was so me – I devised a way that I could indeed take it: by thinking of it as reparations. Hadn't I suffered incalculably for my toxic upbringing, and hadn't my mother been responsible for most of that toxicity?

All of which was much more than Cathy needed to know, or would be able to make sense of. No, I was lying to myself again. It was pretty obvious she'd be able to make sense of nearly anything the world threw at her. Except her own predicament.

★   ★   ★

With 'Wuthering' continuing to do very brisk business, Kate went on *Top Of The Pops* without being given adequate time to prepare, in a sheer black top, red trousers, and black stilettos that didn't exactly say Cathy (Earnshaw, the character to whom the song gives voice). Shown a playback of her performance, she famously declared that it was like watching herself die. *Could they not see that, if she were going to do things properly, she would need time?*

Well, they could, but could she, reciprocally, not understand that it was absolutely imperative that she make hay while the sun shone? Europe loved her song about Cathy and Heathcliff, and EMI jetted her one frantic morning to Verona, Italy, to lip-synch it for them. She walked out on stage. Through the photographers' flashes, she saw a couple of hundred people, and who could have blamed her for mistaking it for her audience? But then the stage revolved 180 degrees, and there she was in a huge circular stadium with more people than she'd ever seen in any one place – and she'd been in Who and Bowie audiences – gaping at her adoringly. You're not in Kansas anymore, gal, nor in The Rose Of Lee in Lewisham. She managed to mime her song, bowed, and, before she knew it, was back at Heathrow. It was all like some mad fairy tale!

The unmistakable one hit wonder's album would eventually go as high as number three, and be certified double platinum. Even America would notice. "The chorus of 'Feel It' is more erotic," the once-proud *Crawdaddy* lied, "than any of . . . Donna Summers' pathetic panting."

I refuse even to speculate why whale sounds bracketed the opening track, 'Moving', which served notice that, to get to whatever she was trying to express, we were going to have to learn not to be distracted by the fervent affectedness of her singing. And once having done so, good luck, as the lyrics, often glaringly horrid ("The stars that climb from her bowels/ Those stars make towers on vowels"), were almost always incoherent. (You rarely know who's speaking in a Katesong, or to whom, or for how long. Full lyrics have been included with all of her albums, but it's no use knowing what the words are if you don't know out of which characters' mouths they're meant to be coming, innit?)

All that said, the melodies of several choruses – 'Strange Phenomena' and the West Indian-inflected 'Kite' – were so swoon-inducingly pretty that you could forgive her anything.

It's troubling to imagine why she scrupulously avoided sounding nine years old only in 'The Man With The Child In His Eyes'. Glaringly badly written in places, it won you over in the end with the inexpressible beauty of Kate's singing. Why, oh, why, did she not sing like this more often?

The chorus of the coy, delightful 'Them Heavy People', played in large part as a sort of West End stage reggae, wasn't only melodic, but used highly unusual intervals without appearing to be trying too hard – a very good trick indeed. But A. Powell should have forbidden her to sing the title song in that key, as you quickly lost sight of everything but how stratospherically high she'd got. Smacked of exhibitionism.

Elsewhere, as in 'Feel It', 'L'Amour Looks Something Like You' and 'Room For The Life', in which poor Ian Bairnson was allowed a very, very brief Brian May impression, her melodic gifts were apparently down in Oxford Street getting sarnies.

In 'Oh To Be In Love', the earliest of her songs (along with 'Wuthering', of course) to look as cynically at romantic love as anyone had looked at it since Felice and Bordeleuax Bryant wrote 'Love Hurts' for the Everly Brothers, she introduced her trademark trick of seeming to be taking the piss out of herself when she dropped for a moment into her lower register. The word "baby", as a term of address, had never been sung less convincingly (or was it more mockingly?) in Western pop than in 'James And The Cold Gun', which, had it been a per-formance on the West End stage, would rightly have been vilified as merciless scenery-chewing.

Listening to the album in the 21st century, it's nearly impossible not to be reminded by 'The Saxophone Song' of Lisa Simpson's far superior 'Sax Man'. And the naff close-miked drums throughout made very clear that if Hugh Padgham hadn't come along with gated reverb and ambient miking a few years hence, someone else would surely have had to.

★ ★ ★

I've tried to atone for my sins against poor Mary Priscilla Enser, but have never gone quite so far as my best friend from my modelling days, who, at any party, would seek out the most ill-at-ease looking person on the premises and devote the balance of the evening to making him or her feel pretty and witty and charming. While recognising that the beneficiaries of his altruistic displays were undoubtedly hugely grateful for them, I thought there was something distasteful (I would, wouldn't I?) about how he was using them as a medium for the expression of his own wonderfulness. *I have no real interest in you, and would much prefer to spend my time trying to pull the prettiest girl here, but behold my selflessness.*

My atonement took the form of urging Babooshka (had their been even the tiniest chance that I would come, on the spur of the moment one day, to call her by another nickname?), when she was herself in the fourth and fifth grades, to do far better than I'd done. If you stick up for people who are being picked on, I told her, not only are they going to love you for it, but those doing the picking will as well, though it might take them a while to admit it. Even kids, with their rapacious sadism, respect those who go against the flow. The easiest thing in the world (I knew from experience!) is to be one of a mob tormenting somebody. But even those doing the tormenting will recognise your courage.

It didn't work, largely, to hear her tell it, because she was often the one being ganged up on. Oh, how I loved hearing that.

Hoping to build up some credit for her, I volunteered to help tutor kids in her class, and offered after-school acting lessons. I spent a lot of time at her school. The clothes and slang and haircuts were a bit different from my own, 37 years earlier, but the sadism was exactly the same. The two most passive – and thus most eagerly tormented – boys in her class were, respectively, its brightest and most imaginative on the one hand, and its handsomest on the other. Their brightness and gorgeous-ness did them no good whatsoever. If it wasn't the long-eyelashed little hip hop fashionplate who spent most of his time in class drawing pic-tures of motorcycles, it was the severely damaged son of an abusive alcoholic biker (so I was told) who was forever humiliating them in front of their classmates.

The teacher allowed me to address the class on the subject of courage. (Yes, yes, I know. Like getting an albino to address it on the joys of tanning.) I pointed out to them that it took lots more courage to stick up for someone on whom lots of others were picking than to join the latter group. They all looked at me soulfully, all except Jack the little hip hop fashionplate and Karl Biker's-Boy, the compulsive actor-out.

I formed a club, The Kindness Club, and offered membership to everyone in class who'd be brave enough to stick up for somebody being tormented by lots of others. I unveiled the certificate of member-ship I'd designed. They all thought both the idea and the certificate way cool. When even Jack openly aspired to membership, I was giddy with delight.

The next week, Jack demanded induction on the basis of having stopped a fistfight on the playground. His teacher took me aside and informed me that, while Jack had indeed stopped it, he'd also started it, apparently so he could stop it. And he'd taken his time about it. Karl continued not to want to know, and to spend every available moment assaulting Will, the handsome boy.

The following Friday afternoon, when I arrived to collect her after school, I learned that my daughter had had an especially rough week. Jack had passed up no opportunity to tell her that he thought the Kindness Club really stupid. And when she didn't tell him to fuck off, but instead took exactly the route I'd have taken at her age, the passive one, he'd become ever more vicious.

There is nothing new under the sun.

7

Bathing For A Tart

I ACHED to ring Nicola, but knew I couldn't. What I had to do now was pretend I didn't want her. Or was it? Would she interpret my silence as indifference, as I hoped, or as resignation, which would have been fatal? I had an idea. I'd send her a text message saying I'd ring her as soon as I got home from Ibiza. Assuming she knew that Ibiza was where rich men went with their lovers, she'd be consumed by jealousy. We'd see how she enjoyed the taste of her own medicine.

Naturally, I wouldn't actually go to Ibiza, which sounded like my idea of Hell – a place where armies of drunken little Brits in their early twenties staggered around trying to shag, but more often succeeding only in vomiting on, one another, to the accompaniment of one of the sorts of music I hate most, that in which the bass drum, playing four to the bar, is actually very much louder than the vocalist. *Thud! Thud! Thud! Thud!*

Or maybe I would go. Wouldn't it do me a world of good being surrounded by physically perfect young specimens who'd drunk themselves into a state of candour as vicious as children's? If I dared to waddle among them, they would no doubt jeer so loudly as to be heard on the Spanish mainland. I would buy a local handicrafts gift for Kate. It was just what I needed.

I got on-line, and found the website of a company that, if I departed later that afternoon, would fly me back and forth to the island for hardly more than British Rail charged for a return ticket to Birmingham. At those prices, I felt confident that the plane would be full of randy eighteens-to-thirties who'd titter brazenly at the sight of me taking up the two seats I knew I'd require, and then, after they'd had a few drinks, jeer openly. I sent Nicola the terse text message I'd had in mind on the train to Gatwick. She didn't respond, and I dared to imagine her being too overcome by jealousy for the job.

There were a lot of kids on standby apparently. Once everyone had taken his assigned seat (or, in my case, pair of seats), the riff-raff were admitted to the plane. A large blond kid with tattoos enough for himself and three mates and a pierced eyebrow, a haircut like that which David Beckham had sported for approximately 48 hours in 2001, and the manner of a moron, stopped beside me and asked in perfect Mockney of the seat beside me, " 'Ere, is that one free?"

I told him it wasn't.

"Looks free to me, innit? Who's sitting in it, then?" I wouldn't have imagined him capable of satire, but there you are.

"Both seats are mine. For obvious reasons."

"What a wanker!" he marvelled, "just throwing your money away." He called across the plane to a similarly cretinous-looking mate, climbing over someone to an unoccupied seat he'd spotted. " 'Ere, Chris. Fancy this. Bloke's bought two seats, and there's only one of him!"

"Maybe he likes a bit of room to stretch out in?" the girl with a large nose just across the aisle from me offered.

My moron gaped at her forever. Then, as he determined that he probably wouldn't try to shag someone so nasally overendowed even at the end of a long night's drinking, his lip curled in disdain. "Who fucking asked you, you minger?"

An air hostess, sighing, arrived to escort him to a seat several rows forward. My moron glared back gloatingly at my defender as he followed her. It's been my observation that such people nearly always imagine themselves to be in a position to gloat. Afraid that my defender might try to chat with me, I buried myself in the Martin Amis paperback I'd bought at the airport. As usual, I didn't much enjoy it, even though there could be no denying his ability to write gorgeous, gorgeous English, and felt guilty about it. The failing was surely mine, rather than Martin's.

I got so fed up that I closed it, sighing, without even marking my place, and leaned over to look out of my window. There was nothing to see. I made the mistake of turning toward the aisle. She was waiting for me, the big-nosed girl, with an expression that said, *Please don't hurt me.* I pretended she hadn't really registered, that I was looking all over the plane. But I hadn't the heart for such heartlessness, and nodded at her in acknowledgement.

Her name was Indira. She was studying to become an orthodontist. "I reckon anybody who can straighten teeth will never starve in Britain." Her own teeth were exemplarily straight and white. I supposed that orthodontia students were able to have their teeth bleached at a significant discount. Her moustache was faint, but not so faint that you didn't notice it right after the remarkable nose, and even before the wonderful teeth. She addressed me as *sir*. She seemed to be travelling alone.

I could feel a Diane Geller situation coming up. Back in junior high school, when I commonly summoned the nerve to invite pretty girls to dance, I never actually spoke to them as I shoved them gracelessly across the dance floor. If anything, poor Diane Geller was as Semitic as the girls I fancied were blonde (often artificially, but that made it even better for me), as short and thick as they were tall and slender, as eager as they were aloof, as dowdy as they were tawdry. And here she came cutting in on the surfer girl beauty I'd been studiously ignoring while shoving her around the dance floor, tapping her on the shoulder to indicate that she wanted to dance with me.

Surely every eye on the premises was fixed now on me and Diane Geller, and every mind attached to the eyes thinking, *They suit each other.* Oh, the unbearable shame.

A better person than I – a decent person, a person not destined to become a corpulent grotesque later in life – would have seen the song out. But not Leslie Herskovits. Eight bars after losing his surfer girl, Leslie Herskovits abruptly let go of poor Diane Geller's hand, mumbled, "Excuse me," and ran for the gym, there to be picked last for an impromptu game of basketball. The memory of all of which made me absolutely ravenous, of course.

I imagined Indira's whole life. I imagined she'd never been asked out, much less made love to, and that she was on her way to Ibiza because she'd heard it was impossible not to get shagged there. It broke my heart, and it wasn't my problem. Even we self-loathing grotesques have our standards.

Well, I was going to do better by her than I'd done by poor Diane Geller. I was going to be forthright. My message would be cruel, but my tone kind.

"Listen, darling," I interrupted her. "There's something I need to say to you right now, before we even converse any more. Attraction is a strange, inexplicable phenomenon. Who can say for sure why one person finds another attractive? Is it something inborn, or something learned? I don't pretend to know. What I do know is that, although I find you personable and vivacious, and assume you're very intelligent as well, and even though I appreciate your trying to intervene on my behalf when that moron tried to take my second seat, I just don't think it very likely that I'll ever come to fancy you."

I'd actually done the right thing. It was exhilarating. And she was coping with it! All the fears we carry around within ourselves of others not being able to deal with our candour? Maybe most of them are ill-founded! The look on her face hadn't changed. There were no tears in her eyes.

"Oh, I don't think I could ever fancy you either," she said. "You're far too old for me, for a start. And I'm actually going on holiday with my boyfriend, Ranjana. He's our co-pilot, you see. I'm flying free."

We waited for our luggage together, Indira and I. When her bag came, and she left with it, the blond idiot with the pierced eyebrow and his mate Chris came over. I expected the worst, and got it. "We don't fancy yours much," they said, and then roared with laughter. Everyone seemed to be looking at us. For a long moment, I considered whirling round and seeing if my ripping the stud out of his forehead might make the blond idiot a little less generous with his opinions, but of course I didn't.

★   ★   ★

It occurred to me on the taxi ride to my hotel that, aside from the locals, I might be the only person on the island over 30, or anywhere near my size. It occurred to me I needn't have come to Ibiza to feel alienated, but then remembered I'd come so I could tell Nicola without lying that I'd done so. I had told more than three lifetimes' share of lies by the age of around 35, and was commonly caught out and humiliated. I tell the truth now not because I'm any more noble, but because I've come to realise you usually get caught anyway.

By the time I got up to my hotel, my clothing was sticking to my skin. The lobby was full of blazing red British young people in shorts and the agonised expressions of hangover sufferers, although in some cases it might well have been sexually transmitted infections making them so miserable. "I'll never raise another pint to my lips," a tall, skinny ginger-haired boyo moaned in the cadence of Cardiff. "And you can quote me."

I went out and found a tapas restaurant, where I ordered *aceitunas aliñadas, alcachofas a la vinagreta, canelon de atun, tostadas de pisto, tortilla española, patatas ali-oli, ternera asada, plato combinado, jamon iberico, salpicon de marisco, salmon ahumado, ensalada rusa, pimientos asados, patatas bravas, pincho de pollo, champiñones a la plancha, pincho de solomillo, queso de cabra, croquetas de pollo, calamares a la plancha, gambas al ajillo, pulpo a la plancha, patatas a la importancia, salmon a la pimienta, raxo adobado, mejillones a la marinera, chorizo y morcilla, almejas en salsa verde,* and *vieiras a la plancha.* I'd have ordered something else, but that's all they had on the menu, and only celebrities can order off the menu.

The *pulpo* and *chorizo* were so delicious I had a second portion of each, and then wasn't only unable to eat anything more, but probably in greater pain than the hungover kids in the hotel lobby. But of course I deserved to suffer, if not to be gaped at as a quartet of waiters were doing. "*Lo siento,*" one of them apologised. "But it is such pleasure for us to see a British person enjoying our cuisine. Most of your young compatriots come in wanting only chips and lager. It is like spitting in the face of the chef's mother. Sometimes we want to cut their hearts out and stew them until tender in the chef's special tomato sauce."

I suppose I looked aghast. The waiter laughed. "We would not serve such a dish to you, *señor*. We reserve this dish for those of your young compatriots who dare to order real Spanish cuisine." I didn't bother telling him I wasn't a Brit.

By the time I got back to my hotel, the hungover young people were beginning to perk up with the help of cold *cerveza*. A couple of them managed to get in the lift with me, and were kind enough not to remark on how little space I left them. I went to my room and had a fitful *siesta*. The melody of Mr. Acker Bilk's 'Stranger On The Shore' kept running through my mind. I wondered if it had been that to which Diane Geller and I were dancing when I abandoned her so cruelly. Teenagers in those days would occasionally be caught dead listening to music their parents liked, or even dancing to it. I made myself throw up and was able to sleep.

The street outside the hotel was already an Hieronymous Bosch painting come to life when I woke. Bare-breasted girls whose DNA doomed them to a premature capitulation to gravity, and who thus would have been well advised to keep their tops on, were being chatted up by slobbering boys who three or four pints earlier wouldn't have had the cheek to chat up any girl, even one with floppy tits. The more attractive boys and girls had found one another, as they always manage to, and had their tongues down one another's throats, though a few removed them occasionally to vomit. There were boys bellowing foot-ball songs, and other boys peeing in such numbers against the walls of nightclubs charging £40 cover, but which included one very watered down drink, that the bouncers didn't even try to stop them. There were couples shagging in the doorways of closed shops. There were drunken girls menstruating unashamedly like Marilyn Monroe in the street while crowds of boys made animal noises of encouragement. There were sunburn victims writhing in agony on the pavements, and friends trying to cool them off by pouring beer that had cost £6 a bottle on them. The sizzling sound of the cold beer against the inflamed skin was enough to make one vomit. It was in all ways every bit as awful as I'd expected, and slightly worse, and just what I deserved.

I wiped my mouth on the lank blond hair of a boy who reminded me of Chris from the aeroplane, and headed, as my genes compelled, for the same restaurant where I'd had lunch. I lived as a boy with my parents in Los Angeles, a very large city on the west coast of America. It is not known as a restaurant city in the same way that San Francisco is, but even then it had a few million residents, and thus a great, great many restaurants. And from the time I was around five until I left home at 19, my parents only ever ate at one, the Chatam on Westwood Blvd. in West Los Angeles. Never mind that it couldn't have been more mediocre. They'd gone there in 1951 or something, and neither felt overcharged nor been poisoned, so it was there that they went forever after, content with the very low level of pleasure they'd been taught in childhood was their due.

Kate Bush is known to have been a vegetarian from an early age, but thought to have taken to eating fish sometime after the release of *The Red Shoes*. She has, over the years, endorsed several organisations seeking to end barbaric treatment of animals, but has resisted the temptation to introduce her own line of frozen vegetarian ready-meals. I for one would fill my freezer with them without hesitation. But it, like *The Red Shoes'* follow-up, is apparently not to be.

Years after the Chatam restaurant went under, a victim of changing tastes, and was supplanted by a restaurant whose menu wasn't printed entirely in Olde English script to suggest its elegance, my parents' tendency to stick with the tried, true, and not very good got them in trouble when they decided to get a professional in to landscape their back yard. He was known to drink, and to disappear for weeks at a time while one's back yard remained uninhabitable, but he'd done the Andresens', across the road, and the Jendens', a few doors up from the Andresens'. According to my mother, he was the only landscape designer in the city. When she told me this, I went through my usual repertoire of gestures of disdainful incredulity. I suggested, in my familiar cuttingly sarcastic way (learned from the best – her!) that in a city whose population had grown to three and a half million, he quite possibly *wasn't* the only landscape designer. She got that weary, hurt look that I was to see more and more in her early seventies, when I realised with increasing clarity how she'd poisoned me as she became ever more abusive, and said, "Well, he did the Andresens' and the Jendens', and I didn't want to do a lot of looking around." Meaning that, as ever, she chose the devil she knew.

And got exactly what one might have predicted. The guy dug up their back yard, planted a few trees and some ground cover, and disappeared for the better part of a month, not returning my parents' ever-more-plaintive phone calls, in which, far from threatening to take him to court or something, they appealed to him, like children to an unyielding father, from a position of absolute weakness and supplication.

I was visiting them one Saturday afternoon when he and a couple of his illegal immigrant crew, whom he almost certainly paid far less than the minimum wage, actually materialised in the back yard, and hurried out to confront him. Very far from apologetic, he was openly defiant. Had he promised my parents that he would finish by such-and-such a date? No, he hadn't. Therefore, he wondered if they could stop leaving messages on his goddamn phone machine.

We stood there glaring at each other, and then I grabbed his ponytail with one hand and awarded him a smart uppercut to the chin with the other, sending him sprawling backwards. His jaw broken, he moaned for the Mexicans to help him, but for the minimum wage he was paying them, did he really expect them to take on a force of nature like me? I kicked him in the ribs, feeling a couple cave in. He whimpered for me to stop. I brought my foot down hard on his abdomen. There was no air left in him. I spat on him. I told him if he didn't show my parents the respect they deserved, I'd find him, wherever he tried to hide, and beat him so badly he'd hardly be recognisable as human.

I wish.

What I really did was tell him – not plaintively, but glaring right back at him – that I really hoped he'd be able to find a way to finish the work soon. And then I turned on my heel and walked back into the house.

Remembering all of which made my blood sugar level drop so precipitously that when I got to the restaurant, I frantically ordered everything I'd had for lunch, except the *almejas en salsa verde*, which I hadn't much liked the look of, and then a couple of *raciones* as well. I was the only non-local in the place. The waiters beamed at me almost adoringly enough to make up for my childhood. The food was delicious, but I hardly tasted it. What I tasted was the pain of having let my parents down, and having humiliated Diane Geller.

A quartet of young British idiots came in, loudly. They were led to a table and offered menus, on which they gave up quickly. "'Ere, Ramon," their spokesperson demanded slurredly, "can we just get some fucking chips and sausages? And I'm talking proper sausages, not bloody spicy wog ones. And make it quick, all right, mate? We want to have time for a proper dessert. We're having crumpet."

His three pals absolutely shrieked with amusement. Crumpet! Oh, what a sidesplitter!

They did the nearly impossible – ruined my appetite. I wasn't yet two-thirds of the way through my *chorizo*. My waiter looked broken-hearted.

I headed into the thick of the mayhem outside, and by the time I'd got 20 steps from the door had been handed 20 flyers telling me about the low booze prices and sex-starved nymphets awaiting me at various local bars and clubs. I'd have been handed many more if those handing them out hadn't abruptly turned away at the sight of me, repulsed by either my girth or my age. But the mini-skirted, knee-high-booted reps-gone-wrong who stood in the doorway of every bar and club in Sant Antoni couldn't have found me more attractive, waving at me like shipwreck victims at a rescue helicopter. I hadn't felt so popular since my Marcel Flynn days.

I hadn't come to Ibiza to feel popular.

Desperate times called for desperate measures. As I passed a bar called *Tu Madre La Puta*, I overheard a trio of bare-chested young Scots with Sir Alex Ferguson tattoos advising the girl in front of it that they'd come in only if she gave each of them a rim job. Without a moment's hesitation, she knelt on her pile of flyers before the least repulsive of the three, and reached for his zip.

As I rounded the corner into Del Progres, I was set upon by a mob of swarthy little Hawaiian-shirted men with shifty eyes and pencil moustaches, Iberian wide boys who addressed me as *jefe* and *amigo*, and one another as *puto*. "Lowest prices on es on the island, *jefe*," hissed one, apparently referring to ecstasy. "When my hashish is gone, *amigo*, it's gone," predicted another, "and at these prices, it's going to be gone soon." A third wondered, "Charlie, *jefe*?" I wasn't quite sure what he was asking, and so just gave him the curt smile I had developed back in London for vendors of *The Big Issue*. I hoped he hadn't mistaken me for a mate. If he had, wouldn't he wrongly accuse his mate of having given him the cold shoulder?

Out of the frying pan and into the fire. "Fake Louis Vuitton handbag for *la mujer, amigo*?" offered a little local with a gold incisor and a glass eye. "Can't tell it from the real thing. Guaranteed. She love you for it, *amigo*." I had the feeling that if I didn't at least appear to consider the offer, I might get knocked over the head.

Sifting through the guy's wares, I nearly fainted to discover that they included the *Earthrise* videotape from 1992, featuring not only Kate and Peter Gabriel singing 'Don't Give Up' in superimposition, rather than

hugging one another in front of a solar eclipse as in the far more familiar, far less collectible, version, but also Kate's brief appearance in *Spirit
Of The Forest*, along with other stars as diverse as Debbie Harry, Lenny
Kravitz (with whom she would at no point be linked romantically), and
LL Cool J. I'd been trying to get my hands on it for over a decade. The
guy wanted 50 euros, and was flabbergasted when I handed them over
without a trace of hesitation. He claimed he'd meant to say 75. I said 50
was all I'd pay, and that he should throw in a fake Louis Vuitton
handbag. He did, eagerly. I thought maybe Kate would enjoy having it.

I put the precious tape into my shoulder bag and turned into Del
Progres proper. Finding a place to step on which someone hadn't
vomited, or wasn't lying unconscious drooling out of the side of his
mouth, was no easy undertaking, and every couple of seconds a
drunken young reveller, stumbling over one of those already passed
out, hurtled by at an alarming rate. It was rather like walking across a
firing range.

A crowd of hooting drunken British youth had formed around a girl
with bare breasts, though mere bare breasts hardly seemed enough to
attract a crowd in this nightmarish place. Then I realised she must be
lactating, as she was squirting milk into her admirers' mouths. I shud-
dered with revulsion. A wobbly young lout with the emblem of
Blackburn Rovers tattooed on his forehead accosted me. "What's the
matter, mate? You a poof or summat?" But our confrontation was
short-lived, as he proceeded to lose consciousness and pitch face
forward into what I hoped was a pile of dog poop, but was probably
human. "This," another lout felt called upon to advise me, "is the most
fun I've ever had."

I spotted a *botega* window against which no one was throwing up or
peeing, and went to collect myself against it. A large group of
bare-chested buffoons suddenly began to swarm like excited honey
bees to my left. I drew closer to investigate. The strongest, best-looking
boys, those likely to protect their young with the greatest ferocity, had
pushed themselves to the centre of the swarm, and were flexing their
pectorals and lats and biceps, flashing their dazzling white smiles, frantically preening. Their fleshier, less gorgeous brothers had to be content with trying to suck in their guts, and saw that it wasn't Pamela
Anderson in their midst, or Holly Valance, or Danii Minogue, but a
small, dark-haired woman.

It was Indira from the plane, smiling shyly, looking mostly at the
ground between her feet, clearly embarrassed by the preening she'd
inspired, but clearly enjoying it too.

71

She noticed me and waved. I thought those who hoped to mate with her might tear me to pieces for it, but she managed to push her way through them to me. We were backed up together against the *botega*. Testosterone perfumed the humid night air. I knelt so she could shout into my ear. She had to shout to be heard over the braying and bellowing of the mob.

"Ibiza's jolly good fun, isn't it, sir?"

"If you enjoy this sort of thing," I said. "Where did they all come from?"

"Dunno," she said. "It's been like this since I stepped out of the hotel."

"But what about your fiancé, the co-pilot?"

The most overheated of her suitors had dropped his shorts and pants and was now pole dancing polelessly in front of her, stiffening while the others chanted, "Wood! Wood! Wood!" and trying to clap in time.

"He was knackered," Indira explained, "and fancied a nap. And what he doesn't know won't hurt him, will it?" In all the world there are few things more unnerving than an ugly woman attempting coquettishness.

A topless girl with enormous bovine breasts stared at me in what I mistook for horror for a long, tense moment, and then threw up on my trainers. "Why don't you fucking move then, Jimmy?" her severely sunburned mate demanded in the thickest Glaswegian accent I'd ever been able to understand.

Move was exactly what I did, as hurriedly as my girth would permit. By the time I turned into my hotel's street, I was drenched with sweat and gasping. The bar was still serving, but there was no one in it to serve. No, I was mistaken. There was a girl – no, a woman, definitely a woman – in her mid-thirties, almond brown from the sun, artificially blonde, hoop-earringed, and heading my way, cigarette in hand. "Buy a girl a G&T?" she asked in a Home Counties accent, revealing that she had more teeth than space for them.

"If you put out your fag," I said.

"Health fanatic?"

Not by a long chalk. I just can't abide the smell, or the stupidity. It says right on the pack Smoking Kills. I know there are those whose response to that is, "Well, something's going to at the end of the day, so why not enjoy yourself until it happens?" Such people apparently haven't watched anybody die of lung cancer, as I have (in a very compressed way, on television). And where's the pleasure in waking up in the morning feeling as though you are being stabbed in the chest?

"Allergic to the smoke," I said. It's easier. I'm not sure it's even possible to be allergic to cigarette smoke in the same way it is to be allergic to pollen or cats, for instance, but people usually don't question you. She shrugged and stubbed her cigarette out in an ashtray on another table.

She had smoker's breath, inevitably, but was pleasingly candid. She pretended to be interested in me, but one of the few things I've figured out for myself over the course of my adulthood is that nearly everyone is much happier talking about him or herself than hearing about me, and she was no exception. She'd first come to Ibiza nine years before, on holiday, at age 19. I reckoned it was the sun and cigarettes that made her look a lot older than she really was, or at least admitted to. The contrast of dark brown skin and pale blonde hair was striking from a distance, but up close, you could see she was already quite leathery. She'd enjoyed herself so much on her first visit that she signed on to become a rep for one of the many British companies that flew young people over, sheltered them, kept them drunk, and flew them home, all for a relative pittance. Her affection for the island was such that she didn't resign even after discovering that her unwritten job description included fellating various senior male staff when they flew over from Britain to ensure everything was running smoothly. She became the mistress of a club owner who she reckoned I must have met, as he'd long since lost the club and taken to peddling fake Louis Vuitton bags and charlie in Del Progres. At 24, she found herself too old to get another rep job, and turned in desperation to prostitution.

Did I fancy a shag?

I found her leathery skin and longing glances at the ashtray in which she'd stubbed out her cigarette distasteful, but fancied continuing our conversation a bit first. I could tell she thought I was winding her up. When she realised I wasn't, she got a little misty for a moment.

"It gets so lonely here sometimes, with nobody to talk to. The locals won't chat to me because of how I make my living, and the Brits are either too drunk to make sense or too hungover to want to. And I feel about 100 years older than most of them. Are you sure I can't finish my fag?"

It wasn't easy for a tart on Ibiza. The British boys had the British girls to shag, at no charge. The locals seemed to prefer 16-year-olds who looked 14. If I didn't change my mind, I was going to be her first trick in the past 10 days.

It was shameful, but I felt that gave me a bit of leverage. I asked if she'd tell me that her name, undisclosed to this point, was Nicola.

"Why not?" she shrugged. I asked if she'd be willing to ridicule me before the actual act, and there it got dicey. She asked why I'd fancy such a thing, and what she was meant to ridicule me about. I answered her first question first. "Isn't that obvious?"

She looked wary, which in turn made me worry that she might bolt at any second. "That you're a bit of an . . . older bloke?"

"Well, you can use that as well, but just look at me. My weight, Nicola! My weight!"

"Oh," she said, rather less decisively than I'd have hoped, "of course."

"I mean, aren't you worried that if we shag with me on top, I'll crush you to death?"

She looked at me for a long moment, and sipped her drink, took a deep breath, and said, "You're mad if you think I'm going to let somebody your size get on top of me, mate."

Wood!

As for the ridiculing part, I admitted I didn't know why the thought of her re-creating some of the most awful moments of my life – and I was getting an idea! – aroused me. It just did. Maybe there was something wrong with my DNA. God knows there was.

I told her I'd need 20 minutes to have a bath. She looked at me with something resembling fondness, and addressed me with it as well. "You don't need to bathe for a tart, darling, and at the end of the day, that's all I am."

I explained that, tart or no, I couldn't bear the thought of not smelling fresh with a woman. My mother had been sent home from grade school for her woeful hygiene in the days when her family couldn't afford hot water, and I'd have been betraying her memory, even though she remained alive, by not bathing. But there was a less noble part of the equation too. While I bathed, I hoped that Nicola might be able to find a couple of handfuls of grass cuttings somewhere.

That changed her tune. "I don't know what you have in mind, darling, but it's definitely going to cost you a bit extra. Christ knows where I'm going to find bloody grass clippings. You sure sand won't do the trick?"

I told her I was more than happy to pay whatever she thought fair. We parted.

I remained excited throughout my bath. Indeed, thinking about the grass she'd come back with, and the awful things she'd call me while she made me eat it, it was all I could do to keep from manipulating myself into no longer requiring her services.

She was longer than I'd expected. A drunken boy had asked her to rim him, and she'd got him to agree to pay 50 euros for it. He'd passed out before he'd counted out 30 of them. She'd taken them for her time, and then the rest of what he had on him.

She took off her clothes in a couple of smooth, effortless motions. It wasn't the sight of her naked, but that of a couple of handfuls of grass cuttings on the bureau that had me shivering with excitement. I asked her to put her shoes back on. She complied and looked at me expectantly. "I suppose," I said, "that you find the idea of physical intimacy with me inexpressibly disgusting."

"Yeah," she agreed. "I suppose I do."

I waited. But so did she.

"I reckon you find my obesity nothing short of obscene," I suggested.

"Obscene," she agreed. This wasn't going at all according to plan.

"And you're probably thinking that I could bathe for twice as long as I did without getting the glutton pig stench off me."

"Twice as long," she said, finally demonstrating a little initiative, but frankly, not nearly enough.

I could hear the desperation in my own voice. "And to demonstrate your contempt, you're probably going to make me eat those grass cuttings."

"Eat them? Oh, right. Yes, that's exactly what I'm going to do." She sighed as she turned to the bureau, but I was too excited now to care. I got down on hands and knees. I offered her my face.

"Eat it, you disgusting fat pig," she said, which was obviously really good, but she just left her hand there, as though expecting me to eat from it voluntarily, like a tame stag in Richmond Park or something. I had to put my face in her hand and rub against it before she got the idea. But when she finally got it, oh, what heaven on earth! "You disgusting fat grass-eating pig," she said. "You obscenely obese glutton pig stench!"

Oh, how I adored it – and her, for making it possible. After I finished, I told her I'd pay for her time if she'd just lie beside me.

"There'll be no additional charge, darling." She apparently thought it sweet that I didn't want her to get dressed and piss off the second I finished. She'd been lonely herself. She put her head on my shoulder without my asking for it. I'd had no idea when she was atop me how gorgeous her hair smelled.

We just lay there silently for several minutes. She rolled over on her side and supported her head on her hand. "This isn't my business, darling, and if you don't want to talk about it, just say so, but I don't understand about the grass."

"I don't understand it either. Most people want to forget the most humiliating moments of their lives. People like me find it incredibly exciting to relive them in an erotic context. I honestly don't know why that would be."

"Maybe you're trying to restage the humiliating event to have a happy outcome or something. And what could be a happier outcome than the ultimate erotic pleasure?"

I turned to face her, to marvel at the intelligence I'd never dreamed she had.

"I went back for a year when I was 21," she explained, "and read psychology at Roehampton University. I was thinking of trying to become a psychotherapist." Much as Kate herself had as a teenager! And this a woman who'd have rimmed a drunken yobbo for 50 euros!

The world is such an inhospitable, stupidly unfair place. Everywhere you look, talented, clever, energetic people struggling to get by, and numbskulls running countries.

I asked if she'd come back to London with me. I've always fallen in love too fast, and was too old to stop. She said she was flattered, but that she'd come to adore the sunshine.

She had to get home. It turned out she'd had the Spanish club owner's daughter, whose unusually understanding paternal grand-mother looked after her when Nicola, as I continued to call her because it turned out to be her real name anyway, was out making a living. She gave me her email address, and we promised to stay in touch. I wasn't sure I believed her about being called Nicola.

I could hardly sleep that night for the braying and bellowing and screaming and laughing and crying and gurgling and surprisingly loud projectile vomiting of the alcohol-, es-, hashish-, charlie-, and unpro-tected sex-abusing 18- to 30-year-olds a couple of blocks away. But it would have been unfair to blame my insomnia entirely on them. Thoughts of the wonderful cruel things Nicola had said to me would probably have kept me awake even if everyone else on the island had suddenly had his larynx removed. How I would have missed her already if she hadn't been so eager to give me her email address.

8

Her and Her Vision

IT cost me an arm and a leg, but I couldn't bear the thought of another day and night on Ibiza, and tried to buy a couple of seats on the first flight back to London on any airline that flew there. The chirpy young woman at the ticket counter affirmed that there were indeed a couple of seats unsold, but that they were at opposite ends of the plane. When I asked how she envisaged me fitting in only one seat, she looked confused, and then said, "Well, like anybody else I suppose, sir." I didn't appreciate her sarcasm. I booked only one seat and hoped, against hope, for the best.

God knows how, but I managed to squeeze into a single seat, between two 18- to 30-year-olds who winced in agony at every noise, and who for that very reason nearly didn't survive takeoff. But as we ascended to our ultimate cruising altitude, they perked up enough to converse. After swearing me to secrecy, the one on my right, Denis, a much-tattooed marketing student from Exeter University, described the idea that was going to make him a millionaire. He was going to start a company, called Body Doubles, that would recruit kids to get tattoos for footballers and pop stars who had no room left on their own epidermises, but had much they hadn't yet expressed. I thought it might be cumbersome to have to be perpetually accompanied, but Denis believed that no modern athlete or top recording artist lacked an entourage anyway. He expected that other students like himself would find getting proxy tattoos an easy and enjoyable way to make extra dosh, especially since they would get to do most of the things the stars themselves did.

This had been his fourth visit to Ibiza, and by far the one he'd most enjoyed. "I don't think I've gone longer than five hours anytime in the whole week without throwing up," he related proudly. If he'd thrown up rather more often than he'd been shagged, well, that hardly meant he'd had anything less than a crackin', wicked time. He had indeed heard of cirrhosis of the liver, but believed that one owed it to himself to enjoy life to the full. "We've all got to die of something, innit?" Anyway, he believed that receiving a liver transplant in middle age probably made one irresistible to women, and at exactly the time (around 37 or 38, in most cases, he thought) they would probably cease to regard one as a potential sexual partner. "Not all of them, mind you, but a certain kind, blondes in their early thirties? Absolutely."

Concluding that poor Denis's cirrhosis wasn't of the liver, but of the cerebrum, I pretended to be asleep for a few minutes, during which I turned in the other direction.

Chloe, to my left, had also been to Ibiza for four consecutive holidays, and had come home pregnant the previous three. For that reason, her parents had tried to talk her into an alternative destination this time, but when she'd threatened to top herself, they'd reneged. She had found such threats very effective in getting what she wanted from her parents, but foresaw a time when she might actually have to jump off a building or something to retain credibility. She asked me to find out if Denis found her fit, as she found him. I thought they were well suited, but would never have been able to forgive myself if I'd heard they'd reproduced, and pretended once again to have fallen asleep.

Kate's 'Eat The Music', from her *Red Shoes* album, began going through my head, and I wound up spending the balance of the flight thinking about my own history of eating.

I don't know about Hannah Bush, but cleaning was my own mother's idea of a good time. It wasn't tricky or intimidating, and it made her feel in control. There was rarely a moment during my childhood when you couldn't have performed surgery on any floor in the house.

Cooking was my mother's idea of no fun at all, and we didn't eat well. We had the same few meals over and over and over – one night fried fish (heated up by my mum in the oven, but very often not quite enough), a jacket potato, and frozen peas and carrots, the next meatloaf (with a hard-boiled egg in the middle), a jacket potato and frozen corn, the third baked chicken, a jacket potato, and frozen mixed vegetables, the fourth tuna noodle casserole with crumbled potato chips on top. Then the cycle would repeat. Never a sauce. Rarely a herb. (When my dad took to bringing pizzas home from a place near where he worked when I was around 12, I thought them absolute ambrosia. Oregano!) Rarely a fresh vegetable. Sometimes Jell-O with canned fruit suspended in the middle. We ate like federal prisoners.

The tragic thing was that she had real talent. Every couple of months she would make a *bolognese* sauce from scratch, and it would be exquisite. The house would smell like Heaven. As I've mentioned, I loved sports from a very early age, but on days my mother made *bolognese* sauce from scratch, I could hardly be coaxed outside.

My dad was the world's tidiest and least discriminating diner. Meatloaf with an egg inside? Yum! Inadequately heated frozen fish? Yum! Baked chicken without anything resembling a sauce? Rapture. He kept everything on his plate in neat little districts. While chewing, he would nudge his peas and carrots into perfect parallelograms. Order had to be maintained until the last forkful!

We finished every morsel. I could no more have left food on my plate than my dad could have let his corn kernels drift into the mashed potatoes, not when my parents had been teenagers in the Depression. My mother, whose family had been unable to afford adequate hot water, had been sent home from grade school for being dirty. We did not – *could* not! – waste food, however boring and flavourless, however full of it we might be.

After the dishes were done, we would congregate around the TV, and everyone's palates would perk up at last, as my mother broke out the cookies. She baked well, though I could have done with far fewer sponge cakes, and had the most exquisite taste in supermarket cookies. Whether home-made or bought, they were invariably the most interesting, flavourful part of the meal by far, and we gorged on them, washing them down with cold milk while watching situation comedies about wonderful wholesome families with mothers who wore pearl necklaces to do the hoovering and didn't habitually cut their husbands to shreds with their tongues in front of the children.

We'd go out for hamburgers every week or so to spare my mother the drudgery of turning on the oven and heating up frozen fish and frozen vegetables and baking a potato. A place called Woody's Smorgasbord allowing you to put your own condiments on your grilled burger appealed hugely to my parents, former Depression teenagers forever on the lookout for a bargain. And when Woody's introduced its special five-for-the-price-of-four Thursday nights, we were there every week. My dad and I each had to eat two, and I was only 10. But there was a job to do, and there could be no shirking. One didn't eat for pleasure, or until full, but to maximise his savings.

The inevitable happened. I got tubby. Ordinary beige jeans (my mother refused to allow me to wear the blue jeans that were the virtual uniform at my school) ceased to fit. I needed a size called husky.

But my school lunches! Oh, I ate like a king. For other boys, a single slice of some horrid grey lunchmeat between two slices of white bread.

But for Leslie Herskovits, great huge thick fantastic sandwiches with bologna from an actual delicatessen, a thin slice of last night's meatloaf (on its own it couldn't have been less flavourful, but juxtaposed with the actual delicatessen bologna, it was absolute ambrosia), and lettuce, all between two slices of actual bakery rye. My classmates could hardly believe their eyes.

But I wasn't only . . . husky, of course. I was also the only boy on the playground in tastefully juxtaposed beige jeans and brown shoes, rather than the inevitable blue jeans and black shoes, and was reflexively passive. And oh, the fun my classmates had with me. At lunch, pretending to imagine that I might try to snatch their sandwiches – two slices of packaged white bread with a single slice of horrid grey lunchmeat between them – no one would sit within 10 feet of me.

All these decades later, I am, in most ways, the same person I was then, the same lonely, alienated little fatso.

It could have been worse. I realise that. I didn't change my eating habits. My mother continued to cook like someone who hated cooking, and we continued to fill up on cookies. But by the time I reached 10, and playing sports (ineptly!) at every opportunity, I'd somehow got quite slim. The horror that was junior high school was only a couple of years away. There I noted what life was like for those flabby boys who had something entirely too much like tits.

It could have been very much worse for me. And it was quite bad enough.

As we began our descent, I found myself wondering if Kate was likely to have eaten boxty (that is, potato griddle) cakes, an Irish favourite, as a child, as I assume her mum Hannah had eaten them back in her native County Waterford. I pictured Hannah teaching Kate the age-long Irish doggerel about them, namely

> *Boxty on the griddle, boxty in the pan.*
> *If you can't make boxty, you'll never get a man.*

I wondered if champ, that quintessential Irish favourite, made of the humblest ingredients (potatoes, scallions, milk, salt, and lots of butter) were a big Bush favourite. I wondered if the Bushes had nibbled on treacle bread when they sat around singing ribald Victorian sea shanties on warm spring evenings, as my own family had sat around stuffing itself with cookies as we watched situation comedies that depicted American family life as something very different from our own.

And then we were back at Gatwick.

★ ★ ★

Delighted with the brisk sales of Kate's debut album, EMI threw her a champagne reception in Paris. When the record kept flying out of the shops, they not only threw her a big party at St. Katherine's Dock, in the shadow of Tower Bridge, but also chipped in on an expensive Steinway piano for her rehearsal room. They carped about Jay, who'd given them stick for plastering her erect right nipple all over the fronts of buses, continuing as her manager, and wondered, pointedly, if, when she finished her champagne, she would like to get right to work on her *next* album. *Would you mind terribly catching your breath some other time, love?*

They wanted to release 'Them Heavy People', even though it found her revelling, as no British pop singer had ever dared to, in her discovery of Gurdjieff, as the follow-up to 'Wuthering', but she thought it would reinforce the popular misconception of her as a novelty act, and didn't have to weep this time to get them to release 'The Man With The Child In His Eyes' instead. It proved another jolly good choice, reaching number six. In years to come, it would prove her most-recorded song, with everyone from Dusty Springfield to Natalie Cole trying their luck.

She flew to Tokyo to perform 'Moving' at Budokan. It quickly went to number one in the Japanese charts. She made a TV advert for Seiko watches and flew home, telling the press the little white lie that on her forthcoming second album she would be rather more a rock singer. She discovered that she was now unable to walk through an airport without people stopping her to say how much they loved her. She came from a loving home, and was never observed being less than gracious and accommodating.

Sounds dispatched a writer to puncture the myth of her being cordial all the time. She was unfalteringly cordial to and around him, and he had no choice but to report that it was no myth. The noted rock photographer Barry Plummer shot her atop the lion-skin rug in which she used to stash change at her family home. It struck many as an odd choice for a new vegetarian. EMI wondered if she might like to get to work on her second album. If she liked, she could record in the south of France, and think of it as a working holiday.

* * *

Mere mad months after the release of *The Kick Inside*, Kate and Andrew Powell and various KT Bush Band stalwarts flew to Nice, on whose outskirts they set up shop in a studio recommended by Dave Gilmour. The girl who hardly two years before had been speechless with delight on discovering the miracle of overdubbing wanted engineer Jon Kelly to tell her in detail about every facet of the recording process. She made no bones about looking forward to a day when there would be no Andrew Powell standing between her and her vision. The temerity of the man! Delighted with her first vocal on 'Wow', he'd tried to discourage her from singing it 40 or 50 more times.

They brought the tapes back to AIR Studios, above Oxford Street, and replaced a lot of the KT Bush musicians' parts with those played by the crew from the first album. One imagined that the KT Bushmen were something less than exultant. In that way of hers, Kate continued to offer to pop out for sarnies, and someone would have to remind her that she could no longer skip down Oxford Street without countless strangers stopping her to tell her how much they loved her, or to plead with her to stop controlling their thoughts via microwave transmissions to their dental fillings.

The resulting album, *Lionheart*, was another hit, albeit not quite on the scale of *The Kick Inside*. For me, it had all the debut album's faults without half its charm. Rather than that blazed by 'The Man With The Child In His Eyes', Kate had seemingly chosen the path of implacable preciousness. On 'Hammer Horror' and 'In The Warm Room', she sounded for all the world like the star of a cabaret staged by patients of a mental hospital. Her pitched screeching on 'Fullhouse' was enough to send the unconverted running for cover, as too, to a lesser degree, was the excruciating pun that provided the title of the severely over-arranged "rock" number 'Don't Push Your Foot On The Heartbrake'. She continued to seem compelled to make fun of herself every time she dropped into a traditionally adult vocal register.

The lyrics remained confusing. 'Wow', whose chorus, with the addition of a few cellos, might have evoked the Summer of Love Beatles, seemed to be about a gay lovey too sexually voracious to succeed as an actor, but who could tell for sure? We found out only a few words into the partially yodelled 'Kashka From Baghdad' that the protagonist was gay, but if you imagined Kate to be about to say something interesting about the plight of sexual minorities in repressive Muslim or other societies, you were out of luck. The arrangements were forever sacrificing rhythmic flow for cleverness. If 'Oh England My Lionheart' was enough to make one want to immigrate, the Brecht- and Weill-ish 'Coffee Homeground' made him long for temporary deafness.

But you had to hand it to her: she was uncompromising – it was impossible, in fact, to think of another recording artist to the right of

Captain Beefheart, for whom Kate made no secret of her admiration, more disinclined to make things easy for his or her listener. Years later, *The New York Press* would suggest, "Bush is a genius, and geniuses do over-reach. Some of her stuff [has been] awful, paint-peeling noise."

I became a fervent fan in spite of my significant reservations about her music when I realised how alike we were. Screeching, writing lyrics that no one on earth had a prayer of understanding, she virtually defied people to like her music. I, desperate to spare myself the heart-break of inexorable rejection, had taken in adolescence to defying people to like me, all in. Where Kate screeched, I was endlessly judg-mental and caustic. I could have devoted myself to Captain Beefheart, of course, but there was always a slim chance he didn't realise how dif-ficult his music was. Kate, on the other hand, had composed and sung 'The Man With The Child In His Eyes'. Anyone who could make music that beautiful but who chose instead to give us 'Fullhouse' had to be trying to keep the world at arm's length just as frantically as I.

*   *   *

Arriving back at Gatwick from Ibiza, I suffered an unpleasant hallucina-tion. When you go past Customs and emerge into the terminal proper, you invariably see a mob of mostly swarthy middle-aged men, nearly all of them in suits, holding aloft signs bearing the names of the passengers they're meant to collect. But for a moment it appeared to me that all their signs said, *You should have stayed abroad, Fatso.* I stopped in my tracks, nearly causing a collision. I was so relieved to see an elderly couple behind me waving excitedly at one of the sign-holding drivers that I nearly threw my arms around them.

London as a whole hadn't changed much since I'd been away, but it was probably foolish of me to expect that it might have.

Mrs. Cavanaugh was just serving lunch when I got home. It looked delicious. I chatted while I ate with one of the other boarders, Mr. Halibut, whose name I'm not making up. He had a very dry sense of humour, and it wouldn't have been out of character for him to have shortened his name from Halliburton, or something, but of course I had no way of knowing. At close to 80, his main passions in life were Kate's *The Sensual World* album, which he played at least four times per day, and hating the actress Elizabeth Hurley, whom he regarded – and this was invariably the second thing he told anyone about himself – as a talentless gold-digger.

On my sole visit to his rooms, he'd shown me the scrapbooks of Hurley clippings he maintained. One was devoted almost entirely to articles about the christening of the son she'd had with some American scumbag movie producer who later refused to acknowledge paternity. All the biggest celebrities in the UK had attended, which was more than the American scumbag had done. Old people are commonly believed to be intimidated by digital technology, but Mr. Halibut spent up to six hours per day looking for Hurleyana and maintaining the website he'd devised to express his passion, *hurleyhatred.com*. In nearly a year, the site had received only 221 "hits", or visits, which I thought said more about the level of interest in Hurley than in Mr. Halibut's handiwork, which was really quite good. The portal page, for instance, contained an animation that he'd had to purchase and then learn a complicated programme to make.

I knew asking him about the website might ruin his mood – he'd originally expected it to be so popular that he'd be able to get cosmetics and hair care companies to advertise on it – but we were beginning to have more silences than chat, so I threw caution to the wind. He claimed not even to pay attention anymore to how many hits he was getting. "I do it for the pleasure it gives me," he said. "I wouldn't give a monkey's if nobody at all visited." It was clear he was lying, and I made a mental note to visit his site more often. I figured I'd been responsible for around 150 of the previous year's 221 hits.

He didn't fancy dessert, and said I could have his. When he went upstairs, Mrs. Cavanaugh told me she reckoned she must have been responsible for around 200 of Mr. Halibut's hits. It occurred to me we were both probably wildly overestimating. It was wonderful to be home.

She asked me to let her know if I saw Cathy, who'd missed dinner last night and not been seen since. Mrs. Cavanaugh had recently been horrified to learn there were men who preyed on girls with eating dis-orders, and that, like paedophiles, they made many of their contacts over the Internet, luring their victims to clandestine meetings with promises of no food.

9

The Final Brutal Affirmation

WITH me firmly on her side now, but unaware of it, Kate toured Australia and New Zealand and dutifully expressed great esteem for the Aborigines. She appeared on *Saturday Night Live* in America at guest host Eric Idle's invitation but didn't take the country by storm. She came home to learn she'd been voted *NME*'s number two Pin-up for the year and *Sounds*' number two Female Sex Object. Debbie Harry was in her prime. Kate seemed not to have much enjoyed the long flight, and would soon be described as frightened of flying.

She might have been a bit iffy on performing live as well, but turned out to have been girding herself for it. Fully a year before actual rehearsals began, she, Del, or Paddy took to conferring for hours with Simon Drake (no mere EMI promotion man, it turned out, but a magician as well!) in his Chiswick home about ideas for visually enhancing the presentation of songs on the first two albums. Now she began seriously visualising a 150-minute multimedia extravaganza in which every song would be a one-act play in itself. There would be supplementary dancers, Simon's illusions, and no fewer than 17 costume changes. She would call it nothing less modest than *The Tour Of Life*, and it would be like nothing anyone had yet seen!

Was she serious? Oh, very. Fully four months before opening night, she began rehearsing with the musicians (The KT Bush Band, with Preston Heyman replacing Charlie Morgan, bolstered by three additional players, including guitarist Alan Murphy, and two female singers) at Greenwich's Thameside Woodwharf Studios, then with dancers in Covent Garden, and finally with the entire cast of thousands at Shepperton. By mid-March, weeks before the first show, the tour was sold out.

Over the course of the 150-minute performance, Kate would never actually leave the stage, but rather disappear behind a huge metal egg that rolled on and off as needed, and that would sometimes accommodate her in its plush red chocolate box-like innards. When first we glimpsed her, she was in a blue Lycra leotard. By 'Them Heavy People', she was in a trench coat and fedora. Moments later, in 'Egypt', she was a gypsy, and then, for 'Strange Phenomena', in a knackered top hat and tails. Later, for 'James And The Cold Gun', she was a homicidal cowgirl. It was positively dizzying!

And iconoclastic! On 'Hammer Horror', for which she was joined on stage by the show's choreographer, here dressed as an executioner, she didn't sing at all, but concentrated on dancing and pulling faces. Years before they became commonplace, her crew had rigged up a remarkable microphone harness out of ordinary wire hangers like those used by dry-cleaners. There were startling lighting effects, smoke and dry ice mist, and, for the fetishists in her audience (no one turned away!), PVC costumery and Kate herself in black leather for 'Don't Push Your Foot On The Heartbrake', which she thought of as her Patti Smith song.

There was wholesale feigned violence – here Simon Drake trying to murder Kate and push her into a barrel marked Pork, here (in what one couldn't help but view as a comment on how little she'd enjoyed playing the instrument) human-sized violins beating her to the ground, here, at the end of 'James', her gunning down every fellow in sight. There was Jay's poetry and unmistakable overtones of those paragons of wholesomeness *Thoroughly Modern Millie* and *Singing In The Rain*. In 'Oh England My Lionheart', sung by Kate in a huge flying jacket on a stage strewn with dying airmen (owed so much by so many!), there was stirring patriotism. And finally, after she'd gathered up some of the countless gifts her audience would surely fling over the footlights to her, there was Kate ending the performance waving as though from the deck of an ocean liner while we who adored her cheered and whistled and clapped along with the thunder of Heyman's drums.

A photographer managed to sneak into one of the final dress rehearsals at the Rainbow Theatre in Finsbury Park. Roadies removed the foolish boy's film from his camera and growled at him menacingly. A distraught Kate berated him for trying to spoil her surprise. The BBC readied a 15-minute report on the tour for *Nationwide*. Granada TV planned a show of its own. Everything seemed to be coming up roses. The unofficial opening night, at the Poole Arts Centre in Bournemouth, left everyone feeling exhilarated – until they heard that, when he'd gone to the top of the auditorium to perform an "idiot check" – that is, to ensure that no gear had been mistakenly left behind – lighting man Bill Duffield had fallen head first 17 feet onto concrete. He was in a coma, and would die a week later. Kate considered cancelling the whole tour, but was persuaded to go on with the show. The next night, April 3, 1979, she made her official live debut at the Liverpool Empire, half a mile from the Cavern Club. At the end, the audience applauded her so enthusiastically that she told them she wished she could do the whole tour in Liverpool, though it would hardly have been fair to her fans in Stuttgart.

By all accounts, the show was magnificent, defiantly silly at times, just like her music, wildly over the top, but a bona fide extravaganza by any measure, grand fun. "The most magnificent spectacle I've ever encountered in the world of rock," *Melody Maker*'s man equivocated. "Kate Bush is the sort of performer for whom the term superstar is belittling."

She played the Birmingham Hippodrome, Oxford's New Theatre, the Southampton Gaumont, the Manchester Apollo, the Sunderland Empire, Edinburgh Usher Hall, Newcastle's City Hall. She was a week at the London Palladium. There was the odd audience member who was fatally disappointed that Kate didn't chat with the audience between songs, but it would have broken the spell. And the press remained ecstatic. "Sometimes teeter[ing] on the farcical, but . . . never short of compulsive to watch," marvelled the man from *Sounds*, whose vocabulary at that point seemed to lack *compelling*. Only that scurrilous curmudgeon Charles Shaar Murray of *NME* demurred, sniffing, "The trouble is that she's completely entranced with the idea of her own stardom," inspiring an unprecedented shitstorm of protest.

★　★　★

Cathy turned out not to be with an anorexiaphile, but atop my bed, unconscious. With my box of Cypramil beside her. And all but one of the little tablets punched out. She'd probably had 13 or 14 of them, and who knew what else.

Panic. Awful doused-in-ice-water, nauseating panic.

She had a pulse. That much was certain, and very good indeed. I headed for the stairs. But no. I had to keep a level head. I had to do things in the proper order. Remembering that she might have been on my bed since the night before, I was struck by how deeply unfair it was that I should feel I had only milliseconds to do the right thing. I phoned for an ambulance. The dispatcher was really good, and got me calmed down enough to be intelligible very quickly. I put the phone down and panicked all over again. Should I have asked if I needed to give artificial respiration? I'd worried in the past about some horrid old person or homeless type collapsing right in front of me and needing it, for how would I be able to bring myself to put my mouth on that of someone of obviously deficient hygiene? Given the way her breath smelled, I might not even have managed it with poor Cathy.

She was breathing! What was I thinking? But now I had to get downstairs and tell her mum. Oh, why me?

I got downstairs as quickly as I could. It wasn't very quickly, of course. Mrs. Cavanaugh was drying the lunch dishes. I told her she had to come immediately upstairs to my room. The blood drained from her face. She was up the stairs in a third of the time it had taken me to get down them. She was on the phone when I finally reached her. "I don't care if you've already got one coming," she was shouting down the phone. "I want you to send another. What if the first one breaks down?"

The point was moot. The ambulance I'd phoned for had already arrived. She was down the stairs at the speed of light, and the paramedics up them. They listened to Cathy's heart with a stethoscope. They pulled one of her eyelids back and shone a light into her eye. They took her pulse. "She'll be all right," the one with multiple studs in his ear lobe said. "We'll just get her stomach pumped and she'll be all right." They lifted her onto their stretcher as effortlessly as they might have lifted a cat.

"Yes," Mrs. Cavanaugh said. "She will be all right. You'll see to it."

"You can count on it, missus," the other one, the one with no piercings, affirmed, and then they were gone.

★ ★ ★

No model remains in demand forever. Even if public taste doesn't change, the creative directors of the big advertising agencies certainly do. They feather their own nests by convincing their clients that prospective customers and clients are fed up seeing the same old faces, however wonderfully symmetrical they may be, however dominated by fantastic cheekbones, and that, if they're smart, the clients will rely on experts such as themselves to pick the next face the public will adore. One month absolutely everyone wants you. The next, everyone agrees you're overexposed, and you're lucky to be hired to model underpants with your back to the camera. But I never took money for sex, not even when the alternative was soul-destroying monkeywork.

For around nine months after my last Marcel Flynn campaign, mine was the face and body everybody thought would sell their product or service. Then Mark Pringle, nine years my junior, and very much more chiselled-looking, and later Andrew Chen, 14 years my junior, with a better-defined six-pack, and half-Chinese at a moment when New York's and London's hottest creative directors all seemed to imagine in unison that consumers were feeling sinophilic, effectively put me out of work. My agent Rona, who'd discovered me when I was hitchhiking, asked if I'd consider escorting a woman from her temple to a big charity event for a tidy sum. I said sure, and away I went.

Phyllis Liebowitz had been the second (that is, trophy) wife of a guy, may he rest in peace, who'd made his fortune catering for location film shoots and then, God forbid, died of a massive stroke on the golf course at 71. On that first date, I heard about the poor devil and his untimely death until it was coming out of my ears, but apparently managed to look interested, because the next week she asked Rona if I could accompany her to a friend's daughter's wedding. When I reminded Rona that I was a model, and not a gigolo, Rona gently pointed out that I was a model for whom none of the creative directors were asking any more, and that Phyllis might be willing to pay me 20 per cent more than the first time. It wasn't as though single Jewish men handsome enough to have modelled for Marcel Flynn were growing on trees.

Phyllis did indeed agree to the higher fee. I overheard her telling two women at the wedding that she was seeing me. When they asked if I were as good in the sack as I was easy on the eyes, Phyllis just winked at them in what they could hardly have been blamed for interpreting as the affirmative. Later, while she danced with a former business partner of her late husband, one of the two women asked if I might be available to escort her to a friend's daughter's *bat mitzvah* the following Friday evening. I got the feeling she was less interested in me than in the idea of upstaging Phyllis. In early adolescence, I'd never have dreamed that women – even those almost old enough, at least biologically, to be my mother – would fight over me. Now, in adulthood, I discovered myself embarrassed by their doing so.

In her big Lexus sedan on the way home, Phyllis made it clear that, for what she was now paying me, she thought she ought to be getting more than just my wit and charm and good looks. I had no girlfriend at the time – I was a few weeks shy of meeting the woman who'd become Babooshka's mother – but was still mortified by the prospect, far less on moral grounds than on practical ones. Put simply, I was afraid I might not be able to get aroused, and would be humiliated. Which was what poor Phyllis wound up feeling, even though I told her – sincerely! – that she was by far the most attractive 49-year-old woman I'd ever known. Through her angry tears she informed me that around the time she'd met her late husband, may God rest his soul, somebody like me would have been lucky to get 90 seconds of her attention. At 32, it was difficult for me to imagine that anyone aged 49 had ever been much younger than 47 or 48, and even harder to imagine that they'd ever been a universal object of desire. At 32, I was very stupid.

Phyllis turned out to have a vindictive side, and told Rona I'd made inappropriate advances. Rona was livid. It took me days to convince her of my innocence. By the time I finally did, it was too late to get her to ring the other one to say I was available for her friend's daughter's *bat mitzvah* after all. I earned less that week than the homeless guy who sat in front of the local supermarket with his multiple missing teeth and a Starbucks cup into which someone occasionally tossed a few cents and a wad of chewing gum from which all the flavour had gone.

Rona was only a couple of years my senior, but came from a different world. In hers, one stuck staunchly to one's own kind. Gentiles dated and married gentiles. The coloured, as she called them, dated and married the coloured. Most importantly, Jews dated and married Jews. My family identified themselves as Jewish only sporadically. My mother enjoyed imagining that anti-Semitism was ongoing and nearly as widespread as in her youth, when she could remember her parents being turned down as tenants because of their ethnicity. She seemed to derive a strange sort of pleasure from imagining that certain restaurants wouldn't serve us, though this seemed, in the end, to be based on purest whimsy. When out in public, she always spoke the word *Jewish* in a whisper, apparently for fear that gentiles might otherwise glare at us censoriously. In municipal elections, presented with a ballot listing endless candidates for offices he'd not even heard of, my dad made a practice of voting for those with Jewish surnames. No Friedman, Rosenberg, or Silverstein failed to get his vote. I studied to become *bar mitzvah* solely because my only friend at the time was going to do it, leaving me with no one to hang with. And I reckoned – mistakenly, it turned out – that I'd make some money on the deal, it being customary to give the little pipsqueak who'd just read some Hebrew in a thick California accent and pronounced himself a man a wad of cash for his trouble.

Decades later, my sister, who hadn't spent 45 seconds of her life in Hebrew school, suddenly turned into Rona *redux* and specified in her advertisements on on-line matchmaking sites that she was interested in hearing only from other Jews, though I think she probably said *Jewish people*. (*Jew* sounds so brazen somehow, so militant, *Jewish person* so gentle, so genteel. A Jew will swindle you at his delicatessen if you don't watch him like a hawk. A Jewish person is someone you'd meet for cappuccino.)

Rona held her nose and got me dates with gentiles. When it came to me, there was no telling the two ethnicities apart. The gentile women wanted sex with me no less than poor Phyllis had, and were no less irate when I spurned them, always for the same reason. The nastier ones attributed our lack of relations to my being a fag, a cocksucker, or, in one memorable instance, a fudgepacker. The more vulnerable ones wept inconsolably, imagining my rejection of them to be the final brutal affirmation of their lack of allure. I came to hate the whole business, and got out of it for a while.

I got a job typing enrolment forms at the university. It couldn't have been more boring. My co-typist was Whitney Houston's double – that gorgeous – but no fun to chat to. I had to amuse myself by giving everyone (except those with extremely common names, for whom it was apt to cause problems) a different middle initial than the one he'd applied with.

The job might have been my downfall. Most of the other typists were women, nearly all of them overweight, nearly all of them with photos of multiracial toddlers on their desks, nearly all of them with boxes of chocolates close at hand, boxes whose contents they'd commonly decimate over the course of a shift. I think the idea was to try to compensate for the work being mind-numbingly boring with the intense sensual pleasure of chocolate.

I have reason to believe that Kate has had very much the same idea at several points in her career, while working too hard in the studio. Kate is wrongly thought to have come at one point to weigh 18 stone. I am rightly thought, if only by myself, and now you, to have gained three pounds in my month as a typist. Rona asked me pointedly if I'd gained weight. I hadn't felt a big blubbery embarrassment since age 10. It promised to be a very long time before I ever felt anything else.

★　★　★

I'd have got a taxi to the hospital, but I wasn't sure which one Cathy had been taken to. I'd only just finished lunch, but was very, very hungry. I went downstairs to wait for Duncan and Gilmour to get home from work. I felt I owed it to them to relate what had happened. And then I felt I didn't, as I certainly hadn't encouraged their sister to look through my things and take my Cypramil. And then I felt once again that I did. If it hadn't been for my bloody fat man's self-loathing and depression, there'd have been no Cypramil for Cathy to find, at least in my room.

Duncan and Gilmour came home moaning about the heat. "It's the nutter," Gilmour observed with a snort when he noticed me. His more gracious elder brother asked if I was all right. I told him I wasn't, and burst into tears. I related how I'd found Cathy on my bed, and how their mum had gone with her in the ambulance.

The next thing I knew, Gilmour had his hands round my neck and I couldn't breathe as he screamed, "I'll kill the nutter! I'll fucking kill him with my bare hands." I'd have expected Duncan to be very much stronger than his younger brother, but it took him – and me! – what seemed hours to get Gilmour's hands off my throat, more than long enough for my whole painful life to pass before my eyes, not a pleasant spectacle.

"At the moment Mum needs us most," Duncan shouted, "you decide to go mental on me? Wally! Prat! Come on, let's get over there."

I asked if he thought I might be able somehow to squeeze into the back of their van, and here came Gilmour again, even more intent than before on strangling me. "We could get 10 of you in the bloody van, you fucking loon!" And here, before my eyes, came my whole life again, that woeful cavalcade of shame.

"Maybe it's better if you keep the home fires burning," Duncan, still kind in spite of his exertions, in spite of his emotional upset, suggested, and I agreed.

It's funny how the mind works. You try to think about something – anything! – other than that which is causing almost unendurable stress, and what comes up? Russell Crowe in *The Gladiator*, the famous opening scene, in which he advises the Roman legions he commands, "At my command, unleash Hell." At the time my daughter took me (with the utmost reluctance) to see the film, the line struck me as especially cool, on a par with, "Are you feeling lucky today, punk?" But the more I thought about it, the more ludicrous it seemed. Did it not go without saying that, with hundreds of bloodthirsty Goths, or whatever they were, across the ravine, waiting to do everything in their power to repel them, the Romans would hit them with their best shot? Is it conceivable that Maximus, Crowe's character, might have said, "At my signal, unleash considerable unpleasantness, but let's not go overboard, shall we?"

I hated myself for my self-amusement at a time like this, and then for wondering if Nicola had wondered why I hadn't phoned.

I don't know how she did it, but Mrs. Cavanaugh actually made dinner, and then came to each boarder's room in turn to apologise for it being so late. I didn't even acknowledge the apology, but just put my arms around her. She cried, just for a moment, very softly, a woman of incomparable restraint. She blew her nose softly into a facial tissue and sat on the edge of my bed, the bed atop which I'd found poor Cathy. The hospital had determined that Cathy hadn't taken my Cyp at all, but had lost consciousness owing to her extremely low blood sugar level. They were feeding her intravenously, and had every expectation of her surviving, though there was no question about her needing to take in nourishment. "It wasn't your fault," she said. "I want you to know I don't hold you responsible."

"But if it weren't for my stupid self-loathing and depressiveness," I said, "there wouldn't have been any pills in here for her to pretend to take."

That sounded odd coming out. Mrs. Cavanaugh and I looked at each other, and she burst out laughing. And once she'd started, there was no stopping her. She absolutely howled. Gasping, she slid off the bed onto the floor, which made her laugh all the harder. I couldn't help but respond in kind. If you'd walked past my room, you'd have thought it had been occupied by the Lunatic Liberation Army. And then, of course, when she had no more laughter left, Mrs. Cavanaugh found more tears, and was absolutely wracked with sobs.

At last she was exhausted. She dabbed at the corners of her eyes with her facial tissue, said what any woman in the English-speaking world would have said at that moment ("I must look a mess"), and sighed back to her girlhood. We could hear Mr. Halibut listening to *The Dreaming* for a change in the room below mine. Kate got nearly all of 'Sat On Your Lap' sung before Mrs. Cavanaugh finally spoke. "In a way, you're kindred spirits, you and Catherine, both of you unable to see yourselves as you are." I couldn't be sure what she meant, but this wasn't the time to ask, I didn't think.

She sighed again, this time back to before her conception. "Can you imagine what it would be like for me to lose her?"

Vividly. At that point, I hadn't heard my Babooshka's voice in 18 months.

10

The Pain Of Our Estrangement

ALMOST as though on cue, Babooshka put on a great deal of weight at exactly the moment her interest in boys blossomed. Almost simultaneously, her mother persuaded the Swiss electronics millionaire she'd married after me to pay for her to have a face-lift and her breasts enlarged. Having endured all the pain the surgeries entailed, she'd then bought a wardrobe to show off her new figure. When they'd go shopping together (and she rarely wasn't going shopping), in her extremely skimpy Lycra shorts and extremely tight Lycra tanktop, teenage boys would make loud sounds of approval. Bab would be mortified with embarrassment. I would sympathise with her, and tell her I thought it was really insensitive of her mother, and Bab would hate me for it.

I'd adored her not merely from her first breath, but from the moment I learned she was growing inside her mother's womb. Her birth transformed me. For a long while there, I not only didn't loathe myself, but actually felt ever greater self-admiration, as Babooshka brought out kindness and patience and generosity I'd never dreamed I had in me.

And none of it was nearly enough. There was a Saturday afternoon when she was around two and a half that we spent together, just the two of us, because her mother was at the art gallery where she "worked", if you'd call sitting at a desk doing crossword puzzles work. I was crazy with adoration for my daughter, and did everything I could think of to make her happy, but she sulked and pouted all afternoon in spite of what I did. When she saw her mother's car turning the corner into our road, it was as though the sun had broken through the clouds. My daughter was transformed, radiant now with joy.

Her mother and I divorced. We'd come to be unable to bear one another. Trying to be responsible, I'd taken a legal word processing job that made the earlier one typing enrolment forms seem exhilarating in comparison. I got up at 05.20 every morning so I could be at the bus stop at 06.20, and arrive at work in San Francisco, 50 miles to the south, at 08.30. After a very long day of being treated with naked condescension by smug young attorneys, I'd ride the bus nearly two hours in the opposite direction, and arrive home at around 19.30. Whereupon I'd almost invariably find my wife watching crap television (reruns of really excruciating late Sixties sitcoms, that sort of thing) and drinking with her parents, my in-laws, who'd as good as moved in with us. Knowing that I had around 180 minutes in which to have dinner, exercise, play with my daughter, and try to do some work that might, in some way, turn into a lifeline out of the professional nightmare I'd been living before I had to get to bed to be up at 05.20 the following morning to repeat the whole process, I'd ask my wife if she'd had time to make some dinner.

Wasn't she entitled to relax a bit, she'd demand petulantly.

I got myself a little flat in San Francisco and drove up to collect Bab every Friday evening, and took her back to her mum's and grandparents' every Sunday night. The time I had with her was by far my happiest. But it wasn't so happy for her. No matter how gentle and adoring I was, no matter how attentive, she always made it clear that she greatly disliked being deprived of her mother's companionship even for 48 hours.

I challenged the divorce decree I'd passively accepted in the beginning because I wasn't in any shape to put up a fight. Under the terms of the amended settlement, my wife had to drive my daughter half the time, and began bringing her down to San Francisco on Saturday mornings. At the sound of the bell ringing, I'd whoop exultantly, and run down the stairs three at a time. And when I reached the ground floor and flung open the door, my daughter, crying, would be hiding from me behind her mother – her mother who, when the going in our marriage got tough (at least half because of me, I admit now and admitted then), refused to consider couples counselling. *But it isn't just us*, I said. *We have a daughter to think about. Our splitting up is going to affect her for the rest of her life.* Nope. My wife couldn't be bothered.

And it was my wife to whom my daughter clung for dear life.

Fifteen years after the fact, the memory of that continues to hurt nearly more than I am able to express.

And it never went away. I'd hide my pain from Bab, and soon have her laughing again. We'd have wonderful times. I'd take her to the playground in the square between the big hotels at the summit of Nob Hill, a magical place, and push her endlessly on the swings. She'd gasp with laughter at the thought that I was pushing her so high that, if she wanted, she'd be able to jump off the swing right into the living room of a flat in one of the elegant old buildings that surrounded the square, and find out what they were having for dinner. I'd carry her on my shoulders all the way to North Beach, where, on a bustling Friday or Saturday night, we'd walk along Columbus Avenue watching the Italian chefs frantically cooking in their open kitchens, and smell the delicious smells. I'd remain for hours on the verge of tears of joy, only for my daughter to advise me, at a moment of peak exultation, "I want Mommy."

A great man once sang, ungrammatically, "If you love somebody, set them free." If I'd been a better man, maybe I'd have let my daughter have her way. What I did instead was let her see how much she hurt me, and try to point out all the ways in which Mommy let her down. Shame on me, and what an extremely high price I'd wind up paying.

My daughter reached school age. Every other Friday afternoon, I'd drive up to collect her from school, and every other Friday afternoon the look on her face would confirm what her mother had related she'd said, that she wished I were the kind of divorced daddy you were always hearing about, the kind who made plans with his kid and then didn't show up. Every other Friday afternoon, another broken heart.

She was her mother's daughter, extremely bright, but with an apparently congenital aversion to having to work very hard at anything. Trying to do for my daughter what I'd come passionately to wish someone had done for me at her age, I taught her things. I did what Kate's brothers and dad did for her – taught her to write poems and songs, how to compose melodies and then harmonise them. I taught her to sketch. We spent huge amounts of time in the car travelling back and forth between my city and her mother's, and I decided we should devote some of it to learning Spanish. Bab resented all of it.

Her mother, who had earlier taught her how to use a remote control device to change television channels, now taught her to have fake fingernails professionally affixed to her real ones, how to have highlights put in her hair, how to spend lots of time at the mall shopping for cute new outfits, and then, by example, how to walk out of another marriage, but not, as noted, before her Swiss electronic millionaire third husband (there'd been one before me, without children) could pay for her cosmetic surgery.

As my daughter fought her way through adolescence, lusting after boys who found her too fat to ask out, going through friends as some people go through paper towels, often finding herself without any, things got ever rockier between us. I tried to teach her some small sense of responsibility by requiring her not to leave mounds of dirty laundry on her bedroom floor. She hated me for it, and Mommy eagerly assured her that it was my nature to be tyrannically controlling. (Hadn't I, during our marriage, always tried to ensure that we showed up for dinner with friends reasonably punctually, rather than the 45 minutes late that had long been her norm?)

I accepted part of the blame for her girth. As I looked back, I saw with horror that I'd routinely used food as a medium of comfort over the years. She felt awful about having been rejected by yet another friend? Well, why don't we see if a Baskin-Robbins ice cream cone makes the pain a little more bearable? She felt awful because her mom's greatest interest was in attracting the attention of much younger men at groovy night-clubs in San Francisco? Well, why didn't we go and have dinner at her favourite Chinese restaurant?

I didn't accept only the blame, though. I also accepted the responsibilities of trying to set a good example for her, and of facing up to the problem. I ate as though preparing for a famine, but worked out daily at the gym. She made plans to go with a gay classmate to a dance at her school. The afternoon before the dance, she burst into tears at the thought of being the only girl there who hadn't been legitimately invited by a boy. It felt like a knife in my heart. I consoled her as best I could, but didn't leave it there. Not wanting her to have to suffer in the same way again, I pointed out, with the utmost gentleness, that she was very beautiful (as indeed she was), but that a lot of boys weren't seeing that because she was overweight. I'll never forget the look of rage and shame and betrayal she gave me.

For a moment I was speechless. Then I delivered a message of hope. She was undeniably overweight, but the solution was very, very simple. She needed simply to eat less and exercise more.

Now there was only rage in her eyes. Undeniably overweight? Well, how was it that her friends (the two she cited were even more bloated than she) thought she looked just fine? And what if she didn't like going to the gym? It was remarkable how disgusting and uncool she was able to make it sound. What if she didn't like sitting around in a moth-eaten sweater caked in snot, reeking of cat urine?

Mommy wasn't much help, of course. Mommy was Victoria Beckham skeletal without having set foot in a gym in around seven years, since I'd got her to go with me for maybe a week back in Los Angeles. (She'd enjoyed it for a short while because she looked really cute in her spandex leotard, and knew it.) If Mommy could be skinny without working out, why couldn't my daughter?

What Mommy could do was teach her the importance of having her hair and nails professionally looked after at regular intervals, and how to put on make-up. My daughter is artistic, and was good with make-up. Her hair looked fabulous when she got back from the hairdresser. And if her fake nails made her feel more confident, then all the better. But compared to her bloatedness, none of it mattered much. The boys unanimously looked past her to her more lithe classmates. And my daughter suffered terribly.

★ ★ ★

In every city to which the *Tour Of Life* travelled, Kate bravely confronted the press, and proved rather less puckish, but also less churlish, than the acknowledged master of the rock star press conference, Bob Dylan. When Piccadilly Radio asked her how much money she'd made, she claimed to have no idea. One can picture Dylan replying, "£14,230.55." They asked if she'd come to live in luxury, and she assured them she'd been living in the same flat for years. What would she take with her if consigned to a farmhouse on a bleak Yorkshire moor? Friends, cigarettes, tea, music, and two cats. Dylan, in his prime, would surely have included Anita Ekberg and a light bulb.

After the final performance of the British part of the tour, in Edinburgh, various stars of the show repaired to the pricey fish restaurant Cousteau's, only to realise that over-zealous fans had followed their coach and were apparently intent on watching them eat through the window. Fearing they might freeze to death, kind Kate took them some wine and signed autographs. Back in London, there was a soiree at the Dial 9, with guests including The Tubes' Fee Waybill and David Bowie's PA.

The country simply couldn't stop talking about her. The *Daily Star* speculated that Zoodle and Pyewacket were past lovers on whom she'd cast a spell. (Are you in there, Al?) Word got out that no heterosexual British male would want to miss her performance of 'Wow' on BBC-TV's *The Abba Special* on the evening of Good Friday, *The Daily Express* promising nothing less than "wanton erotic gestures". The *Daily Mail*'s editorial cartoonist depicted Margaret Thatcher, as Kate, inspiring Prime Minister Callaghan to gasp. She was indisputably iconic now.

Gnashing its corporate teeth, sulking unashamedly, EMI announced that she'd declined its producers' invitation (ungrateful little cow!) to record the theme song for the forthcoming James Bond film *Moonraker*.

It turned out she'd seen fit instead to record the theme for *The Magician Of Lublin*, warmly received at film festivals and avoided like the plague by British filmgoers.

The show headed for Europe. Kate's throat felt crap, so four songs were cut from the programme in Stockholm, Copenhagen, Hamburg, and Amsterdam. A doctor in the Swedish capital advised her to use her voice only on stage. Her training with Lindsey Kemp came in handy as she began communicating in mime. People started responding non-verbally, with their own impromptu sign language, as though she wasn't just momentarily mute, but deaf as well. Sometimes people can be so adorable.

She got her voice back and the tour proceeded to Stuttgart, Munich (where the Circus Krone stage was nearly obscured by the thousands of red carnations the audience tossed onto it), Cologne, Paris (in the Théâtre des Champs Elysées, where G.I. Gurdjieff himself had once been boffo), Mannheim, and Frankfurt before returning for three additional nights at the Hammersmith Odeon, one of them a benefit for Bill Duffield.

At that performance, it was Peter Gabriel and Steve Harley who came out in trench coats and trilbies for 'Them Heavy People' rather than Kate's usual dancers Gary and Stuart. The audience was beside itself with delight, and somehow remained so even during Harley's solo turn. In the end, as the three stars sang 'Let It Be' (and not, as those already fatally fed up with Paul McCartney's vague ode to hopefulness might have preferred, 'Gimme Dat Ding') together, Harley got the audience to sing along as though at a football match and Kate wept.

★   ★   ★

One Sunday afternoon, I drove Babooshka and her gay male classmate and friends to the cinema on the understanding that the classmate's mother would give them a lift home. Five minutes after the film ended, my daughter was on the phone to me. Classmate's mother wasn't answering her phone. I was right in the middle of something I needed to complete, and told her to try her friend's mother again in a few minutes. Ninety seconds later, the phone rang again. Classmate's mother still wasn't answering, and they were getting bored just standing around. Then take the bus, I suggested. The bus was safe, inexpensive, air-conditioned, and only rarely had anyone on it. It came every 15 minutes.

From her reaction, you'd have thought I'd told her we'd henceforth eat nothing but kitty litter.

I conferred with her mother, admitting that I was worried by how very much our daughter had come to take for granted. I believed it horrifying that she wouldn't even consider public transport. Her mother's response was to buy her a car of her own the week she became eligible to drive. And I was the controlling one.

From when she was two and a half and I got my first place in San Francisco, I had always encouraged my daughter to think of where we lived together, even if it was for only two or three days a week, as Bab's and Daddy's house, and not just Daddy's. Now she started leaving messages on my answering machine on Thursday nights advising, "I don't want to come to your house tomorrow, Daddy."

Beside myself, I consulted psychotherapists. None of them was quite able to explain my daughter's great attachment to her mother, whose first priority, now she was free of the Swiss electronics millionaire, with a substantial chunk of his fortune in a new bank account bearing only her name, was to display herself in groovy San Francisco night-clubs. Her highest aspiration seemed to be being taken for a contemporary by much younger men.

My daughter spoke to the psychotherapists with the utmost reluctance. Before one appointment, she pretended, in the waiting area when she arrived late with Mommy, that she didn't know me. It felt as though my heart was being ripped out without an anaesthetic.

Mommy hooked up with a smug-seeming insurance salesman with a post-ironic quiff who enjoyed taking her to groovy Eighties-themed night-clubs. My daughter, who'd grown accustomed to having Mommy to herself, wasn't keen. In view of her longer and longer absences from . . . my house (one I'd moved to from San Francisco, considerable inconvenience be damned, largely so my daughter wouldn't feel I was taking her away from her few school friends every weekend), I told her it hurt me seeing so much less of her than New Boyfriend. Her response was not to see or speak to me at all for three months.

I hid from the pain of our estrangement as far away as I could get, in London, and then went back and was reconciled with her. Indeed, her relationship with New Boyfriend had become so uncomfortable that she asked if she could move full time into . . . my house. By agreeing instantly, I later realised I was doing exactly what I'd so often accused Mommy of doing – enabling Bab simply to run away from a problem she didn't want to be bothered with facing. But the pain of our estrangement, and then the elation of our rapprochement, had rendered me incapable of thinking clearly.

I blew it. I insisted that she regularly take her dirty laundry down to the hamper – not actually wash it, mind you, but just take it down in anticipation of it being washed. She wasn't living with Mommy now, but seeing a great deal of her. Every day after school, she'd stop by the boutique in which Mommy, absolutely without ambition, was working as a 48-year-old salesgirl, albeit one who, in a flattering light, might be mistaken for 36. Every day she'd try to talk Mommy into banishing her apparently philandering new boyfriend. Every day, Mommy would lie and say she'd think about it, and my daughter would arrive home in severe emotional disrepair, very often in tears. And every day I would do everything in my power to console her.

I phoned my ex-wife. Whereas she seemed disinclined to leave New Boyfriend, and whereas talking about it invariably upset my daughter terribly, I asked if she'd consider ceasing to talk about him with Bab. What temerity! Imagining that she was going to allow me to hold her accountable for anything! If our daughter was miserable, she informed me, it was because she found life so very difficult under . . . my roof.

I very nearly hit it. Every day I had to clean up, insofar as my daughter's state of mind was concerned, after my ex-wife. And during all this, my daughter was telling my ex-wife how miserable she was with me?

I confronted Bab. She admitted she had indeed complained to Mommy about how . . . controlling I was. And, to my infinite regret, I now did indeed hit the ceiling, telling my daughter that yet again I felt hurt and betrayed.

There was no sign of her for days. It turned out that Mommy, that great believer in never actually trying to resolve a difficult situation you can simply run from, had given my daughter the keys to her parents' house nearby, of which she'd enjoy full run, as they were at their other home, in Miami.

I finally spoke to her again eight days later after she called asking for her stuff. I'd put everything in plastic bin liners, which I now let her come to collect. No anaesthetic again. I told her that I'd loved her more reliably than anyone virtually from the moment of her conception, but that I couldn't condone her abandoning our household yet again. If she moved out, it was the end. If she couldn't resolve a conflict with the person who loved her most in the world, what hope was there for her?

She made her decision. Predictably, it was to take over her grandparents' house, where there was no one to object to mounds of dirty laundry on her bedroom floor.

A couple of weeks passed in silence. I phoned to invite her to have lunch with me. She declined. Then she stopped taking my calls. I left messages on her grandparents' answering machine, but she didn't return my calls. I went to London again, but arranged to fly back in time to attend her graduation from high school. She sent me an email saying not to bother because she wasn't going to provide a ticket. I pointed out that this act of premeditated cruelty was something she would probably come to regret for the rest of her life. She didn't listen. I didn't witness my daughter's graduation from high school. I can't begin to describe how much that hurt.

I got over it to the point of being able to send her an email a couple of weeks after the fact assuring her I would adore her with my dying breath, as I'd adored her at her first. She ignored it. I left her phone messages. She didn't return my calls. I sent more ignored emails. I returned to the UK, this time to stay. I liked the gloom. I liked that a London-based agency thought I looked enough like George Clooney to pay me.

I sent more emails – nothing heavy, but just descriptions of what I was doing. All ignored. I sent her a birthday card. Ignored. Her favourite restaurant in San Francisco had been a hip North China place called Firecracker, whose signature dish was called Firecracker chicken. Someone in the UK manufactured Firecracker chicken-flavoured crisps. Thinking it might bring a smile to her beautiful face, and maybe soften her heart a bit in the process, I sent her an empty packet. She ignored it.

Finally, after seven months, I heard from her. She curtly demanded to know what had become of the CD containing the installation software for her favourite computer game. Throughout her adolescence, I'd felt as though between the rock of alienating her even further and the hard place of not accepting the responsibility of getting in her face when she behaved shamefully. Should I do yet another Neville Chamberlain imitation, or risk extending her silence by telling her what I thought of her email?

I must have written 20 drafts of my eventual response, in which I told her that I felt very sorry for her, as one of two things would be true. Either she would, later in life, be overwhelmed by feelings of guilt and shame for the way she'd treated me and others who'd always been there for her, or, worse, she'd remain the person who'd sent me that spiteful email after months of cruel silence, after not allowing me at her high school graduation.

I received no response, and another 10 months passed in silence.

My sister, who'd always been sweet and generous with Bab, and whom Bab had always liked, tried to get in touch, not on my behalf, but her own. My daughter wouldn't respond to the messages my sister left at her college dormitory. Unlike me, my sister could stand the sound of my ex-wife's voice, her former sister-in-law's. But when my sister phoned to try to get my daughter's direct number, my ex-wife, who hated me for being controlling, refused to divulge it. And more months passed without my so much as hearing the voice of the person I loved most in the world.

The first night my daughter came home from the hospital, I'd burst into tears as I held her in my arms and thought of all the cruelty and pain from which I'd be unable to protect her. I'd sworn to her and myself that if I did nothing else with my life, I would find a way to be a wonderful dad to her.

Every hour of every day, her silence reminded me how badly I'd failed in that which had mattered most to me in my lifetime, and every hour of every day, though of course you couldn't see it with the naked eye, I got a little bit fatter, a little bit more repulsive.

I didn't have to imagine what it was like to lose a child. I knew from the inside. But I wasn't going to get into it with poor Mrs. Cavanaugh. We'd only wind up weeping all over one another.

She turned out to be no stranger to depression. During her own childhood, her mother had sometimes gone 72 hours virtually without speaking. She'd lie in bed staring in terror at the ceiling, hardly able to breathe. When either Mrs. Cavanaugh or one of her brothers asked what was wrong, she'd say, "Hurts too much," through clenched teeth. I didn't have to imagine that either. I knew from the inside what it was like not to have a single thought over a day's course that didn't hurt. But Mrs. Cavanaugh finally left me on the shore with the revelation that her mammy had eventually become unable to get out of bed even to use the toilet. They'd had to put her, at age 44, in diapers.

Even in my most ferocious depressions, even when my eyes and ears and nose and fingertips told me I was in my bedroom, but something greater than the sum of my senses told me I was in Hell, even when the sound of Kate Bush singing 'And Dream Of Sheep' could not ease the agony, I never peed myself.

I nearly laughed, as it occurred to me how the famous Monty Python sketch in which a succession of rich Yorkshiremen try to top one another's claims of humble origins might be rewritten for depression sufferers. No more *You had a hole? Luxury!* Now *You felt you were in Hell, but were able to retain control of your bladder and bowels? You call that depressed?*

11

Allowing Another His Tears

AFTER Mrs. Cavanaugh left, I spent half an hour looking through the mail-order catalogue I'd received the morning before. It offered some very good prices on digital cameras, and I wondered if I should order one for Kate. But I had no way of knowing if she was one of those easily flummoxed by digital technology. Having received no response to any of the 2,000 emails I'd sent her over the years, I couldn't even be sure that she had a computer. It occurred to me that no one as keen to learn the ins and outs of the recording studio as she had been after *Lionheart* could be a Luddite, but I'd read that Kurt Cobain, said to be able to build an amplifier from scratch, had been so confused by the manual accompanying his video camera that he'd never figured out how to power it with its internal batteries, and had had to keep the camera plugged into the wall when he photographed his baby daughter. It might well be that Kate was implacably adventurous in the studio, but fervently technophobic out of it, and if that were the case, my gift might serve only to remind her of her own shortcomings, which, of course, was the last thing I wanted. In the end, I wound up ordering another pair of earrings for her.

Exhausted by my deliberations, I turned on the TV, and discovered with delight that *Megastar*, on which poor Jez from Overeaters had flirted briefly with fame, had been reincarnated as *Fab Lab*. It was early days, and the comically inept, self-deluded contestants hadn't yet been banished from among those who could actually sing a bit, and who would be sequestered in a mansion full of hidden video cameras while they were instructed in the ways of the modern pop star by a succession of vaguely familiar Eighties has-beens trying to revive their own careers by being seen on television. Everyone was singing solely for the patronage of the four judges, not yet having to hope, as they would when the competition really got going, that the public would phone up to vote for them.

One of the judges, a record producer from Oop North, exuded endless delight in his own stupidity as he reduced a succession of terrified-looking girls to tears with his brusque dismissals. I got the awful impression he imagined himself candid, rather than brusque. The worst part was that all the judges seemed to be responding enthusiastically at random. They'd tell Genoa she was foolish to imagine she'd ever sing for anyone other than Butlin's audiences, and she'd stagger from the room sobbing. Then, a moment later, they'd tell the fog-horn-voiced Stevie, neither as attractive nor as good by any criterion I could make out, including looks, that they couldn't remember ever hearing anything so marvellous.

After a while, a theme emerged: the evisceration of youth. This, unmistakably, was middle age getting its own back. Not one of the judges was younger than 40, and the brusque Northern cretin must have been within shouting range of 60. But the tables had been turned in a big way. The young singers' smooth cheeks and thick, glossy hair, high, firm breasts, vitality, and courage were marched blindfolded before the stupid, smug, greying, talentless judges and, in most cases, cruelly humiliated, yawned at, stopped in mid-verse, jeered at, urged to piss off home to Wigan. Mum and Dad and their mates and classmates had all pleaded with them to audition, not to squander their remarkable God-given abilities? Well, it was simply too ridiculous for words! And how the judges played to the cameras as they fell all over one another, absolutely howling with derisive laughter. See what good your youth and beauty and talent do you now, Smoothcheeks? Ha!

I discovered I was simultaneously quite enjoying it, and hating myself for enjoying it. What a gamut of emotions it elicited. Here my heart broke for the broken-hearted might-have-been superstar, her meticulous Britney Spears impersonation savagely disparaged, weeping uncontrollably as she staggered from the audition room. And here, as the brusque Northern cretin and the smug, posh-accented record company executive beside him flared their nostrils in contempt, I wanted to get my hands round their wattled necks and squeeze until they breathed no more. It was a geek show for enlightened times, and I fell for it hard.

★ ★ ★

By the autumn following her concert tour, Kate was sufficiently recovered to perform with Cliff Richard at the London Symphony Orchestra's 75th anniversary celebration at the Albert Hall. She wore her white dress from the 'Wuthering Heights Indoors' video, the panelled full-length white terylene one, with a chiffon underlay, and performed 'Symphony In Blue', 'Blow Away', and 'Them Heavy People'.

She became ever better chums with Gabriel, who introduced her to drum machines and sampling, and appeared in her Christmas special for BBC-TV. She didn't fail to notice the remarkable way Gabriel's engineer Hugh Padgham had recorded Phil Collins' drums, and would soon use a similar combination of open-miking, gated reverb and warm distortion on her own stuff, to excellent effect. Determined to find the drum machine as rich a source of inspiration as Peter had done, she resolved to write a song a night with it. After fretting for a while that it might drive her mad, she learned to start hearing musical clues in the relentless beats, and soon had 20 songs dashed off.

EMI pointedly wondered if she might like to put them on an album. She would, provided she be allowed to produce it herself, with the help of engineer Jon Kelly. Abbey Road heaved with the flowers with which EMI filled its small, intimate Studio 3 to try to keep her creative. She was said to have gone through much chocolate and Courvoisier, and to smoke John Player Specials like a bloody chimney.

She mostly used the musicians who'd backed her on stage, along with the celebrated piano player Max Middleton, who wore a succession of peculiar hats for the occasion. Paddy, of course, played a great many very exotic instruments. She spent a week each on 'Breathing' and 'Babooshka', not in the ivory tower of the control room, but singing live right along with her accompanists each time, trying to inspire her accompanists. It was said that the staff of the Abbey Road canteen were outraged to the verge of mutiny by the amount of EMI crockery Kate smashed trying to get just the right smashing-crockery sound for the song's end. But when the recording was done, she sent everyone in sight Belgian chocolates. How could one not love this girl?

★ ★ ★

Duncan paid me a surprise visit just before *Fab Lab* was over. "Know what I quite like about it?" he asked. "That the judges don't pull their punches. When somebody's crap, they say so." All my life I've had the feeling of living on a planet slightly different to that on which the rest of humanity lives. It makes me lonely. And hungry, of course.

"I wanted to apologise again for Gilmour," he said. "Even when they were little, he always saw himself very much as Cathy's protector."

I nodded my acknowledgement, but wasn't delighted with the implication that Cathy needed protecting from me. Duncan turned towards the TV, on which an Asian boy with very large eyes was trotting out all of Sir Elton's most familiar vocal mannerisms. "Blimey," Duncan marvelled. The judges were absolutely beside themselves. "I will absolutely stake my reputation on your becoming a huge, huge star," the radio personality judge gasped. There were tears in the corners of the Northern cretin's eyes. "Brilliant," he whispered, loath to let them spill out, "absolutely brilliant."

The smug record company executive with the posh accent rolled his eyes. "Pedestrian," he yawned. "Maybe slightly below pedestrian, but I'll give you the benefit of the doubt."

The fourth judge, the lone woman, usually by far the gentlest, said she'd known straight away the boy had been imitating George Michael, but didn't think he'd done so very successfully, and off he went, his bottom lip quivering. He got outside, to where the show's Scottish presenter, whom we were clearly supposed to perceive as irresistibly scampish, was waiting for him, and absolutely detonated with grief. "My dad's got cancer," he wailed, "and my mum's a seamstress, but she's got arthritis in both her hands and can barely manage the work anymore! I was going to support them and my nan and four little sisters!" The Scottish scamp looked mortified. It was one thing to comfort some little narcissist who'd lost nothing more than her dreams of universal adoration in spite of her breasts being too small and her hips too big, but this – did their contracts compel them to deal with something like this? The kid actually collapsed to his knees, pounding the floor in agony. It was wonderful television.

"Poor little sod," Duncan sniffled, and then he was in tears of his own.

In comparison to most of those I'd been around in the past half hour, both live and on screen, I was Mr. Cheerful. What a very weird feeling.

Duncan got worse before he got better. I put my arms around him. He startled me with how enthusiastically he responded in kind. It turned out not to have to do with Cathy. "I split up with my partner on Monday," he sniffled. "Nearly three years together. And we had a kid. I can't tell you how much we'd been through together, her and me, and now it ends like this." He shook his head and resumed crying. A fat girl was screeching Toni Braxton's 'Unbreak My Heart' at the four judges, who were trying to top one another's comically pained expressions. I reluctantly switched off the TV.

"We met at Addictions Anonymous. Mine was gambling, hers sex. Don't laugh. I didn't know before then that you can be addicted to sex or gambling, but you can. Do you suppose I'd be moving back in with my Mammy at my age if I hadn't spent every spare minute at

William Hill betting on football or whether the bloody sun would shine the next day? We became each other's strength.

"She relapsed a couple of times, once with her ex-husband, of all people, and once with Gilmour. That took some getting over. Her ex-husband who used to beat her up, mind you. But we got through it. And as I say, we had Jennifer. She's autistic. Incredibly clever – you can tell – but they say we may never hear her voice. And we got through that as well.

"Then a few months ago, something happened. Me and Gemma went out and left this young bloke, the younger brother of Gemma's best mate from work, to look after Jennifer. Nice-looking young fellow, and not the sort of teenager who can never quite manage eye contact. Really confident – looked you right in the eye. Shook your hand so you knew you were shaking hands with somebody. What's that word? Charisma, charismatic. The sort of guy that back at school all the boys would have wanted to be mates with, and all the girls fancied."

He refolded his handkerchief. I thought he'd have been happy to have the TV on, so it could distract him. I wasn't so sure that wouldn't have been a good idea.

He sighed and pulled the corners of his handkerchief. "He needed a lift home. A cab might have cost me 20 quid. So I offered to drive him." Another sigh. "I'd never felt anything like that for another bloke. Back in school, if somebody was a poof, I was always the first to give him a hard time. I'm not proud of that, but there was a lot we didn't know back then, and there you are.

"I pulled over. We chatted, not about anything especially sexy. We talked about football, for Christ's sake. He just had this really appealing, charming way about him. Jamie his name was. I leaned over and held him, just held him. He put his arms round me. I kissed him. Got my tongue in. It wasn't like I was forcing him. It wasn't like he wasn't kissing me back. Oh, bugger!"

He was in pain. We both were. Why on earth was he telling me all this? The only thing clear was that he had to get it all out.

"I was beside myself with confusion. He was all I could think about the next three days. Even Gilmour, who's got his own problems, his anger issues and that, noticed something was wrong. I told him me and Gemma were rowing.

"I tried to get Jamie on his mobile. He didn't return my calls. I sent him a text message saying I had to see him. Then I heard back from him. If I didn't give him such-and-such number of quid per week, he was going to tell his dad. He had the text message from me as proof.

"It turned out he was only 17. He hadn't managed to mention that before, and I'd been too stupid to ask. He looked 20, not that I'm any great judge. You know what they say about a man having only enough blood to work his brain or his cock, but not both at once? Well, I was living proof. And I'd thought I'd been a wreck before!

"For three weeks I paid him. But then me and Gilmour had two really slow weeks on the trot, and I had to choose between him and my gambling debt. My gambling debt's to a couple of thugs who'd be just as happy to dislocate my shoulders as get their money. So he rang Gemma and told her the lot. She was livid. She said it wasn't that I'd had somebody else, or even that the somebody else was an underaged boy. It wasn't even that I was spending money she owed for Jennifer's being looked after during the week, when we were both working. It was that I'd lied to her. That's what she said hurt worse than anything."

His voice had become a monotone. He wasn't talking to me anymore, but to the picture-less television screen. "So she packed me in. Said it could never be the same."

Ibiza seemed six months ago. I wanted so much to surrender to my exhaustion. But there was more on poor Duncan's mind, and he reverted to his thousand-metre stare and monotone to tell me what it was.

"What I told you about the babysitter? It was all true. But that isn't why Gems left me. In fact, she quite enjoyed the idea of a threesome. She packed me in because I hit her."

He sat there shaking his head and sighing. "No. I'm lying about that too. I never laid a finger on her. Never even came close. Which is quite odd, isn't it? When I was a sprog, it seemed my da must have walloped me 20 times a day. I was forever black and blue. He said if I didn't tell my teachers I'd stumbled on the stairs, I'd get worse. I think some of them must have suspected, but they couldn't be bothered with it.

"It wasn't all bad, I suppose. It made me fearless at school. I reckoned there was nothing the hard lads could do to me that my dad hadn't done already. I was a crap fighter, but I wasn't afraid of anybody. I was respected for that.

"Mammy finally divorced my dad just before I turned 15. Gilmour was a little chap, of course. Da had been walloping Mammy for years. She began walloping back when I was around 12, but he was much bigger, and he'd done a bit of amateur boxing as a lad. It wasn't until she started carrying a paring knife with her at all times that he finally laid off a bit. I was there the first time she stuck him. Got him a good one between the ribs. You should have seen the look on the bastard's face. I wish I'd had a camera, but I was lucky just to get something to eat. He gambled too. Maybe it's a genetic thing. Maybe it's in my bloody DNA.

"So I grew up thinking might makes right. Well, not really thinking it, not sitting down with my chin in my hands like that famous statue and saying, 'Hmm, yeah.' More accepting it as the way things naturally were. So I'd have expected myself, when me and Gems got together, to use my fists on her. Never, though. Not once. I'd have felt a complete coward.

"I wish it had worked in the other direction. In her house, her dad used his tongue instead of his fists. I'd spend five minutes around him and Gems' mum and want to run screaming out of the house. You'd never met a more sarcastic bastard. I don't think I was ever round their place that Gems' mum didn't wind up in tears. And Gemma inherited her dad's abilities. By the time she'd finish with me, I'd be in tears, near enough. And I still never laid a finger on her.

"It was that I'd lied to her, like I said in the first place."

We talked about how Gemma's early life had, in at least one key way, been exactly like my own, with one parent habitually slicing the other up with his tongue. I told him I thought he should be very proud, given what he'd witnessed as a child, of not having abused his wife. I even managed to tell him I'd have given anything to be able, as he was, to say I hadn't backed down from fights in school. I told him how I'd spent my early life feeling deeply ashamed of myself in that regard. I even told him about the aftermath of the football game at Montgomery High School. I'd never told anyone before. My voice broke. And then the dam. It was my turn for tears.

He didn't put his arms around me, and I was grateful. Years ago, the girlfriend who succeeded my wife accompanied me to a session with a couples counsellor. When I burst into tears about something, my girlfriend reflexively threw her arms around me. When the smoke cleared, the counsellor asked her to consider what she'd done. In a way, she acknowledged, it's compassionate to throw your arms around someone in pain, but in another way, can't it be seen as an unwitting attempt to contain them for one's own benefit? When they put their arms around someone at a moment like that, people almost invariably say, "There, there. Don't cry." But why, beside sparing one's self the discomfort of seeing another in terrible pain, should that be? Crying's an incomparable release. Crying's cleansing. It may well be that telling someone who's just burst into tears not to cry is even worse than patronising them by telling them to cry, to go ahead and let it all out. What colossal arrogance for anyone to imagine that it's ever his place to "allow" another his tears!

Duncan didn't put his arms around me, didn't feel called upon to give his permission verbally for me to cry, didn't tell me not to cry. He put his hand lightly on my leg, patted it almost imperceptibly, as though to say simply, I'm here.

12

Absolute Bastards

I KEPT my mind off Nicola by becoming ever more addicted to *Fab Lab*, tuning in twice a week hoping to see the young singers I loathed being reduced to tears by either the judges' ever harsher pronouncements or the public's antipathy. At the end of every edition of the programme, three contestants who'd received the fewest votes of support from the viewing public were marched first before the four judges, who picked one to spare from banishment. Then those for whom the public had voted would decide which of the remaining two to spare. All of this was accompanied by music portentous enough to have been composed for a film about the siege of Leningrad, or for *Who Wants To Be A Millionaire?*

By the time a contestant faced his peers, he was usually shaking visibly, and often glistening with sweat. The little speech they gave to their fellow singers was always the same. "I did the best I could with my song, and all I ask is that you vote from the heart." As opposed, I guessed, to the gall bladder, kidneys, or cerebrum. I particularly enjoyed the banishment of the self-infatuated little male model type from Oldham who'd tried to demonstrate his versatility by performing an old Elton John number with much batting of his long eyelashes and the odd wildly incongruous hip hop hand gesture. He reminded me of a boy in my junior high school who, in signing my yearbook, had got my name wrong. A boy that popular could hardly be expected to remember all the wallflowers' names, could he?

For a moment, it appeared as though he'd foil me and maintain a stiff upper lip, remain gracious and brave to the end. But then, when the vacuous blonde (what else?) presenter asked if he expected to miss his fellow contestants, he burst into angry tears. "After they've voted me off? No, I won't miss the fuckers a bit!" It was a great, great moment in British pop history, and television history as well.

They had him on again briefly to apologise at the conclusion of the following week's programme. This time, as he explained that the pressure had got to him, and that he was in fact extremely grateful for the opportunity *blah blah, blah blah*, his tears seemed sad, rather than furious. But then, quite wonderfully, he lost his composure all over again after the vacuous blonde asked what he'd been doing – winning a karaoke contest in his local. Those who'd voted him off still stood to win a lucrative recording contract and a year's stay in a luxury flat in St. John's Wood, and he'd won a karaoke contest in a pub in Oldham. "It isn't bloody fair, is it?" he howled. "I can sing better than all but two of the remaining boys, and I'm loads better looking than either of them! That's got to count for something! It's fucking *got* to!"

A part of me hoped that the next evening's news would reveal he'd either topped himself or broken into and wreaked mayhem in the house in Hertfordshire where the surviving contestants were sequestered, but I had to be content with the most recent horror in the Middle East.

★ ★ ★

Kate's heretofore unerring sense of what was commercial faltered. EMI wanted to release the buoyant 'Babooshka' as the first single from *Lionheart*, but she insisted on 'Breathing', in which she came out against the idea of a nuclear holocaust. BBC TV's *Nationwide* invited her on to talk about the song, and showed most of the controversial video she'd made to promote it, which was rather more than could be said for those craven wusses at *Top Of The Pops*, which asked its viewers to be content with only the video's beginning. On Radio One's *Roundtable*, Ian Dury, Kid Jensen, and Anne Nightingale all agreed that nuclear holocaust wasn't a very good thing at all, and that Kate's song made a powerful case against it. (Years afterwards, Kate would perform 'Breathing' perhaps the least antic song ever written, at a concert benefiting Comic Relief. To add to the hilarity, the pedal of her piano stuck halfway through the song, resulting in her exploring tonalities she'd gone on stage with no intention of exploring.)

'Breathing' reached only number 16. 'Babooshka' made the Top 5. No one could have blamed EMI for saying, "Told you so," but there is no evidence of their having done so, probably in significant part because the album that contained the two tracks proved to be the first number one by a British female solo artist (if only for a week, after which it was dislodged by Bowie's *Scary Monsters*).

For me, *Never For Ever* was only a very small improvement on

Lionheart, solely on the basis of 'Babooshka', with its irresistible chorus, and 'Army Dreamers', which benefited from a pleasing acoustic guitar motif and wasn't over-arranged, even though its centrepiece was an annoyingly coy lead vocal. 'Violin', with its balls-to-the-wall guitar solo, dude, contained more vocal mannerisms than Lene Lovich managed in her entire recording career. 'Egypt' similarly evoked a mental patients' cabaret. If Kate actually stayed in her lower register for several bars in succession in 'The Wedding List', she more than made up for it with the munchkin backing vocals of 'Blow Away (For Bill)', which pretty much forfeited any chance the song had of being touching. 'All We Ever Look For', featuring a synthesiser pretending to be someone whistling, timpani (just, apparently, for eccentricity's sake), and footsteps walking back and forth across the stereo landscape, recalled Brian Wilson at his least accessible.

★ ★ ★

The mountain of flesh and Cyril rang (they'd got my number from directory enquiries!), and invited me to lunch at their home. I told them I'd feel awkward, not having been invited by Nicola herself. They said I shouldn't, as it would be only the three of us. Nicola was . . . away.

If anything, the mountain of flesh was even huger than the first time I'd visited, but also very much more welcoming. Her interactions with her poor husband reminded me of my own parents' no less than before. "Cyril," the mountain of flesh decreed as soon as he'd admitted me to the house, imploring me under his breath for a fag, "why don't you go out in the garden and smoke a few fags or something?"

"Because I haven't got any, love," he finally managed, warily. "When did they stop being forbidden?"

She ignored the question and rang a little bell on the little table beside her. What looked like a proper English butler, but was probably just a newly retired neighbour enacting a fantasy of submission, appeared. "Smithson," she said, "you will roll my husband three cigarettes."

"I'm afraid I've quit smoking, madam."

"You've done nothing of the sort, Smithson. Three cigarettes. And we will have our starters now."

Smithson, blushing, led the excited Cyril, who seemed unable to believe his good fortune, out of the room.

"You're probably wondering why Smithson didn't answer the door," she correctly surmised. "What, and deny Cyril the exquisite pleasure of trying to cadge a fag? But enough of Cyril. We were surprised not to have seen you around. It was our impression that you rather fancied Nicola, unseemly though it certainly was for you to do so, given the discrepancy in your ages."

I mumbled the usual lies about having been busy. She demanded to know what I'd been busy doing. Attending to personal business, I told her. But still she came, wanting to know what sort of business. Watching *Fab Lab* and overeating, I thought. "I'm afraid I'm going to leave it at personal business," I said, smiling, disliking her.

She sighed. Smithson tiptoed into the room with a trayful of food. "Not yet, Smithson," she said. "Do send my husband back in."

"Very well, madam," Smithson sighed, hating her. "He's only halfway through his second fag, though, madam. Shall I . . ."

"*Now*, Smithson," she interrupted him emasculatingly. "Just now!"

Poor Cyril reeked of his truncated pleasure, but I soon twigged that was the whole point. The mountain of flesh fanned the air in front of her and pulled a face. "What a vile, vile, vile habit! Honestly!"

"I'm sorry, darling," Cyril began. "It's a very difficult habit to . . ."

"Shut it, Cyril. And keep it shut!"

He shivered with humiliation and clasped his hands in front of him, head bowed. I felt right at home. "I won't beat about the bush," the mountain of flesh said, turning back to me. "I should like to start seeing rather a lot of you, your time-consuming personal business permitting, of course."

"Well," I improvised, "when Nicola gets back from wherever she is, I expect you and Cyril and I will indeed be seeing . . ."

"As of 48 hours ago, she's at a fat farm," the mountain of flesh interrupted, picking three large bonbons from a huge box beside her. "In California. It's said to be the best in the world, with an incomparable rate of success, and its own jargon. I do know it's costing Cyril a bloody fortune. She'll be there several more weeks.

"But Nicola isn't a part of this particular equation. It's you and me I'm talking about. For whatever sordid little reason, you're attracted to fat women. They don't come any fatter than me. On her return, if this place is all it claims to be, Nicola will be only a fraction of her former size. Hence, it's obviously me you want to have an affair with."

Leering, she first pulled her top sheet down and then the hem of her dressing gown up, revealing herself to be wearing black nylons with lace tops. I thought I might faint. I hoped I would.

"Don't tell me you haven't thought of me since we met," she said. "Don't tell me you haven't fantasised about diving into me, as though into a heated swimming pool. Because I simply won't believe you."

I was vaguely conscious of Cyril, where he stood, gasping. But I had to devote most of my attention to willing enough blood to my brain to keep me standing.

"I'm very flattered," I finally began.

As you know already, it was hardly as though I hadn't been yearned after in my time, inconceivable though that might have seemed to anyone who saw me that day, or who'd known me as a kid. Just before and during my tenure as the face of Marcel Flynn, I'd turn up at the dentist for my biannual cleaning and all the hygienists would suddenly remember they had appointments they wanted to confirm out in the reception area. Returning from the gents' in a restaurant, I'd stop conversations in mid-word at tables where only women were seated.

At the ends of two job interviews (for soul-destroying temporary office jobs), my female prospective employers asked me to stand up and turn around for them. Having not been noticed at all when I yearned for it most, I had to admit that I sort of enjoyed being objectified, and believed I could understand why some women enjoyed being lap dancers. Indeed, when I found out how much Chippendales dancers could earn in tips, I actually rang them up to find out about audition-ing, only to learn they wanted guys who could dance and had well-developed pectorals. Dreamboat though I seemed suddenly to have become, I was disqualified on both counts, unless, on the former, they counted the tentative foxtrot I'd done at junior high school sportsnites.

"You may excuse yourself, Cyril," the mountain of flesh snapped at her husband, who bolted without further encouragement.

"He's headed for the loo," the mountain of flesh sighed, "for some feverish self-stimulation. This was all for him, you know."

I knew no such thing.

"Don't flatter yourself, Mr. Herskovits. You're attractive enough, I suppose, in a sort of vulgar, film starrish way, but I'm a one-man woman, and Cyril's that man. Since I got like this, conventional coitus has been pretty much out of the question. For him, my trying to pull someone right under his nose is the next best thing, bless him."

It was confusion I was woozy with now, and not revulsion. She sussed that as well. "He's the best thing that's ever happened to me. I mean, I really do dislike smoking, and really do wish he wouldn't, but the disdain and sarcasm and harshness? All for him. He asks for them. When we first started, I thought it was . . . perverse, I suppose, treating someone you loved like that. But isn't real love giving the other person what delights him most?"

★   ★   ★

Chastened, but enlightened too, maybe a slightly better man for the experience, I proceeded to my second meeting of Overeaters Anonymous. All the originals except Nicola were there, the hostile ones no less hostile than the first time, along with a pair of notable new additions. The more enormous was the more notable. She'd made herself up to look newly exhumed, with very pale pancake make-up, dark purple lips, and violet eye shadow. Her opaque contact lenses were the colour of milk. She wore as much eyeliner as the Mexican gang girls of my youth, but hadn't been content merely to outline her eyes with it. She'd also used it to draw upside-down crosses on the outside corner of each eye. She'd braided her long hair, and then tied multiple long pieces of fluorescent pink yarn to each braid. Her clothing combined filmy black see-thru bits with PVC with black fishnet. It looked as though she'd slashed her stockings with a razor before putting them on. The shoes Boris Karloff wore as Frankenstein's monster were dainty and feminine compared to her boots, with their seven-inch crepe platforms.

She wasn't going to have to change for Halloween. In her sort of desperate, please-notice-me way, she was magnificent.

Her sidekick was far less so. She'd dyed her hair jet black, lavishly outlined her eyes, and was wearing rings not just in both nostrils, but at the outside corners of both eyebrows as well. She'd skipped the pale foundation make-up, though, and thus looked the very picture of robust good health compared to her chum. She might have bought her clothing, all black though it was, at British Home Stores.

But the main difference was in how they carried themselves. The more striking one's body language said she was quite happy to be the centre of attention. Her sidekick's was that of a lifelong wallflower, one quite accustomed to being ignored while pairs of blokes chatted up her more notable friend. I wanted to go over and embrace her, but the look in her eyes when they briefly engaged my own said I ought not to.

It turned out this was their first meeting, and for their attendance to have been the idea of the more striking one, who called herself Dahlia, and weighed 15 stone even though she wasn't quite five feet tall. Her major weakness was melted butter apparently, into which she loved to dip everything she ate.

She introduced herself quite volubly. At 13, she'd shown remarkable gymnastic ability, and there'd been talk of sending her to Eastern Europe to train with a top coach. But then she broke her collarbone and discovered that she liked dancing even more than gymnastics, and singing better than either. By 14, she was winning every karaoke contest staged in Lewisham/Southwark/Greenwich, and by 15 was singing and dancing in the chorus of a West End show, earning more than her butcher father. After an aide to one of the hottest managers in pop saw her in the show, she found herself shortlisted for the mixed group of five the manager was putting together. Of the nine girls competing for three slots, she finished fourth, but no sooner had she talked the West End show into taking her back than one of the three girls chosen for the group was discovered to have a child, and was sacked.

"I was actually stupid enough to be over the moon about it," she said, twisting a strand of fluorescent pink yarn around a finger. "If I'd known what lay in store for me, I'd have run out and had a sprog or two of my own."

Crinolyn, the bolshy mum of teens, wasn't much amused by this. Dahlia's sidekick, whose name and weight we still didn't know, and would wind up never knowing, noticed, and turned out to be more aggressive than her defeated expression might have suggested. "What's your fucking problem, you great fat cow?" she asked Crinolyn. Whereupon both of them got to their feet as quickly as women of such immensity can, and began lumbering menacingly toward one another, only for heroic Graham, our leader, to waddle between them.

Once having caught his breath – which, considering how compressed his lungs were by the fat surrounding them, he did surprisingly quickly – Graham laid down the law to Dahlia's sidekick about no name-calling. "We're here to support each other," he said, "not to cause each other more pain. The thin world does enough of that without any help from us." Dahlia's sidekick resumed looking morbidly sullen.

Dahlia began to continue her story, but Jez E. Bell suddenly blurted, "I know who she is. Just look at her! She's one of The Condimettes!"

Even Crinolyn was impressed. Even I was. There'd been an 18-month stretch just before Y2K during which it seemed The Condimettes were never not at number one. They'd been huge in Europe too, and Asia, and Australia. (We Americans, who hadn't liked Robbie Williams either, begrudged them a single hit, and then ignored them.) I remembered reading an article saying that a doll modelled after one of the five was the gift requested most by little British girls. They appeared in adverts for everything from cosmetics to driving schools to soft drinks. They must have made £100 million pounds each.

"And I bloody hated it, almost from the first day," Dahlia told us. "Oh, the dosh was lovely at first, but you get used to it very quickly. And you soon find out that you can't go out to spend it, not without a mob of slobbering subhumans with cameras converging on you and shooting off their flashes in your face. And what they did to me wasn't even the worst part. It was what they did to my family. My dad couldn't go into the garden for a quiet fag (mum doesn't let him smoke inside) without the telephoto lens boys going mad in the trees they'd been waiting in. One day I was going to take my niece Louisa into London for a day of fun. We took one step out of the door and the flashes blinded us. Louisa was so frightened she wet herself. She's been too ashamed to come out of her bedroom ever since.

"They broke up my mum and dad's marriage. One of the tabloids got photos of dad and his secretary on the beach in Blackpool while he was meant to be in the States on business. Another published photos of my sister and her best mate's husband. There was no hiding from them. Nobody was safe. And it was all down to me. If I'd been content to stick with the karaoke contest circuit, or even on the West End stage, none of this would have happened."

"I don't know what you're complaining about," Crinolyn, the voice of working-class non-empathy said, looking to Boopsie and Graham for their approval. "Poor little rich girl, with your millions, with your half-dozen houses and your cars. I wouldn't be surprised if you had your own bloody plane. Well, stop your moaning. It's sickening."

"Maybe you'd like to step outside and repeat that," Dahlia's sidekick challenged her, reaching into her handbag for a can of hairspray that she brandished like a hand grenade.

"How about if I repeat it to your mother, you hideous fat bitch?" Crinolyn said, laboriously climbing once more to her feet, finding it rather harder this time.

Graham gasped as he regained his own feet. "Crinolyn, what I said to Dahlia's sidekick applies equally to you too. Name-calling is right out, for old members as well as new." It seemed less Graham's rebuke than her own breathlessness that made Crinolyn sit back down.

"You see," Dahlia said, "this is exactly the problem. Everyone thinks if you've got dosh, you've got nothing to moan about. But that's stupid. Does a rich person with inoperable cancer have anything to moan about?"

"Shut it!" Boopsie snapped, shocking everyone, including herself.

"My auntie died of breast cancer last year. I won't have you making light of it."

"I wasn't making light of anything!" Dahlia protested. "I'm hardly in a position to make light of anything, am I?" She glanced around, hoping that someone – anyone! – had enjoyed her little joke at her own expense. I might have been the only one who got it. But she remained defiant.

"I won't apologise for my misery," she said. "If you lot want to believe that nobody with money has any reason to be miserable, be my guest. Just don't come running to me when, after you become pop and film stars in your own right, and the tabloid press make your life a living hell, you discover the dosh is a small consolation."

Nobody got that one either, not even her sidekick, still glowering at Crinolyn. It was clear to me, though, that she was a born entertainer.

"Sod it," she decreed in disgust. "Let's say I had no good reason to be miserable, but that I was anyway. I wanted to be left alone. I wanted the people I loved to be left alone. I had to do something unforgivable and get sacked. It seemed to me, and still seems to me, that our culture can forgive nearly anything over time, except two things – being fat and being old. I reckoned by the time I got even marginally old, my loved ones' lives would be wrecked beyond any hope of repair, so getting fat seemed my only recourse.

"You know how some stars put ludicrous demands in their contracts, like Jennifer Lopez? No one's allowed to refer to steatopygia in her hearing. And she specifies a maximum circumference for the caviar in her dressing room. If any egg is found to exceed that maximum, she's legally entitled to cancel her performance. Well, I didn't go mad like that, but I demanded that my dressing room be stocked with chocolate gateaux and this special ice cream the Americans had formulated just for prisoners of war on the verge of starving to death. Ounce for ounce, it's the most calorific substance known to man."

The front of poor Jez's shirt was getting wet. "What flavours are on offer?" he wondered, salivating prolifically.

"They only do vanilla, which does get a bit boring. But I'd have a roadie melt a couple of boxfuls of Godiva chocolate to pour over it as a sauce."

For a short, exquisite moment, we were all of one mind, lowing rapturously for that which Dahlia described. Someone walking past might have thought we were Buddhists.

"As you can imagine," Dahlia continued, "I began putting on loads of weight. At first our managers tried to pretend it wasn't happening,

Herself. *(LFI)*

Kate would later reveal: "I was unhappy at [St Joseph's Convent Grammar School] and couldn't wait to leave." But not without enough O-levels to spell *boot* five times. *(Omnibus Press)*

East Wickham Farm in Bexley, where Kate enjoyed her girlhood, isn't very far from where Keith Richard and David Bowie enjoyed their boyhoods. There's obviously something in the water. *(Barry Plummer)*

Like David Bowie before her, Kate studied mime with Lindsey Kemp. *(Mick Rock/Starfile)*

An early EMI press shot, albeit not the one that had young men hurling themselves in front of London buses.

Kate with her mother Hannah and brothers Paddy and Jay, all of whom played their part in her music. *(Mirrorpix)*

Kate performs 'Wuthering Heights' on *Top Of The Pops* in entirely the wrong clothing.
(BBC Photo Library/Redferns)

Michael Palin is pleased 'n' privileged to inform our heroine that the readers of *Melody Maker* voted her Britain's top female singer in 1979 for the second year running, this in spite of all the infernal screeching on *Lionheart*. *(Hulton Archive)*

Live in Copenhagen, a city in a Scandinavian country known for its furniture and breakfast pastries, in 1979. *(Jorgen Angel)*

When it came time to perform live, Kate clearly remembered taking dance lessons. *(Rob Verhorst/Redferns)*

With Rowan Atkinson, not exactly Peter Gabriel in the sexual charisma department, collecting their *NME* award for The Secret Policeman's Ball, October 1980. *(Mirrorpix)*

Our vegetarian heroine apparently saw nothing untoward about posing with the family's lionskin rug. *(Hulton Archive)*

Kate with comedian Lenny Henry and a pair of *Spitting Image* puppets, signing Comic Relief books in London, October 1986. *(PA Photos)*

Kate in make-up for Experiment IV, 1986, hardly her most flattering image. *(Geoff Portass)*

At the BPI awards with Peter Gabriel, with whom she collaborated on 1987's 'Don't Give Up'. *(Richard Young/Rex Features)*

At Elstree for 'The Big Sky' video shoot, wrapped in Baco-foil. *(Julie Angel)*

On stage at the Amnesty International concert, 1987, with, among others, early benefactor David Gilmour, here playing bass guitar. *(LFI)*

Kate with long-time partner and drum programmer Del Palmer at a Pink Floyd party. They've long since parted company. *(Richard Young/Rex Features)*

A rare public appearance for the over-40 Kate, at the 2001 *Q* awards, where she picked up the award for Classic Songwriter and endured John Lydon's approbation. *(LFI)*

Kate accepts her 'Outstanding Contribution to British Music' award at the 2002 Ivor Novellos. *(LFI)*

and the press went along. I was on the cover of *Loaded* looking like I'd actually lost weight. What they'd done was put my face on somebody else's body. You can do quite amazing things in Adobe Photoshop if you know your stuff.

"When we were on *Top Of The Pops*, they hid me behind three male dancers. It was ages before anyone twigged. The irony being that it was the tabloid press that wound up being my salvation. *The News Of The World* got photos of me sunbathing nude in my back garden. You might have seen them. They put them on the cover with the caption *Disgusting Horrible Beached Whale Sighted in Islington*.

"I didn't leave it at that. I secretly hired a PR firm to try to get me slagged. It was exactly opposite to what they normally do, and they quite enjoyed it. I became the butt of jokes in the routines of stand-up comedians and chat-show hosts. There was a whole website of jokes that began, 'If Dahlia of The Condimettes was any fatter . . .

"But I hadn't accounted for public support. Our management changed a few words in its boilerplate press release about clients who'd been exposed as alcoholics or substance abusers or paedophiles. You know, the usual bollocks about how, with the right treatment, they hoped I'd be able to get my life back on track and rejoin the group, *blah blah blah*. But the public, who according to all reports, will soon be as obese as America's, weren't having it. Our management were . . . what's that word again?"

"Inundated," her sidekick, still glowering, contributed.

"Right. Our management were inundated with letters of support, letters threatening never to spend another penny on Condimettes product if I got sacked. The papers were full of it for a few days. It was either me or Ulrika Johnsson and that TV bloke who she said had raped her. Didn't anyone see it?"

"I think I may have," Jez claimed, but I got the impression he'd come to fancy Dahlia, as we all had by that time, and was trying to curry favour.

"I had to throw caution to the wind," she continued. "I pretty nearly doubled my calorific intake. From the moment I woke up in the morning to when I had to go on stage, I'd be forcing chocolates down my throat. I passed 16 stone like it was standing still.

"It nearly killed me, but it worked. The PR firm did a deal with an inventor of computer viruses. The virus sent multiple emails to every address in a person's address book with the subject line Don't Let The Condimettes Sack Dahlia! It took a few days, but finally it created the backlash effect we'd hoped for. They got in the girl I'd originally replaced. She'd put her children up for adoption in South America, and they'd all been taken.

"But I couldn't stop eating. My loved ones' lives were going to take years to repair, if they could be repaired at all, and that was terribly upsetting, and I'd come to associate the feeling of being full almost to the point of throwing up with accomplishment. I discovered I couldn't stop eating." A single, perfect tear sneaked as though on cue from her eye. "Which is why I'm here."

Show a group of nine-year-old American girls a photograph of an adorable kitten and they will all sigh "aww" in unison. The women of Overeaters Anonymous now impersonated those American girls, as they got up and converged on Dahlia, covering her with love.

Her sidekick, ignored, tried to pretend she didn't notice. I imagined she did a lot of that. I am cowardly and cruel, venal and vain, mean and misanthropic, with more to be ashamed of than I will ever be able to catalogue. I behaved shamefully towards my parents and have been abandoned by the one person in the world whose love I want most. But I didn't pretend I didn't notice Dahlia's sidekick's discomfort.

I tried to strike up a conversation. "That thing you're not allowed to mention around Jennifer Lopez – steatopygia? What is it, do you suppose?"

This was a girl with no sense of proportion. She gave me the same look she'd given Crinolyn earlier, while brandishing her hairspray. "I don't fucking know, do I?" she snarled. "Why don't you invest in a fucking dictionary?"

Everyone went on about his or her own problems a lot less extensively than the earlier meeting I'd attended. I got the impression everyone was anxious to buy Dahlia a drink. I felt very much a fifth wheel, as I suspect I have from the moment of my first breath, and demurred. *Fab Lab* would be on soon, and how would it feel if I left it unwatched?

★　★　★

That evening's edition of *Fab Lab* was the most enjoyable I'd seen so far. I'd somehow failed to see any of the earlier performances by the contestant Evelyn, who immediately became my favourite. Several contestants' hair stuck out at odd angles, but you got the impression they'd spent ages getting it to do so. Evelyn, on the other hand, seemed to have done his best to get his hair to lie down in an orderly way – and failed dismally. The others had either been graceful to start with, or had been attentive when the guy celebrated for having choreographed such top acts as Wicked Fytt dropped by the Lab to show them how to move when they sang. All four of Ev's limbs seemed to be moving in time to a different drummer. Except for the big Welsh boyo who roared and the Nigerian-surnamed girl who seemed to imagine that she sounded like Aretha Franklin, all the others crooned. Ev croaked and rasped and gurgled and, at the least appropriate moments possible, bellowed. He was Sid Vicious reincarnate, except without the fatal stupidity, and absolutely criticism-proof.

After each of the others performed, the judges would analyse their performances in detail, objecting to this flat note, to that hand gesture repeated once too often, to the other lyrical nuance left unexpressed. After Ev regained his feet, none of them could do anything but giggle. "I don't know if it's music," one of them said, speaking for me, "but I do know I was entertained."

At the programme's end, Ev proved one of the public's favourites. It was enough to restore one's faith in a British public that had first rallied behind Dahlia and then capriciously discarded her like laddered tights: every time I'd watched, the nasal Aretha wannabe had been among the bottom three, only to be reprieved by her fellow contestants. Once again she had to be thrown a line, this time by the judges. Now it would be one of two other girls who was sent packing, either the tearful, blandly exquisite Genoa, whose boyfriend played rugby, or the terrified-seeming Andrea from Leeds, who was nearly as gorgeous as Genoa until she opened her mouth and exposed the dental equivalent of Evelyn's singing. This time the judges were the ones who reprieved the nasal Aretha wannabe. It was very much of a piece with the analyses they delivered after each performance. They seemed to decide which performances to praise – except the sublime Evelyn's – strictly at random.

Someone rang on my mobile during a commercial break. It wasn't someone whose number I had programmed in, which is to say it wasn't Nicola. Hers was my only number. Nor did I recognise the voice, which seemed that of a man trying to sound like a woman, or practising to audition for a Monty Python reunion. "Les Herskovits?" he or she asked. I confirmed it. "You're a mate of the former Condimette who now calls herself Dahlia, or at least a member of the overeaters group she just joined?" When I asked who wanted to know, he or she put the phone down on me.

In any event, the other *Fab Lab* contestants would now have to choose between Genoa and Andrea, but only, of course, after each of the potentially condemned addressed them. "I did the best I could with my song," Genoa intoned solemnly, "and hope you'll vote with your hearts." It occurred to me that, her gorgeousness notwithstanding, I might not have longed to impregnate her even before the anti-depressants knocked my libido unconscious.

But I didn't think long about Genoa because Andrea was now flying in the face of tradition. Tears raced one another down her cheeks. "All I've ever wanted, ever since I was just little," she said, "was to be a famous singer, and not for me. For my mum. She had a promising career started before her accident.

"I know some of us have had a bit of aggro. I apologise for that. It was probably my fault. I think you know what a perfectionist I am." She swiped the tears from her face. "If you'll vote me through to the next round, I'll do anything you ask. Do with me what you will. I'm pretty, aren't I? I mean, I know my bum could be a little narrower, and that I need orthodontia. My dad's a labourer. My mum's disabled. We didn't have money for that sort of thing. But they did their best for me. They couldn't pay for me to have my teeth straightened, but I never doubted their love."

She was overcome by sobbing. The camera showed a succession of close-ups of the gobsmacked other contestants, the judges, poor Andrea's friends and relatives. Her mum, in her wheelchair, was in such agony that she'd thrown her head back and was gasping to breathe. I could imagine that, in the control room, the director was already trying to envisage where he'd display the awards he'd win for this. It was great, great television.

Andrea regained the ability to speak, and addressed another of my favourite contestants, a short, spiky-haired girl from Somerset who was never seen in anything more feminine than combat trousers and T-shirts. "Chris, I know you fancy me. I've seen how you look at me. I've never done it with a girl. Until now, my religious beliefs would have made that impossible. But if you'll vote for me, Chris, I'm yours to do with what you like. Chris, *please*. This means so much to me! This means everything!"

The sycophantic little Scots cheek merchant who was the show's main presenter recovered his own power of speech, and told Andrea to wrap it up. She let out one last laceratingly plaintive *please*, and bowed her head. The blandly exquisite Genoa put her arm around her. Andrea put both arms around Genoa, buried her face in Louisa's chest, and shook with sobs.

Those of us at home saw a great many commercials.

The show returned. There were seven contestants. When Genoa received her fourth vote, the one that propelled her to the next round, she reached for Andrea to console her. But Andrea slapped her hand away. She addressed those into whose midst she would never be allowed to return now. "You bastards. You absolute bastards. Do you suppose that even one of you is singer enough to sweep the floor of my bloody dressing room?"

The little Scot took a tentative step toward her. She froze him with a look of the purest malice and turned back to her betrayers.

"If I live to be 100, I'll find a way to hurt you as much as you've hurt me. I promise you." And then a pair of security guards big enough to have moonlighted not only as bouncers at clubs, but as the clubs them-selves, materialised to escort her away while I, misanthropic enough to have found a fellow human being's meltdown terribly amusing, giggled until I gave myself hiccoughs.

13

Lurking In The Hedge

I THOUGHT I heard a giggle just outside my door, and wished I were 10 stone lighter so the floorboards wouldn't creak if I tried to sneak over to it. Remarkably, they were fairly quiet anyway. I crawled very slowly, muffling my hiccoughs as I got nearer so whoever it was wouldn't be able to tell I was approaching. I finally reached the door and got as quietly as I could to my feet. I worried that whoever it was would hear the pounding of my heart, but no one seemed to be scampering down the hall. I swung the door open.

It was a shaven-headed guy with an earring and a pierced eyebrow, sharp-featured, blue-eyed, early forties, hawkish, not someone whose pint you'd want to accidentally knock over, in a Ben Sherman sports shirt, pressed jeans, and immaculate Nike trainers. The top of a tattoo peeked out from above his collar.

I decided to pretend I was on my way to the loo. "Can I help at all?" I asked.

"I'm from . . . the council," he said, lying transparently. "It's my job to ensure that boarding houses . . . aren't being used as havens for asylum seekers. Any around here, mate? If there are, you'd better tell me."

Downstairs, Mr. Halibut poked his head out of his door. I saw no recourse but to invite my eavesdropper into my room. He seemed embarrassed by the idea, but finally shrugged and accepted. I asked if the council had provided him with any identification. He was so interested in everything in my room that he didn't hear the question. He seemed to be trying not to fail to notice anything. I asked again. He furrowed his brow and reached for his wallet, only to think better of it.

I gently admitted my impression that he wasn't from the council at all. I wouldn't want to get anyone with a pierced eyebrow angry. But I apparently hadn't been quite gentle enough. He glowered as though about to leap up and head-butt me. But then, to my infinite relief, he broke into a big grin, an abashed one. "I'm a journo," he admitted. "Well, a part-time journo, a moonlighter. I'm a builder mainly. But I do a bit of journalism after hours."

It turned out he was a freelance contributor to *The News Of The World*, and had been since he'd happened to find himself in the same off-licence as Declan Worst and observed the supposedly recovering alcoholic former West Ham striker buying a gallon bottle of Stolichnaya. "They paid me £100 for that, and away I went."

He hadn't produced anything quite as juicy – or as lucrative – since, but had found he enjoyed the work, and certainly preferred it to "rowing with the missus," as he put it. "She takes it personally that I'd rather be down the pub getting bladdered with mates or beating up asylum seekers than watching programmes about the bloody property ladder with her! I'd have divorced her ages ago if it weren't for our prenuptial agreement."

It occurred to me that it might have been him who'd rung before and sounded as though auditioning for Python. And I was right. But he'd done all the sheepish grinning he intended to do, and now glared hawkishly at me as though to demand, "What of it?" Similarly, when I asked his name, he demanded, "Who wants to know?" as though there were more than two of us in the room.

He was interested in me only to the extent that I might be able to provide some saleable goss about Dahlia. When I said I couldn't, he looked furious, and then grim. "Another evening down the drain then," he mused bitterly, toying with the hoop in his eyebrow, making me a little squeamish. "Geezers on the Liz Hurley team are making a grand a week, some of them. And here I am stuck in the bloody fourth division."

He seemed in no great hurry to leave. "Where am I going to go? By the time I get back to Plaistow, they'll be taking last orders. You know what the bloody tube is like."

I took pity on him. I had a couple of bottles of Budweiser downstairs in Mrs. Cavanaugh's fridge. It wasn't any more flavourful or robust in London than it had been back in California – it tasted like beer-flavoured soda pop wherever you drank it – but it reminded me of home. I asked if he fancied a pint. He told me he'd sooner drink bloody gnat's urine, but apparently only because he felt culturally compelled to. Then he eagerly accepted my offer.

Swill though it was, the Budweiser made him more sociable, and I felt able to ask if doing the sort of work he did ever made him ashamed. He was incredulous. "Why should it? People need things built, don't they? Without us, people would still be living in bloody lean-to's, like bloody savages, wouldn't they?" It turned out he accepted the odd building job. I gently pointed out that it wasn't building I was referring to, though, but moonlighting for *The News Of The World*. He was hardly less incredulous. "Why should it?" he demanded again. "People need celebrities, don't they? Gives them something glamorous and interesting to identify with, doesn't it? Reading about whose husband Liz Hurley's stolen, or which billionaires she got to be her kid's god-father during their lunch break helps people get through their after-noons at the factory, dunnit?

"And if you're asking me to feel sympathy for the celebrities, save your breath, mate. Nobody forced them to have a hit record or be in a popular film or TV show, did they?"

I was reminded, too vividly, of how, in a tabloid I won't dignify by identifying, one Helen Sanderson, a couple of years before, had offered her readers a shock-horror exclusive. Kate, she speculated, was prob-ably unaware that the six-acre mansion in Berkshire in which she and her guitarist partner Danny McIntosh were hoping to raise what the headline called their "secret son" Bertie far from public scrutiny had been the scene 30 years before of the kidnapping of a 19-year-old boy who lived there with his family. Just the sort of thing parents wanted to hear! But of course no one had forced Kate to have hit records.

"But what about their loved ones," I wondered. "Dahlia told us the worst part by far was her parents and siblings and friends being harassed."

Plaistow belched emphatically, and then waxed sarky. "And I don't suppose any of them had the suss to say, 'Hang on. Maybe this isn't a brilliant idea,' right? Well, bollocks. Anybody who's lived more than a fortnight in this country knows that the tabloid press will quite happily trample anything and anybody standing between it and higher circula-tion." He belched again, more loudly. Budweiser may have no flavour, but no one can say it isn't carbonated.

I asked if I'd be seeing a lot of him. He groaned and said he certainly hoped otherwise. "Dahlia's strictly Page 12 stuff. If I don't get reassigned soon to somebody a little hotter, I'm thinking of packing the whole thing in and going to work for some Albanian mates of mine who import prostitutes from Eastern Europe."

It's an awful thing having no sensitivity to irony, never knowing, without a lot of winking or the like, if someone's winding you up.

★   ★   ★

In the wake of the success of 'Babooshka' as a single and *The Kick Inside* re-entering the album charts, scampish former Malcolm McLaren side-kick Fred Vermorel unleashed *Kate Bush: Princess Of Suburbia*, conceived, he'd reveal years later, as an absurdist novella written from the viewpoint of a pair of psychotic tabloid gossipmongers.

'Army Dreamers', thematically reminiscent of 'Oliver's Army', Elvis Costello's far superior hit of the previous year, became the album's third single, with 'Passing Thru The Air', one of the songs Kate had worked on in Dave Gilmour's home studio years before, on the B-side. Mick Jagger, for whose expressively off-key singing on 'Little Red Rooster' Kate had by now graciously expressed great admiration, churlishly condemned it on *Roundtable* as not his kind of music, but acknowledged that Kate was very nice. Patronising bastard.

Not that the critics were wetting themselves praising the album. One, while acknowledging (incredibly!) that Kate's melodic gift rivalled McCartney's, dismissed the album as "perfection in a vacuum". Elsewhere, *Sounds'* Tony Mitchell, later to move to the fetish-oriented *Skin Two*, sniffed, "It's MOR, it's show business, it's dishonest," in spite of the fact that it couldn't have been less MOR on a bet. (Did he honestly believe this stuff to make few demands of its listeners? *Hello?*) Kate returned to the provinces for the first time since her concert tour for interviews and in-store appearances in Edinburgh, Glasgow, Newcastle, Liverpool, Manchester (where she was thought to kiss over 600 fans), and Birmingham. Back in London, she arrived at her in-store appearance in Oxford Street to find a queue of fans extending halfway to Selfridge's.

The drummer Charlie Morgan gently pointed out that she was now overusing the adjective *phenomenal*, as she'd earlier overused *amazing*, and she was mortified. Years later, it would be *incredible* she'd seem to use in every third sentence. Whatever her word of the moment, she didn't much enjoy the process of being interviewed. Following McCartney's lead (the interview included with his initial solo album was with himself), she told the fictitious Zwort Finkle, "I find it very difficult to express myself in interviews. Often people have so many preconceptions that I spend most of the interview trying to defend myself from the image created by the media eight years ago. Sometimes I find myself saying things to please them or just to give an answer. Sometimes I just burble complete rubbish, and sometimes I feel like a trapped animal. Quite often I go over an interview in my head afterwards and realise I've said something quite contrary to what I believe."

★   ★   ★

Having found, in the harsh light of day, that the mountain of flesh's assurances weren't enough for me, I rang Cyril. My natural inclination, until my daughter was born, had been to care about no one but myself, and after she ceased to speak to me, I went back to it. But I found myself wondering if he was really all right in the face of the mountain of flesh's cruelty.

Smithson the butler answered. "And whom shall I say is calling?" he asked when I requested Cyril. "'Who,'" I reflexively corrected him. Not only a butler, but one who, in trying too hard to speak a butler's impeccable English, spoke it peccably!

"I beg your pardon," he said, censoriously. I explained that *whom* was the accusative form, that it needed to be the object of a verb or preposition, as it was not in the sentence *Who shall I say is calling?*

"Listen, mate," he said after a thoughtful silence, during which he seemed to have decided that he could speak to me candidly, "Fucking him or fucking her, all right? Just tell me which one you bloody want." I simultaneously liked that he felt he could address me as himself, and was devalued by it.

Cyril sounded not merely all right, but positively chirpy. He wasn't content to assure me of his well-being, but insisted we meet for a kebab or a drink. I found the prospect slightly unnerving, though. I can't bear people smoking around me, and out of the mountain of flesh's sight, he would surely be a little chimney. Nor could I imagine what we'd say to one another for as long as it took to eat a kebab, since our previous conversations had consisted almost entirely of his trying to blag a fag and my reminding him I don't smoke. I told him I was awfully busy. I reminded him that getting around wasn't as straightforward for me as it was for people with normal proportions. "Bollocks," he whooped happily. "We're meeting and that's all there bloody is to it."

I'd once smoked myself. I'd worked as a teenager clearing dirty dishes from restaurant tables. The waitresses I assisted always had cigarettes burning in ashtrays in the kitchen, and I loathed the smell. But then, when I went to university, I realised that no one was paying much attention, and that this was a perfect opportunity for me to cultivate a vaguely reckless, dangerous image out of the view of classmates who'd either seen me or heard about me being fed grass.

It occurred to me that Babooshka probably smoked by now. I'd have bet that, in trying to repudiate me in every way available to her, she'd learned to love the hot, carcinogenic smoke in her lungs.

★　★　★

Cyril and I met – he, inevitably, with a cigarette in the corner of his mouth and a replacement in his hand – at a pub near his home, the wonderfully named The Kings Bladder, which seemed, like so much in Britain, to be missing an apostrophe. He leapt up excitedly at the sight of me, and hopped gleefully up and down on the spot as he waited for me to reach him. In the end, he couldn't bear to wait, and ran to intercept me halfway. What a sight we must have been.

He told me I was looking very well. Yet again I cursed my DNA for making me unable to detect irony except in the most blatant circumstances, such as a heroic doctor, newly arrived in darkest Africa to treat AIDS victims after abandoning his lucrative cosmetic surgery practice, being struck down by lightning as he goes out to buy toothpaste.

It was his impression that I might be able to offer some useful tips on going out with younger women, as he hoped to. He based this impression on my having gone out with Nicola. I found this creepy. I pointed out that if I hadn't met her in the overeaters' group, the chances of my asking her out would have been infinitesimal. I told him that our joint membership had made me believe, as I assumed it would make her believe too, that we had something in common. He looked at me quizzically. It made me uncomfortable – and enfranchised to ask how he envisaged going out with younger women in view of his being married to the mountain of flesh. The smoke from his cigarette was getting in my eyes.

"Me and the missus," he laughed, oblivious to my discomfort, the worst kind of smoker, "are husband and wife in name only. I mean, can you honestly imagine me and her having it on?" He screamed with laughter, inspiring scowls all around us, as well, to be fair, as a couple of smirks, and then had to pay for it with several seconds' agonised coughing.

I will never understand how the world works. While Cyril coughed, two guys at the adjoining table stubbed out their handrolleds and lit up fresh ones even while eating the Thai food now being delivered to their table.

"Fucking wog food," one of them growled as he turned his plate in what seemed an attempt to make the stir-fried *ong choi* with yellow bean sauce he'd ordered look more palatable. "God help you if all you fancy's a Scotch egg anymore."

The server, a middle-aged Thai woman, winced, but said nothing. Cyril winced and said a great deal.

"Oi, mate, how about you show a little respect?"

The two handrollers looked at one another. The wog food one asked

Cyril, "How about you shut your fucking gob, you fucking pygmy, before I come over and pull your fucking esophagus out of your fucking bum?" And I'd thought the Thai woman winced before!

Cyril sighed in what at first appeared resignation. I felt my heart beating entirely too quickly. My stomach churned. He carefully stubbed out his fag in a way that suggested he hoped to come back to it, and stood up. His waist and the table saw eye-to-eye. Someone snickered.

"I very strongly suggest, mate, that you apologise," he said, squinting malevolently. The same person who'd snickered a moment before snickered again. Someone else guffawed. If I'd been half a man, I'd have risen and stood beside him. Being who I am, I wanted instead to hide beneath the table.

The publican, bald, prolifically tattooed, and amply spare-tyred – not much to look at, but it's all about how you carry yourself, isn't it? – arrived and scolded the two prospective combatants. "If you lot fancy a punch-up, you can have it in the car park, not in here. You, sit bloody down. And you, eat your *ong choi* and shut up. And we ain't got a car park."

The handroller shrugged and rubbed his wooden chopsticks together, as seasoned diners in Oriental restaurants know they must to avoid splinters. Cyril stayed aloft long enough to suggest it was he who was the more disappointed by the publican's intervention.

Where, at moments like this in my own life, had been those whose interventions might have allowed me to save face in such a way?

But then I discovered it might not have been Cyril whose face was saved. When I asked what he imagined might have happened if the handrollers had come for him, he laughed and said, "I'd have jumped up and down on their faces." During the day, it turned out, he was a foreman at construction sites. Before that, and after his brief career as a jockey, he'd been a full-time thug. "My size really worked for me. I could get into places where a bigger fellow would have been suspected." It turned out, in fact, that he'd just been offered a lucrative freelance thug job. "This bird in some singing contest on television. I understand she was voted out of the competition by the other singers – whose faces she thinks could do with some rearrangement." He cackled delightedly. "If I have time, I'll take it. The dosh is fabulous. And it's been a long time since I did anybody in the music business. And if there's any business full of people wanting doing, it's that one."

He cackled again, more loudly this time. I noticed the handroller who'd stayed out of it earlier, the one having *kaeng khiao wan nuea*, looking annoyed. It took only a glance from Cyril to get him fascinated with his meal.

I realised I'd known Cyril – not literally, of course, but someone just like him – in junior high school, in my not-climbing-the-pole days. Billy Ayres was forever getting into shouting matches with boys big enough to have rested their chins atop his little head. It was invariably the bigger boys who walked away embarrassed. For all anyone knew, Billy might have been as weak as he was tiny, but no one ever tested him. He screamed. His eyes bulged. He didn't express rage, but embodied it. Boiling testosterone must have accounted for 40 per cent of his body weight. I think the universal presumption was that anyone as fearless as that had to be brilliant at some fantastically lethal martial art, or maybe at all of them. He was the Sir Alex Ferguson of another time and place.

But I was wrong about Cyril. He'd been tested extensively, as a bantamweight boxer. He'd been the Territorial Army's champion one year. His record as an amateur was 22–0. Of the 22, he'd won 15 by knockout. He was said to have fists of stone. There'd been talk of his turning professional. At 18, while trying to launch his jockeying career, he was working as a bouncer for Basildon's most popular discotheque "and getting to break four or five big yobs' noses per week."

I looked at him in a new light. And then, seeing him in it, enquired gingerly about his relationship with the mountain of flesh. "The meek-ness and that?" he wondered delightedly. "Just good fun!"

Just as he'd always been good with his fists, he'd always been submissive. "Couldn't tell you why," he mused. "My dad was, God knows. Mum gave him a good verbal trampling every day of my childhood, and I hated it. Maybe my being so aggressive sprang from that, do you suppose?

"As a child, I was like other boys, being the brave defender of the weak female and all that bollocks. But everything changed when I got to adolescence, didn't it? Other boys seemed to want girls they could order about, but I always fancied the ones who wanted to do the ordering. They seemed loads more interesting, loads more challenging."

Just what I would have needed as a teenager. As though any girl wasn't too challenging in the first place.

His mobile rang, and he was transformed. He seemed instantly to get even smaller. His voice lost resonance. His spine seemed to curve. "Hello, darling," he mumbled. "Of course, darling. Absolutely, darling. If that's your desire, darling. Yes, darling. I will, darling."

He beamed with pleasure as he folded his mobile back up. "The missus. On the warpath today. Says she'll cane me when I get home if she has the strength. Brill!"

His accent was fairly common to my newly repatriated ear, but he worked at it. He'd actually been to an expensive public school and learned to speak without parting his teeth. It was there that he'd developed his taste for the cane. "It was one of those schools that thought making you suffer was good for your character," he laughed. I hate people with no talent for bitterness, or at least don't trust them. "We were caned quite regularly for nothing at all really. In fact, I remember getting caned once for not having been caned in the previous fortnight. They reckoned that nobody my age could be that virtuous, and punished me for concealing my misbehaviour so well. 'It would have been much better for you,' the headmaster said, 'if you'd been man enough to admit your naughtiness.'

"They also reckoned that praise stunted a boy's growth or something. The only time I remember ever getting any was while being caned. I didn't writhe or yelp. Matron said, 'Brave lad.' I was over the moon for weeks."

He discovered that he was out of cigarettes, and did the most extraordinary thing – blagged a handrolled from the guy he'd nearly come to blows with earlier, who seemed only too pleased to provide it. I just detest those with no talent for bitterness. Or maybe it was that, once their testosterone levels had got back to normal, the two might-have-been warriors recognised one another's manliness, and admired one another for it. It was a feeling I'd probably never know.

"Odd thing about Matron," Cyril chuckled, "is that I saw her again years later, in a phone box in Wardour Street. Well, not her, but a photo. She hadn't lost her interest in naughty boys. In fact, she seemed to have gone into the business of disciplining them." He screamed with laughter. Soon everyone within four tables of us was helpless with mirth too. If it had been me, someone would have come over and told me to shut up. And I'd have listened.

He had to get home, but wanted to know if I'd enjoy accompanying him on one of his upcoming thug runs, hurting one of the singers who'd voted his new client off her show. "If it were *Fab Lab*," I said, "I might have a problem, as I'd liked Evelyn, at least, and thought a couple of the others seemed quite nice." He shrugged disapprovingly. "In my business, there's no room for moral distinctions. You'd be taking food out of your family's fridge."

I told him I was busy. He didn't believe me. "No, really," I said. "Bollocks," said he. There could be no resisting him, and I wound up agreeing to let him collect me the next morning at eleven.

I had him drop me off at the florist on the high road, rather than at Mrs. Cavanaugh's. After all I'd been through, sending Kate a bouquet of chrysanthemums made me feel much less overwrought. I wrote a note reminding her how much I and countless tens of thousands of others were looking forward to her new album, but decided in the end not to attach it. If she didn't know by now, she'd never know.

Plaistow of the pierced eyebrows and Ben Sherman shirt was lurking in the hedge outside Mrs. Cavanaugh's as I managed to climb laboriously out of the cab that took me home. He seemed disgusted that I was alone. As though there'd have been room in the back of the cab for both me and another person! I asked who he'd have wanted me to be bringing home. "A male pop star not previously known to be a bender," he said, "or, even better, a well-known footballer or rugby player, or, best yet, a Cabinet minister thought to be a devoted family man." I told him I'd see what I could do, but didn't envisage being able to do much, given my devout heterosexuality.

14

Not Thugging, Bluffing

CYRIL collected me promptly the following morning, and we headed for Essex. He was very proud of the black eye the mountain of flesh had given him when he got home from The Kings Bladder reeking of beer and cigarettes. Over the course of our journey, he blagged four fags from our driver, who did a lot of sighing. He pointed out the mansion in which a noted comedian's gay orgies had ended in a young man drowning in his swimming pool. Several motorists had stopped to be photographed with the house in the background. Our driver mused that if the comedian could somehow charge them for the privilege, he'd have made enough by now to pay for his defence. I have never very much enjoyed hyperbole unless I'm the one hyperbolising, but I suppose it's like that for everyone.

Our first visit, Cyril revealed, would be to the home of Genoa, the *Fab Lab* contestant with a perfect face who was forever bursting into tears. Apparently taking after the lugubrious Italian side of her family, she cried when another contestant was brilliant, and when another contestant was crap. She cried when the judges told someone they'd been off-key in certain places, and when the judges said their performances had been faultless. She cried when the public voted for her, and when they didn't. I wondered if she took salt supplements.

According to Cyril, she'd been living with her mum and her older brother since splitting up with her rugby star boyfriend, who'd found the idea of millions of male viewers looking at her tits each week unendurable. Her mum was likely to be at work, while her older brother, a depressive unemployed pianist, was likely to be in bed trying to remain asleep until it was time to die. I was worried Cyril might be required to hurt Genoa, but he assured me that no such thing was the case. "We've got a code of ethics just like anybody else," he assured me, a little defensively, "and hurting women is right out. It's their male loved ones who get it."

136

Genoa answered the door, her face looking very much less perfect in real life than on television, her hips looking very much bigger. When Cyril told her who'd sent him, she tried to close the door on us, but he had his little foot in it. Screaming wouldn't have done any good, as the nearest neighbours were too far away to hear. She did what she did best, and cried.

Cyril asked if her brother were at home. She said he wasn't. He arched an eyebrow at her sceptically and told her he'd hate to think she might be telling a porkie. Rhyming slang seemed to make her cry harder. She looked nervously at the stairs behind her. Sure enough, there came someone who might well have been her brother in his underpants and a knackered grey T-shirt, bags under his eyes, and hair seemingly styled by Jamie Oliver – with a food processor. He didn't smell very nice at all. "Hello, hello, hello," he said, "what's all this then?" Depressives often have the best senses of humour, not that it provides them with any solace.

"I'm afraid your sister's been naughty, mate," Cyril told him. "She helped vote a sort of friend of ours out of the *Fab Lab*."

"*Fab Lab*!" Genoa's brother snorted. "Exactly what music in this country has come to, that. A bunch of no-talents mewling a load of old crap for a panel of judges who wouldn't know real talent if it sat on their laps, and then the tone-deaf public voting for the ones with the dewiest eyes."

Genoa absolutely howled. Her brother rolled his eyes and said, "Not you, Gens. At least you sing in bloody tune. Leave it bloody out for a change, will you?"

Cyril cleared his throat pointedly. "If you two are done squabbling, maybe we can get to the reason for my and my colleague's visit, which is to cause a bit of grief around here."

"Ha!" Genoa's brother exclaimed. "The bigger challenge would be to make it stop for five minutes."

"Hang on," Cyril said, frowning. "Unless I'm mistaken, you're not really experiencing grief, but depression."

"There's such a big difference?" Genoa wondered, blowing her nose into a facial tissue.

"There is, in fact," Cyril said. "Grief, according to *The Penguin Concise English Dictionary*, is deep sorrow, whereas depression is a persistent unhappiness. I think of the difference between them as more or less that between a dull ache and a sharp pain."

Both the siblings snickered. "May I ask what's so bloody comical?" Cyril demanded.

"*The Penguin Concise English Dictionary?*" Genoa's brother asked. "You don't see why a person your size citing that, as opposed to the *OED*, is funny?"

Cyril tried to conceal his amusement, but it was a lost cause. He turned his face away, only to guffaw explosively. The three of them howled. What jolly fun this thugging was turning out to be!

"Right," Cyril finally declared, only to discover, on seeing Genoa trying so hard to suppress her own amusement, that he had more laughter in him. "Right," he said again, and this time managed to look grim. "Time to pay the piper. I understand the gentleman's a pianist?"

"In theory," Genoa's brother admitted sourly, "but not in practice anymore. Packed it in. A real musician can't make a living in this country, not unless he's happy to play rubbish. And I wasn't. You know who makes fortunes in this country with their music? Little twerps who don't know the bloody bass clef from the treble. 'Oh, you want to hear some naff Elton John song while you drink, some ghastly Barry bloody Manilow? Well, here, let me play one for you.' Bollocks!"

I'd edged over to the siblings' CD rack. As subtly as I could, I determined what they had in their collection. Not a trace of Kate, but Tori Amos's *Under The Pink*. They deserved whatever Cyril might do to them.

"I'm afraid I'm going to have to break a couple of your fingers, mate," Cyril informed the brother. Genoa gasped, and burst into tears. "Please," she said, "not that! I'll ring the producers! I'll see if they'll me switch my vote."

"Go right ahead," her brother said, holding both hands out to Cyril. "Break them all if you like. They're not doing me a bit of good, are they? Help yourself!" Now he was in tears too.

"Bloody hell," Cyril said, pushing the hands out of his face, getting angrier and louder with each new syllable, roaring at the end. "Why does everything have to be so difficult?"

Well, the neighbours might have heard *that*. The rest of us were stunned. I couldn't have said that I'd never seen anyone so angry. I'd seen Billy Ayres back in junior high school. I've seen Sir Alex Ferguson.

Genoa's brother was the first to regain the power of speech in the face of Cyril's detonation. "It's all right," he said, offering his hands again. "Honestly."

"Simon, don't, please!" Genoa said, grabbing his hands.

"We're off," Cyril informed me in a tone that invited no negotiation. "This tosser's barmy. She's suffering enough having him for a brother."

He took my elbow and we headed back to the cab, only for Cyril to stop halfway and turn back to his might-have-been victim. "Get help, mate. Don't lie around in your own faeces moaning about how unfair the world is. Of course it's unfair. Of *course* it is! But there are pharmacological solutions for the likes of you, serotonin inhibitors and that. Get a bloody prescription! Stop being the black hole your poor sister has to pour endless love into, and never gets anything back! Blimey!"

I found that quite eloquent. In a film, Genoa's brother would have been duly chastened. But this was no film. He got just as emphatic as Cyril. "Selective serotonin re-uptake inhibitors? I've tried 'em!" he shouted, his face contorted with anger. "I've tried 'em all! And they don't bloody work! Luvox? Tried it! Paxil? Tried it! Zoloft? Tried it! Celexa? Tried it! Lexapro? Tried it! You know the one thing I can always count on them to do? Make it impossible to ejaculate! Do you know what it's like to shag when you can't ejaculate, you self-righteous little *Penguin Concise Dictionary* wankfest? It's bloody torture! It doesn't take you long to go off shagging entirely. And guess what that is? It's bloody depressing!" He was hopping with rage by now, literally hopping. I supposed it was the most exercise he'd had in weeks.

"Walk a mile in my shoes, you ghastly little pygmy! Walk a bloody kilometre!"

Cyril had nothing left to fight back with. We got in the cab and were gone.

Once again my expectations were confounded. I'd have expected Cyril to be upset, or at least embarrassed. But he was about as perturbed as if he'd been told that a pop group he hadn't heard of had postponed the release of its next single by 12 hours. I lack resilience of my own, and dislike it in others.

★　★　★

Kate kept her mind off the distressing news that spandex-clad American rock vixen Pat Benatar had covered 'Wuthering Heights' on her *Crimes Of Passion* album, almost certainly confusing many of her fans a treat, by going to see Stevie Wonder in concert. Hardly less transported than she'd been by Lindsey Kemp, she immediately began work on 'Sat In Your Lap', by far her most percussion-heavy track to date. It would later annoy her mightily when people imagined the recorded version to be an attempt to cash in on Adam Ant's tribal drum sound, as she'd conceived both song and arrangement well before the Ants came to be the biggest thing in British pop since whatever immediately preceded them.

Thinking that starting with rhythms would make her music more accessible, she'd encouraged the loyal Del to learn to program her drum machine, which may sound vaguely salacious, but wasn't intended to. She released a rather shrill Christmas single, 'December Will Be Magic Again'. *Woman's World* published her article "How Can You Eat Dead Animals?" *British Cattle Farmer's World* did not, in retaliation, publish an article entitled "How Can You, a Physician's Daughter, Chain-smoke?" There is, in fact, no such magazine.

'December Will Be Magic Again', made Israel's Top 10, but didn't supplant that unspeakable Slade number I won't dignify by identifying by name in the hearts of her fellow Britons, or at least its disc jockeys. Julie Burchill accused her of "coy mysticism". She consoled herself with the rare Perspex and plastic sculpture of John Lennon and Yoko Ono posing for the cover of *Two Virgins* and a copy of the shooting script of *Magical Mystery Tour* she bought at a Sotheby auction of rock memorabilia.

★   ★   ★

My and Cyril's other visit for the day was to be with Ibrahim, also of Essex. Where Genoa was forever inconsolable, Ibrahim was irrepressibly sunny. He'd been one of the least-popular-with-the-public contestants on two of the three editions of *Fab Lab* I'd caught, but each time had reacted almost as though he'd just been named the competition's ultimate winner, showing off a mouthful of enormous teeth, most of which, in contravention of British custom, went in the same direction. When the most querulous of the judges had described his singing as desperately awful, Ibrahim's look had been one of adorable self-censure. When the gentlest of the judges had suggested that he was out of his depth trying to sing rock, and ought to be thinking instead of a career in a boy band, he nodded solemnly, as though this was the sagest advice he'd ever been privileged to receive. He had to be the most gracious teenager in Britain, and here we were en route to cause him pain.

I found that I couldn't bear the idea and asked Cyril how much Andrea was paying him to rough Ibrahim up. He said he wasn't at liberty to disclose that. I bit the bullet and told him I'd pay him 10 per cent more than she was paying him not to lay a finger on Ibrahim. He gave me a look I'd never seen before, sadness mixed with affront. "That's not something I could even consider," he said. "Completely unethical, what you're suggesting."

According to the dossier Cyril had been supplied, Ibrahim lived with his pregnant wife and their six-month-old son in Harlow – not far, I dared imagine, from where Kate had recorded her original demos at David Gilmour's home studio! "I don't like having to give somebody a walloping in front of 'er indoors," Cyril said, "but the really awful ones are when you have to do it in front of his kids as well. Tears your heart out when they start hitting you with their tiny fists and yelling, 'Stop hurting my daddy.' At least with this bloke, his daughter's going to be too young to know what's going on." I had to marvel at his professionalism, even as I was appalled by it. I considered upping my offer, but worried that he'd be grievously insulted.

Ibrahim's young wife answered the door. She looked around 45, and probably wasn't 30 yet. Ibrahim was feeding Poppy. She'd tell him he had visitors. It occurred to me to try to knock Cyril unconscious.

When I was getting in lots of fistfights, I lived in a tract that had been put up in around 72 hours on the site of what had recently been a plum farm. It was a long way for my dad to drive to work, but the only house my parents could afford, and that with substantial help from the Federal Housing Authority. It was in front of that house that, after hitting my next-door neighbour in the trachea, I came closer to winning a fight than I ever had before, or ever would again.

When we moved very much nearer my dad's work, near Los Angeles International Airport, the cowardliness to which my DNA seemed to dispose me kicked in, and I got in fewer and fewer fights. But I still used my fists.

One day when I was about eight, I had a dispute with a classmate who lived in the block of flats next door to our own. It occurred to me to keep my great disgruntlement under wraps. We walked home together. Perhaps 100 yards short of his front door, I told him I'd been given a really wicked (English teenagers of the Nineties didn't invent the use of wicked as a term of praise) Indian arrowhead I wanted him to see. We were both interested, I for about a fortnight, in Indian arrowheads. I asked him to hold out his hands and close his eyes. When he did so, I socked him in the nose with all my might. He ran home in tears, bleeding all over himself. The memory of which fills me with shame, and makes me want to punish myself with food.

I realised, as we waited for Ibrahim to finish with his daughter, that the years had made me much less confident in some ways. Even if I somehow got Cyril to close his eyes, and hit him with my best shot, wasn't there a chance, given his background as a prize-fighter, that he'd get up off the pavement and retaliate so enthusiastically with his fists of stone that I'd be recognisable by the time he was finished with me only by my dental records?

I was going to let it happen.

The Ibrahim who arrived finally at the door bore little resemblance to the one I was accustomed to seeing on *Fab Lab*. On *Fab Lab*, his fantastically dishevelled hair was a source of endless amusement for the cheeky little Scots presenter. Today, it couldn't have been tidier. He was without the stubble I was used to seeing him with on TV. And he wasn't smiling. He was extremely not smiling.

"Who are you and what do you want?" he demanded, rather less graciously than I'd have expected. "I've got emails from fans to answer. I've got a daughter to finish feeding and a missus to get another bollocking from even though I don't deserve it."

"I'm afraid you've been naughty, mate," Cyril told him, slipping his little foot inside the door. "You helped vote a sort of friend of ours out of the *Fab Lab*."

"What? Andrea, do you mean? She was crap. Good riddance to bad rubbish. Now piss off." Trying to close the door on us, he discovered that Cyril's foot was in the way. "Move your fucking foot, you little pygmy git," he suggested thoughtfully, "or I'll fucking break you in half."

Cyril was the absolute picture of nonchalance. "Well, actually, mate," he said, "I don't expect you will." He lit a cigarette. "I was the Territorial Army's bantamweight champion one year. My overall record as an amateur was 22-0, and 15 of those were knockouts." I expected he was going to get to the fists of stone part, but Ibrahim didn't give him a chance, sending him sprawling backwards with a hard shove into the begonias, where he lay in amazed silence.

"How about you?" Ibrahim asked. He glared at me, and in a moment I came to love him for it. He could just as easily have seen the fear in my eyes and burst out laughing. He wouldn't have been the first.

"None for me," I finally managed, trying my best to sound hard. "I was just tagging along. In fact, good luck on the show. It seems to me it'll be between you and Evelyn in the end."

Oh, great, mouth, keep going well after you've said enough. After pretending for a millisecond that you're actually on the same level, now prove that you're not by buttering him up.

But instead of regarding me with contempt born of my feeble attempt to ingratiate myself, Ibrahim became the version of himself one saw on television. "Do you really think so?" he asked eagerly, suddenly seeming 12 years younger. "Cor, that would be a dream come true!"

I found this very unnerving, and was grateful for the distraction when poor Cyril began growling in the begonias. Whereupon, in the blink of an eye, Ibrahim was the other, far less charming version of himself again. "Get him out of the flowers and bugger off," he suggested, and slammed the door in my face.

The cabbie and I coaxed the smouldering Cyril back into the cab. As we got back on the A24, he declared he would suffer no ethical pangs about keeping Andrea's money even though he'd made Ibrahim feel no pain. "I made a good faith effort," he said. "That's all the code compels." As for Ibrahim having made short work of him, he said, "Well, it's been 25 years since I left the Territorials. Do you suppose Mohammed Ali was as good 25 years after he left the ring as in his prime?"

So all the years he'd been thugging, he'd been bluffing?

"Absolutely. We're not like you Yanks, we English. We don't wallop or shoot each other. Most of the time it's about who can beat his chest loud enough to inhibit the other chap's production of testosterone."

15

Something Very Big Indeed

I TOOK the bus to the next Overeaters meeting. It was the driver's job to worry about the possible consequences of someone my size sitting upstairs, and not mine. During the long ride, it occurred to me that I have probably sent Kate more flowers over the years than lined the route of Princess Diana's funeral cortege in 1997.

Just for the fun of it, I tried to compute how much money I'd spent on gifts for Kate in the past 12 months, eventually putting the figure at just over £2,000, which I do indeed recognise (I am no nutter) as well out of proportion to the slightly less than £5,000 I have earned impersonating George Clooney in that same period. I would unmistakably have, when the money I'd inherited from my mother ran out, to send Kate far fewer, or far less expensive, gifts.

The really frustrating part, of course, being that I never received any sort of acknowledgement for the millions of flowers, the rivers of cognac, the countless dozens of books and magazine subscriptions, the shoes and handbags and scarves beyond counting, the hundreds of earrings and bracelets and necklaces, the lingerie on 14 Valentine's Days, I've sent, as my intuition has dictated, to any one of half a dozen addresses I either got off the Internet or induced other Katefans to disclose in trade. In addition to a mansion on an island in the Thames in Berkshire, she was said to have a sprawling Victorian mansion in Greenwich, and a luxury flat overlooking the river in Battersea, and a couple of other places I can't mention because my sources swore me to secrecy.

As I'm sure you can imagine, the other Katefans I trade with exacted very high prices for their information. I had to swap this Dutch guy one of my two copies of the Canadian promotional LP *An Interview With Kate Bush* (EMI America SPRO 282) for the address of her penthouse flat in Brighton, but that didn't rankle nearly as much as having to trade both my only copy of the Canadian promotional record of 'Wow' on yellow vinyl and one of my three copies of the pink and white "marble" Canadian promotional edition of *Hounds Of Love* for her email address.

You might imagine that Kate's silence has been painful for me, and I won't deny that I would be thrilled to the marrow if she found the time to acknowledge me. But there is, in a strange way, a benefit to her silence. While others can only talk about their devotion to her, I can document mine. There are nearly 2,000 items in the special folder in which I save emails I've sent her, and none that I created in which to store her replies. Wouldn't one who loves her less than I have given up long ago?

★ ★ ★

No one noticed me arriving at the meeting, and no one would have noticed me leaving. Everyone was too busy swarming around Dahlia, whose flirtation with Goth had apparently ended in midweek. "It just wasn't me," she explained, and Graham, unmistakably besotted, nearly swallowed his own tongue agreeing. She could do no wrong in his eyes.

He was the first to tell us about his fortnight. Glancing frequently at Dahlia, he told us he thought he was in love, as he hadn't been for years. Wanting to look his best for the object of his affection, he'd taken to going to the gym daily since our last meeting, in spite of the hostile looks he got there, and lost three pounds. By my calculation, three pounds represented about three-quarters of one per cent of his weight, but I didn't begrudge him the round of encouraging applause his exciting news won him. If Dahlia twigged that it was she who'd inspired him, she didn't let on. She spent the whole of his time before us sending a text message.

Boopsie, who'd actually gained half a stone since our last meeting, had good news of her own. She'd been hired to appear in a series of magazine advertisements for the UK's first chain of kebab restaurants. Her agent had predicted that the meteoric rise of morbid obesity assured her a lucrative future, provided her own morbid obesity didn't result in her own morbidity.

Dahlia had even more exciting news. Noting the success of *Fab Lab*, ITV had rushed into production a third edition of *Megastar*, whose success had inspired *Fab Lab* to begin with. The original *Megastar* had launched dewy-eyed, cleft-palated teen heart-throb Daryn Doll, whose anguished yelping had somehow made 'Unchained Melody' and 'I Will Always Love You' hits for the ninth and sixth times, respectively, and Vinod, who'd originally positioned himself as the male Sri Lankan Britney Spears, only to decide that nothing would do but to be true to his own artistic vision, and to take to performing on television in jeans with ripped knees. In the second edition of the show, ten boys and girls had been chosen for two "bands" overseen by two Major Industry Figure judges. The girls had had the biggest Christmas hit of the previous year. The boys had been pulled from their limousine en route to their second public appearance, in Huddersfield, and beaten bloody.

Market research showed that viewers had made their strongest emotional connections during the original competition not only with the cleft-palated Daryn and the club-footed third-place finisher Claudine, but also with a blind boy from Plymouth, a cross-eyed paraplegic au pair from Norfolk, and a pair of Siamese twins from Solihull, exposed as frauds after their second appearance. (It turned out they weren't even fraternal twins, never mind Siamese ones, but merely good friends who reckoned they had come up with a winning gimmick.) Noting which, the producers had decided to call the new reincarnation of the show *Megastar: The Lame, the Halt, and the Blind*, and to restrict the competition to 18- to 26-year-olds with heartbreaking infirmities. And who better to present it than Dahlia, so fat she was barely ambulatory?

For a long while there, none of us hardly mentioned our own problem with food. Nearly everyone admitted to having been inconsolable when Geoff Sparse, the 30-stone 19-year-old circus freak from Northumberland, was voted off. Those who'd heard it (Boopsie claimed not even to own a television) agreed unanimously that his version of 'Unchained Melody' had been at least half again as moving as Daryn's. "But isn't that the world in a nutshell," Crinolyn mused bitterly. "The boy with the cleft palate gets presented to the bloody Prince of Wales. The boy with the glandular weight problem gets shown the door."

Duncan visited to ask if I'd march with him in the weekend's Gay Pride parade. I wondered if he was trying to seduce me, or at least taking the piss. How far did he imagine someone my size would get before I brought the whole parade to a stop, halting the progress of what politicians in my own country had enjoyed calling the Homosexual Agenda? "Well," he sighed, "nothing ventured, nothing gained."

He seemed disinclined to leave. Just for something to say, I asked if he didn't agree that Gay Pride was a poor choice of names. He scowled suspiciously. Doesn't saying you're proud of something suggest that you chose it for yourself? And haven't gays been telling their straight persecutors all along that they didn't in fact choose their sexuality, but simply grew to accept it as something they were born with?

"Gays are fed up with being ashamed of who they are," he asserted. "That's where the pride bit comes in."

"Of course they are, and understandably. But wouldn't they be playing less into the hands of those who accuse them of being wilfully perverse if they called it the Gay Lack of Shame Parade?"

He rose, fatally fed up. "I came in here to extend a bloody invitation, not to play semantic footsie. Blimey." I had my quarters to myself again.

★ ★ ★

Dahlia's show came on. It was true what they said about the camera making you look heavier. She introduced the show's three judges, trading cheerful small talk as though they'd known one another for ages. One was a perpetually startled-looking former disco dolly who'd had a couple of Top 20 hits in the early Nineties. I surmised that the reason she didn't smile when she was introduced was that botox had paralysed many of her key facial muscles. I guessed that, grateful as she was to have something other than cleaning work after having been so long out of the charts, and never in the Top 10, she'd be the one of the three with a kind word for everyone. To her left sat Shania Twain's former assistant make-up artist, to her right a publicist from one of the big record companies. Having duly noted that Simon Cowell had made a fortune being gratuitously brutal to those whose ambitions slightly exceeded their abilities, the makeup artist and publicist seemed impatient to sink their talons into trembling white flesh.

A deaf girl from Darlington sang a few bars of a Celine Dion hit I'd never liked. She wasn't bad for being unable to hear herself. The make-up artist and publicist thought it the worst thing since ethnic cleansing, but the deaf girl, unable to hear, wasn't devastated. Nor, of course, was she heartened by the praise of the former disco dolly, who characterised her performance as crackin'. I got the impression the girl's younger brother, who translated their respective remarks into sign language, might have edited them substantially.

An epileptic boy from Lincoln came on and got through Take That's inevitable 'Back For Good' without a seizure. Indeed, we had to take it entirely on faith that he suffered from the affliction he claimed. The disco dolly thought he was crackin'. The make-up artist said he'd sooner have his ear drums punctured with ballpoint pens than ever have to hear anything so awful again. The publicist, who seemed to be trying to undress the boy with his eyes, agreed with the disco dolly.

"Star quality," he said, licking his lips. "You can't teach it. A singer either has it or doesn't. And Peter has bloody lorryfuls of it."

And then, to my astonishment, came none other than Mrs. Cavanaugh's daughter Cathy, so frail she had to be brought on in a wheelchair. She sang 'Unchained Melody', of all things, and very nearly made it her own. She was really, seriously good, one of the best singers I'd seen on any of those shows. By the end, the former assistant to Shania Twain's make-up artist was crying too hard to say anything more than, "Miraculous!" The disco dolly pronounced Cathy not just crackin', but *really* crackin'. She seemed to be trying to cry too, but her tear ducts were apparently paralysed. The publicist yawned theatrically and said the performance had made him envy the first contestant, the deaf girl. The studio audience howled its outrage. The disco dolly called him a bastard and the studio audience affirmed her judgement with its fervent applause, almost surely the most fervent the disco dolly had ever elicited. You could tell she wanted desperately to smile, but it just wasn't going to happen. You could also tell the publicist thought this could be the beginning of something very big indeed.

The make-up artist saw the writing on the wall. It hadn't been by praising that Simon Cowell had become the richest man in Britain, or at least on the list of the Top 5,000, but rather by making frightened young singers weep. He reacted to the next contestant, a rotund punkish girl from Swansea whose legs, judging by the fact that the platform of one shoe was very much thicker than that of the other, were different lengths, as though she'd invented prostate cancer. She looked nauseated with embarrassment. The publicist wasn't going to relinquish his lead without a fight, though. In his judgement, the girl should have been drowned in infancy. The disco dolly pronounced her crackin', but it was too late. The girl threw up voluminously between her feet, drawing further attention to her handicap, and then collapsed gasping to her knees. Dahlia led her away while a resentful-looking technician ran on stage with a towel for the mess. It was wonderful television, but I didn't see how it could not go downhill from there. I switched off the TV and decided, as I hadn't for months and months, to attempt a walk.

I marvelled at my own deterioration. During my modelling days, it wouldn't have been a mere walk I'd have contemplated, but a wonderful long run, usually ending with a sprint up the La Cienega hill to Sunset Blvd. By the time I reached the streetwalkers who regularly convened on that corner, I'd be awash in my own endorphins, drenched in my own sweat, aglow with brute vitality, eager, at least until the endorphins in my bloodstream got diluted, to take on the world. And now I was wondering if I'd be able to manage a bloody walk round the block.

I found my sweatpants, which I hadn't worn since moving into Mrs. Cavanaugh's, and was astonished to discover I could still get them on. I rummaged through my drawer for a headband, but after getting it on and looking at myself in the mirror, decided it made me look a twat – or, more accurately, more of a twat than usual. I thought of leaving the whole thing for another evening when it was warmer, or cooler, or earlier, or later. I very nearly turned the TV back on, but in the end actually left my room. Oh, the endorphins!

There seemed to be a row brewing just in front of the house. Normally I give rows a very wide berth for fear they'll involve someone clearly victimising another, compelling a choice between doing what I clearly recognise as my moral duty and sparing myself the humiliation of being snickered at by the victimiser.

I was on a bus on Oahu one time many years ago with Babooshka's mother. Yearning for a little solitude, we'd gone out to the side of the island opposite the Honolulu one. On the way back, an amiable-seeming hippie who looked rather like the singer of Jethro Tull boarded the bus and began chatting up everyone in the vicinity. For several miles, he was all peace, love, and implacable geniality. But then he suddenly got bolshie. Noticing the black American couple a few rocks behind him, he began spewing racist bile. It offended me, but I, in my customary responsibility-evading way, told myself that if the couple could ignore it, maybe I should too, rather than trying to be something I wasn't.

It didn't get better. Despairing of getting any reaction from the black couple, the hippie began loudly telling no one at all how he hated Mexicans, and had personally murdered a great many of them on behalf of the CIA. The fact that he was unmistakably mad made me feel slightly (very slightly) better about ignoring him.

He wouldn't be ignored, though. It wasn't only Mexicans he hated, but also native Hawaiians, of whom there was a great many on the bus, and he was going to murder a few of them too at his earliest opportunity. Which declaration inspired a muscular native Hawaiian teenager to leap to his feet and roar, "Shut the fuck up, you crazy *haole* asshole."

The hippie wasn't about to allow a dark-skinned person to speak to him in such a way, and got to his own feet, whereupon the Hawaiian punched him in the nose, but only hard enough (the hippie might have been under the influence of horse tranquillisers or something) to inspire the hippie to pull out a machete with which he might have sawed through the bus's engine.

Here I, thinking always of my own skin, dropped the ball in a way of which I'll always be ashamed. The hippie was between me and the Hawaiian teenager, with his back to me. If I'd been any kind of man, I'd have leapt on him from behind, or at least punched him in the back of the head or something. Instead, I scurried to get off the bus with everybody else. That the Hawaiian teenager didn't perish on that bus had nothing to do with my accepting my responsibility, and everything to do with God paying attention for once.

The situation in the road outside Mrs. Cavanaugh's didn't seem to call for any such intervention, as it was only two blokes shouting at one another with increasing irritation, apparently over a parking space.

They turned out to be a rumpled tabloid journalist with a combover and dark perspiration spots under his arms, and a stylishly dressed young Asian, who'd apparently got his extremely cute Smart into the space in which the tabloid journalist had hoped to pull his prolifically dented early Nineties Vauxhall. "You don't bloody need all that room for such a little car," the tabloid journalist was fuming. "You can park nearly anywhere you like."

The young Asian rolled his eyes superciliously. "Maybe you'd like me to try to find who owns the cars in front of and behind mine and get them to pull closer? Then you won't feel that space is being wasted."

"Why don't you save your sarcasm for somebody who'll enjoy it?" the tabloid journalist snarled. "It isn't that you're wasting space putting your little poofmobile in here. It's that you can park anywhere you like, and I can't, as my car's much bigger. It's simple physics, innit?"

"You're calling me a poof because I'm socially responsible enough to drive a car with a very much more efficient engine than yours, and that can fit in a smaller space? Well, that's to do with your own intellectual deficiencies, which I'm not going to allow you to make my problem."

"Mr. Bigword, aren't you?" the clearly overwhelmed journalist snarled. "Ain't it just like you posh sorts, when it comes time to be accountable for your crap behaviour, to hide behind polysyllability?" One of the small crowd that had formed around them enjoyed the irony of that, but it was lost on the tabloid journalist himself, whose nose and the Asian's were nearly touching now.

"And how exactly did you go about surmising that I'm posh?" the Asian demanded.

Now, as the tabloid journalist's anger switched into a higher gear, their noses weren't just touching, but flattening each other. "You think

150

those of us who work for the tabloids don't know that you glossy peri-odical boys look down on us? Well, we know all too bloody well, mate."

Here, someone much more a man than I, albeit a woman, finally stepped between them. She was Asian too, much darker-skinned than the Smart driver, with glossy, lank hair that reflected the streetlights. "Leave it out, you two," she said in the slightly impatient, but mostly slightly amused tone of an infant schoolteacher. "There's plenty to go round. And she's likely to turn up at any moment now. Is slagging one another off more important?"

The Asian guy looked sheepish, and offered the tabloid journalist his hand to shake, but the tabloid journalist either didn't see it, or did a convincing imitation of not seeing it, as he turned round.

He noticed me. "Come on," he said, loudly enough for others to overhear, "maybe you can help me find a space big enough for my socially irresponsible Vauxhall, which I drive not because I'm keen to deplete the world's bloody oil resources, but because it's the best I can bloody afford with what I make freelancing for the bloody *Mirror*."

How to turn down such an invitation?

I asked who the Asian in the Smart car was. "Freelance for *Posh Filth*," he said, "and maybe a couple of other of the glossy one-syllable gossip magazines by now. Put somebody's work between glossy covers and they reckon theirs has quit stinking. Arrogant little twats."

I felt duty-bound to admit I wasn't really George Clooney, and thus not worthy of being stalked, especially in such inclement weather. He had to look at me to ensure I wasn't joking. "It isn't you I'm interested in, mate," he said. "It's Cathy Cavanaugh. Did you see *Megastar* tonight? She'll be the talk of the country tomorrow morning. Whoever finds out the most embarrassing stuff about her or her family will never have to work again."

It took a while for him to find a space. There seemed to be lots of people looking, none in a Smart. We hurried back and discovered that my road had become impassable. I saw that Mrs. Cavanaugh and Gilmour were at the front door of the boarding house, addressing a small mob, to whose periphery we hurried as quickly as my girth permitted.

"I'm telling you the truth," Mrs. Cavanaugh was imploring them, wearily, but with dread in her eyes, "she's not here."

"Well, can you at least let us come in and have a sift through some of her personal effects," the glossy-haired Sri Lankan woman who'd sep-arated the tabloid journalist and Mr. Smart asked, a little petulantly, a little accusatorily.

"Set one bloody toe inside this house," Gilmour said, "and they'll need dental records to identify what's left of you."

Mrs. Cavanaugh winced. "There's absolutely no reason for you to be taking that tone with us, sir," the Sri Lankan said. "We're just doing our jobs, or at least our second jobs. I, for one, work during the day in IT, as you might have inferred from my ethnicity."

"We have a right to our fucking privacy," Gilmour asserted.

"I would suggest otherwise," the Sri Lankan said. "We in celebrity gossip come up against this all the time. I submit to you that the family forfeited access to the privacy privilege when young Cathy became a contestant on *Megastar*."

"But that was only Cathy," Mrs. Cavanaugh, showing more of the strain with each passing moment, blurted. "What about the rest of us, who've always been rather more circumspect?"

The Sri Lankan sighed, a little patronisingly, I thought. "You really don't read the tabloids, do you, dear lady?"

"The *Guardian*, actually. Occasionally the *Independent* as well."

"Well, if you deigned occasionally to venture out of your ivory tower, you'd know that, insofar as celebrity harassment is concerned, the sins of the father are very much the sins of the child as well, if you see what I mean, and vice versa."

"Mind your fucking tone," Gilmour snarled. I don't think he understood what the Sri Lankan had said, but it was clear to all how she'd said it.

The Asian who'd nearly come to blows with the tabloid journalist intervened. "What my colleague is trying to say is that, in today's celebrity-mad culture, families and friends and even casual acquaintances of celebrities are fair game."

"If you didn't want us to be here," the tabloid journalist contributed, "maybe you shouldn't have let your daughter and sister go on television and break everybody's heart." His tone suggested that he imagined himself being wonderfully clear where the Asians had been opaque. "Now how about just a quick look through her personal effects?"

Before Gilmour could reiterate his ugly threat, there was a commotion behind us. A black Daimler limousine had entered the road from the Vicarage Road end and now, having found it impassable, was trying to back out, only to find its way blocked by several late-arriving gossiparisites. "It's her! It's Cathy!" somebody shouted, and it was Beatlemania revisited, with people all over the Daimler like cockroaches.

The excitement was too much for a person of my proportions. I headed inside, and was able, even though he was clearly desperate by now to break someone's – anyone's – leg, to get past Gilmour, and into the kitchen. In which, to my astonishment and confusion, sat Cathy. My howl of surprise brought Mrs. Cavanaugh and Gilmour running.

Mrs. Cavanaugh burst into tears at the sight of her, and embraced her so hard I thought she'd fracture something. "I thought you were out in that car. I thought we'd lost you for sure."

"She's a decoy," Cathy explained, looking very, very tired, if not at death's door. "I've already signed to a management company, and it's a good thing. They have decoys for all their stars. Good job somebody thought of it, I'd say."

"But that poor girl out there!" Mrs. Cavanaugh, ever compassionate, wailed.

"An asylum seeker. Would have been deported next week if she hadn't done this. It's a cruel thing, but it was entirely her choice. And it isn't like she didn't have a driver and a couple of bodyguards in there with her."

"We taped the show," Gilmour said. "You were deadly. Come watch."

Mr. Halibut, who'd come down to see what all the excitement was about, and I helped Cathy into the lounge, one of her frail arms around each of our necks. Gilmour found the spot on the videotape with her performance, which sounded even better on second hearing. I hadn't realised that the make-up artist and publicist judges' mouths had both been hanging open through the second half of the song. But we never got to the end.

It turned out that what Cathy was wide-eyed with was horror. "Stop it!" she wailed. "Please! Don't make me watch!"

"You were marvellous, love," Mrs. Cavanaugh implored her. "And this is exactly how Kate herself felt after seeing her first appearance on *Top Of The Pops*. She described it as feeling like watching herself die. But people adored it. It changed people's lives, that performance, even if she didn't like what she'd chosen to wear."

She sobbed. "Did you see how fat I looked? Did you see? And on the word *heart*, did you hear I was sharp? Oh, my god. Oh, my god!" She looked at me. "Do you have any more of that antidepressant stuff left?" I shivered with revulsion. She turned frantically to Gilmour. "Kurt Cobain used a shotgun. Can you get one somewhere? One of your mates?"

Mrs. Cavanaugh slapped her. I'd never seen her lose her temper, but who had ever been so sorely provoked? "You will stop this sort of talk immediately, Cathy! Do you hear me?"

The bodyguards in the Daimler could probably have heard her – through bullet-proof glass. She was screaming. "Have you not put me and your brothers through enough already? Shame on you! Shame on you!"

It wasn't enough, of course. As a teenager, Cathy felt that it was her God-given right to put those who loved her through every kind of hell. "Well, excuse me for having an awful disease that I can't do anything about, Mum!" Her eyes filled with tears. "I suppose you'd be screaming at me if I had leukaemia as well!"

Mrs. Cavanaugh reared back to slap her again, but then collapsed to her knees like a marionette whose strings had just been snipped. She wanted to cry, but there were no tears left for her. She just shook her head, back and forth, back and forth.

Cathy burst into enough tears for the both of them. The taciturn Gilmour followed suit. The three of them held onto one another for dear life. Mr. Halibut and I looked at one another. We both seemed to feel like intruders, and went upstairs.

I watched the gossiparisites swarm over the Daimler from my window, pounding on the window, pulling furiously at the locked doors, trying even to open the bonnet. When they realised it was trying to inch back out of the road, a couple of them lay down in its path, whereupon their comrades began chanting, "Their blood will be on your hands! Their blood will be on your hands!" It reminded me of my college days, but the student radicals of the Sixties were much better at it than this lot. Loath to have their legs crushed, the two sacrificial lambs kept slithering out of harm's way. The Daimler's progress was glacial, but unmistakable. By the time the Old Bill finally turned up and cleared a path, it was halfway to freedom anyway.

16

Major Suss

I WOKE up the next morning to an impatient pounding on my bedroom door. It was Duncan, with neither seduction nor Gay Pride on his mind. "You fucking Judas," he howled as I opened my door. "You quisling! You louser!" I hoped I was still dreaming, but there was nothing dreamlike about how he grabbed a handful of my pyjama top and pushed me back into my chair. He threw the morning's *News Of The World* into my lap. Its headline screamed CATE THE GREAT'S BROTHER: A BENDER!

She sings one song on television and is already Cate the Great?

"That obviously isn't the bigger problem," Duncan said, reading my mind. "How could you? How bloody *could* you?"

I couldn't have, and hadn't. And I told him so.

"But you're the only one who could have," he said, "you or . . . the bloke who used to look after me and my partner's daughter. Oh, bugger." He shook his head morosely.

"Well, you might not like them," he finally sighed, "but they're good at what they do, aren't they? Bloody terrific at it, in fact."

"It's their livelihood," I said, "at least those who don't have well-paying IT jobs during the day."

He left and I switched on the television. When I was up in the morning, I especially enjoyed watching editions of *Trina* on which the results of paternity tests were revealed to leering, multiply pierced teen yobs whose misshapen slag girlfriends had accused them. I seemed never to tire of the leering teen yobs assuring Trina that they couldn't possibly be the kid's dad because they'd shagged their misshapen slag accusers only once. Biology seemed to be taught in the British state schools even less rigorously than in my own country's.

This morning's edition, though, would reveal no paternity test results. Rather, its theme was *My Talented Daughter Got Left Out of Megastar Because She Isn't Anorexic*. A tweed-capped working man from

Scunthorpe was telling Trina how his household had gone without such pleasures as cable television for years so that his daughter Julie, indistinguishable from the indignant unwed young mums I was accustomed to seeing, could have singing lesions. But then, when her big chance came, it turned out not to have come at all, as *Megastar*'s producers announced they wanted only contestants with heart-tugging medical conditions.

"Ain't bloody fair, is it," demanded Julie, who apparently imagined her singing voice sufficiently beautiful to compensate for her straggly, oily hair, spots, huge nose, faint moustache, double chin, small breasts, big tummy, huge hips, thick legs, enormous feet, and appalling make-up. Let Britain get an earful of this girl, I thought, and Kylie Minogue can start looking for work as a cleaner or market researcher. "And just because I'm normal-sized."

Trina brought on another guest, an emaciated male bulimic from Reading who'd also sung on the previous night's *Megastar*, though with less spectacular results than Cathy. In his view, it was high time someone other than what he referred to as "gorgeous normals" got to entertain for a living. All the eating disorders in the studio audience – and they were about half of it – applauded as feverishly as their weakness would allow.

"Bollocks to that," proclaimed Julie's dad from Scunthorpe. He apparently looked at Julie through love's eyes. "Who's bloody forcing you to binge and purge, or whinge and emerge, or whatever it is you lot do?" The normals in the studio audience erupted in applause of their own. "Why don't you just eat properly and stop your moaning?"

"It's out of our hands," the male bulimic from Reading began to try to explain, but a punch-up had broken out in the studio audience. Actually, it was a punch-up in theory only, as the emaciated girl combatant had the strength only to cover her ears with her hands while her fat woman antagonist beat her with her handbag.

As security guards pulled the fat woman off her victim, Trina dashed over with her microphone and meticulous coiffure. "Obviously emotions run high around this issue," she said to the fat woman, seeming to hope she would hear the statement as a question.

"Bloody right, they do," the fat woman affirmed, gasping. "I'm fed up with the self-disabled demanding everybody's sympathy."

"Is that true?" Trina wondered, clearly trying to goad her studio audience. Its normals howled, brayed, and bellowed their assent, in many cases waving their fists.

Trina was clearly displeased with the level of blood lust she'd fomented, and I thought how awful it must be for her. She watched tapes of Jerry Springer and Rikki Lake and saw American studio audiences eagerly throwing chairs at one another, trying to gouge out one another's eyes. She tried to inspire mayhem among her own audiences and they were content with a bit of braying.

"How about it, eating disorders?" she challenged the other half of her audience, looking as though she'd sooner have been almost anywhere else. "Are the normals heartless swine?" Weak as they were, the eating disorders' affirmation was very much less shrill.

"Pathetic," Trina said, shaking her head in disgust. "Really feeble." She leaned down into the face of the nearest eating disorder. "You," she snapped. "Is your problem with food something you chose for yourself, or is it as much out of your hands as an alcoholic's problems with drink?"

"I certainly didn't choose it," the terrified young woman muttered.

"Speak up, for God's sake!" Trina said.

"I didn't choose it," the young woman repeated, right into Trina's microphone this time. "It's horrible, Trina. It's hellish, I wouldn't wish it on my worst enemy."

The eating disorders tried once again to roar their assent, but they'd pretty much spent themselves on the last one. Trina let her hands drop to her sides in disgusted resignation, a commercial for a feminine hygiene spray came on, and someone tapped faintly on my door.

It was Cate the Great herself, predictably beside herself, feeling, she revealed, as though on a runaway train. She was obviously in no condition to be confronted about her appalling question about my Cypramil the night before. She'd come home from her brief hospitalisation almost seven pounds heavier than when she left, and even menstruating again. But she appeared as she sat before me to have lost all seven pounds again, and maybe a couple more into the bargain.

"My mate Judith just rang," she said. "She's in *The Sun* today, about how she's made more suicide attempts than any other girl her age in Britain. She was so embarrassed that she tried again this morning. And it's my fault."

"Really? Since when do you write for *The Sun*?"

"Don't be sarky. You see what I mean."

"Did you do anything more than sing really well on *Megastar*?"

"I sang crap. I was so sharp you could have sliced bloody cheese with my performance."

"Do you get the impression anybody minded?"

"They just felt sorry for me because I'm fat. Anybody can see that."

"I don't see it, Cathy. There were other eating disorders on. Why would they have felt sorrier for you than for the others?"

She just glared at me. I figured at any moment she'd bolt from the room. But I was mistaken. "You live your life," I said. "If the ghouls at some horrid tabloid choose to profit from your friend's misfortune, that isn't to do with you. It's on their heads."

There was another knock on my door, this one very much more assertive than Cathy's had been. I waddled over to find out who it was. I opened the door to peek out and nearly got trampled by the pair lurking behind it, who entered the room about as diffidently as the Nazis entering the Sudetenland. "Who is this?" the female half, around 22, blonde-streaked, striking, intense, reeking of cigarettes, demanded, glaring at me.

"My mate," Cathy said. I couldn't remember anyone having referred to me as a mate, and I found it sweet and touching beyond expression.

"Welcome to my room," I said, and loathed myself for having done so. I'd intended nine parts censure to one of hospitality, but it had come out sounding almost entirely hospitable. We passive aggressives die a little bit each day.

The blonde girl's eyes hadn't left mine. "What were you telling her?" she demanded.

"I beg your pardon," I said, with a stronger note of censure. Oh, I was standing right up to my intruder now!

She harrumphed in disgust and lit a cigarette. I don't allow smoking in my room, but I thought telling her so would be like a palm telling a monsoon not to get it wet. "You were advising her. I heard it. Don't try to deny it. I've got a witness."

Her companion was about her age, spiky-haired, fleshy, alarmingly pale, so intent on no one's missing the alarming paleness that he'd lined his eyes in kohl, sneering even while he chewed one of his own fingernails, petulant, wretched, infinitely entitled. I didn't have to hear him speak to know he'd do so without parting his teeth.

"He was telling you about ghouls and tabloids," the blonde girl reminded Cathy. She was striking now, around 22, but it was probably mostly because of the fortune she spent on her grooming and clothing. Her features weren't nearly a match for the care with which they were presented – by her mid-thirties, when her hair wasn't as thick and shiny and her neck had begun to crease, she wasn't going to be very striking at all. I was nearly always right about these things. It occurred to me I'd seen her before.

"What else did he tell you?"

Cathy was finding this all very embarrassing. "Nepenthe, blimey. He wasn't advising me. He was giving me a shoulder to cry on. He's my mate." I wanted to embrace her forever for that. I wanted to burst into tears. But I couldn't embarrass her.

Nepenthe continued glowering at me for a long moment, and then sighed, and plopped down adolescently on my bed, from which she informed me that it was important for Cathy not to receive mixed messages. She took out her mobile to see if she had any text messages, and frowned when she saw she hadn't.

"Make yourself comfortable," I urged my visitors. Cathy seemed to be the only one who realised I was being sarcastic. The fleshy pale boy with kohl-rimmed eyes spat out whatever he'd been able to gnaw off one fingertip, sneering no less implacably, and began work on the next.

"Nepenthe's my manager," Cathy informed me. "Since last night. Since I finished my song, in fact."

"A talent like Cathy's comes along once every couple of genera-tions," Nepenthe challenged me. "But the pop music industry isn't just about talent, is it? It's at least as much about having management with major suss. And that's what me and Harold bring to the table." I had the strong feeling she was saying this for Cathy's benefit, probably for the second time in two nights, more than mine.

"New ideas," Harold whined, in exactly the tone and designer-roughened accent I'd expected. "That's what it's all about, innit? Bold new ideas."

I realised where I'd seen Nepenthe – on one of those shows about the children of the very rich, one in which poor little rich girls were seen planning fantastically expensive parties that they often wound up forget-ting to attend, or arriving at six hours late because they'd been dissatisfied with the job their hairdressers had done on their hair, and had had to fly at the last minute to Gstaad to get someone who actually knew what she was doing to do it properly. I'm exaggerating, but not wildly.

I found that the smell of Nepenthe's cigarette made me feel mis-chievous, and asked who else she managed. I always marvelled at people who lit cigarettes before determining if there were any ashtrays about. Nepenthe wasn't pleased to have to go to the window to flick her ashes out. I'd expected that my question would make her defensive, and I was right. "As actual managers, we haven't any experience. And I don't think that's a liability, not at all. Cathy could choose somebody that's been doing a crap job for their artists for years. Of course she could. But what she chose was a team without a lot of bad habits, and with a lot of bold new ideas."

Cathy smirked at me shyly. "They were the first to ask," she said. "There were a couple of others waiting for me outside the studio, but it was too late by then."

"Too late?" Harold demanded petulantly. "You mean you'd even have considered one of those grotty old men out there? Well, if that's what you prefer, don't let us stand in . . ."

"Bollocks!" Nepenthe, staring futile daggers at Harold's trachea, interrupted. "A deal's a deal. A signature's a signature. Cathy isn't going to regret giving us a chance."

Harold flushed with embarrassment, shrugged, and moved onto his left ring finger's nail.

"So what," Cathy wondered, "about *The Sun* printing that rubbish about my mate being suicidal? What are you going to do about that?"

"My dad," Nepenthe said, as though nothing could hope to be more obvious. "He'll sue them. They'll have to apologise, and give your mate a load of money as well."

"But what they printed was true. It wasn't slander, or libel, or what-ever they call it. What bothered me was that if it hadn't been for me, my mate wouldn't have been publicly humiliated like that."

Nepenthe, apparently very displeased that her answer had been deemed inadequate, went back to her mobile phone. "You don't get to the top of the pop music industry without a few people being hurt along the way," Harold philosophised, taking over, demonstrating the great resiliency of the two-person management team concept. I tried, but couldn't resist asking about his own experience. I reckoned he'd run a club.

He'd run a club, semi-weekly at one of his dad's venues. It had nearly broken even. "I think you're either born with the knack for this sort of thing or you're not," he mused. "In my family, entertainment's in the genes, innit?"

I realised where I'd seen him – or at least a younger, American version of him – before too, in junior high school, running (actually, staggering) around the track with the flab on his chest bouncing, inspir-ing torrents of derision from the Boys Who Could watching – a boy even more contemptible than I'd been, a true rarity.

Nepenthe's mobile began playing the melody of a recent hit. She scowled at it, and then grinned. "MegaGlobal Music," she announced with fervent nonchalance. "They want a meeting."

"Let them beg," Harold said in the voice of the boy with the flabby chest, grown up and ravenous for vengeance. "Let the bastards bloody crawl." Cathy shot me a look that asked what she'd got herself into.

But it soon gave way to an expression of complete bewilderment.

"I'm starving," she announced, surprising even herself. "I could murder some eggs and beans and fried mushrooms." I thought this absolutely sensational news, but Nepenthe didn't share my enthusiasm. "Let's not fix what isn't broken," she said. "The public love you on death's door. We'll get you drip-fed if it comes to that. But let's not tamper with a successful image."

I couldn't stay silent, but I did manage to stay civil. "Do you not understand what a breakthrough this is? Do you not understand how important it is that Cathy start eating properly? This could be the difference between life and death!"

Nepenthe didn't stare mere daggers at my throat. She stared hacksaws. "And may I ask," she finally managed, "what you know about the pop music industry? May we know what experience *you* have?"

"From what you've said, just very slightly less than your own," I said, trembling with anger. It seemed that if I went over and punched Harold in the trachea, he probably wouldn't try to punch me back – I have always been reasonably fearless with those even weaker and more submissive than myself. Seeming to intuit what I was thinking, he gnawed frantically at his fingertips.

"Never mind," Cathy sighed. "I've lost my appetite anyway." She'd never looked more frail.

They left together, Harold and Nepenthe each with a hand under one of poor Cathy's bony elbows. I smouldered. The realisation that Harold and Nepenthe might prosper made my intestines hurt. There might have been a time when I'd have assumed that arrogance and naiveté like theirs would guarantee their failure. But I'd seen too many idiots thrive in my day. And what an excruciating spectacle it was, as they invariably took as a given that it wasn't blind good luck responsible for their success, but suss or charm or determination. And then, once having bumbled onto something and made a lot of money, they'd invariably be surrounded by people trying to flatter them out of some of it, which would make them even more arrogant. It was a cruel, senseless world, but the only one into which I'd been born.

★　★　★

Having had recording equipment of her own fitted at East Wickham so she could take her time recording for once – oh, woeful, woeful idea! – Kate resolved to make her fourth album very different from the first three, not only by virtue of the songs having been rhythmically inspired, but by disengaging from poor Jon Kelley, on whom she thought she'd become too dependent. He implored her to reconsider, but, like the members of The KT Bush Band before him, he would simply have to be brave in the end.

She declined to portray the Wicked Witch in the Children's TV series *Worzel Gummidge*, just as she would decline to be cast in a forthcoming West End production of *The Pirates Of Penzance*. (But it apparently got her thinking about Gilbert & Sullivan, witness her evocation of 'Nightmare Song' from their operetta *Iolanthe* in 'Suspended In Gaffa'.)

Taking the occasional break to sing backing vocals on fellow former Lindsey Kemp protégé Zaine Griff's song for the great man, 'Flowers', in the process demonstrating that she wasn't up herself, she continued to work on *The Dreaming* until nearly half of 1982 was gone, and then jetted off to Jamaica on holiday rather than work on her autobiography, *Leaving My Tracks*, which the publishers Sidgwick & Jackson, were absolutely squirming to offer the nation's readers.

They're squirming still. The fact of the book's never having been published didn't keep it from being reviewed, though. *Lives And Works*, an anthology of articles about and reviews of rock personalities, noted, "In this beautifully illustrated book, Kate Bush gives an account of her approach to her work, techniques, inspirations, and lifestyle. An interesting, unselfconscious attempt at autobiography, it does not appear to be written with the aid of a ghost writer [as though that's the sort of thing one could deduce about the autobiography of someone with some small flair for writing!], and is surprisingly fluent." The book was thought to comprise 144 pages of text and eight of photos.

Once back from her dreadlock holiday, she boldly replaced David Bowie on only two days' notice in the Prince's Trust Royal Gala at London's Dominion. While performing 'The Wedding List' backed by Pete Townshend, Midge Ure and Phil Collins, among many others, she was mortified to realise the strap of her dress had broken. A trouper, she gamely covered herself and improvised choreography. And what a good thing the tabloids still weren't reading lyric sheets, as 'The Wedding List' was about a woman scorned putting a bullet in the head of the fellow who'd scorned her when he tried to marry someone else. A fine thing for the Prince to have to hear!

17

George Harrison's Mistress

I'D hardly got rid of Cathy and her new managers when Duncan came again. He was in turmoil because of the revelations in the press of his sexual ambivalence, but not for the reasons one might have guessed. It turned out that half the decorators he worked with had taken him aside, looked around to ensure that no one could overhear, and admitted, "Me too." He'd always expected that interior decorators were prone to erotic inversion, but was shocked – as I was too! – to discover that something like 60 per cent of those who dismantled Britain's condemned houses share the decorators' predisposition, however much interest they may feign in rugby, however much bitter they may swill, however brazenly they may leer at the protuberant new barmaid down the local.

Far from distancing him further from his estranged partner Gemma, the revelation seemed to have given him a shot of B_{12}. Now that she knew it had been to sneak off to gay pubs and the gay aisles of adult bookstores, she no longer seethed with resentment about Duncan's having been out several evenings a week. She'd even sworn to go on a fad diet endorsed by Geri Halliwell, the same diet Catherine Zeta Jones was suing the *Express* for saying she too was on, and to become a regular at the local health club.

The problem being that, apart from the babysitter, I really was the only man in whom Duncan had been interested sexually. It was with the secretary for one of the architects for whom he worked that he'd been spending more and more evenings, Nimalka with whom he'd come to realise he was irreversibly in love.

"She's a goddess," he told me, desperate for my credulity, "right out of the *Kama Sutra*. From Lahore, right? Perfect skin, the colour of tea with exactly the right amount of milk. Thick black hair so glossy you could shave in it. Great huge, sensual lips. Or is it sensuous? I can never remember, and I must have looked it up 100 times. Fantastic great huge breasts – real cover of one of the lad mags ones – set off by a tiny waist. Endless slim legs. Blimey, I'm getting aroused just describing her to you."

I didn't look for myself. God knows I didn't.

"And a sweet, gentle nature. I mean, without that the rest of it would be . . . well, the rest of it would be fabulous, but not so fabulous that I'd have put my relationship with Gems in jeopardy for it.

"Mammy loves her. The first night I brought her over so they could meet, they could have chatted about Kate Bush all night. Nimalka thinks Kate never surpassed *The Kick Inside*. I've seen Mammy get very cross with people who've said that in the past, but Nimalka defended her choices with rare eloquence. That's what Mammy said – 'rare eloquence'. She's the first girlfriend I've ever had who Mammy could talk with about Kate. You should have seen the delight in her eyes.

"Do you know what Mammy told me? That my bringing home girls who didn't know anything about Kate was like a vicar's daughter bringing home a member of the Islamic Jihad. If I'm honest with you, I'll admit I never had a clue she felt so strongly about it."

I asked what the dilemma was, since it was clearly Nimalka he adored, and Mrs. Cavanaugh approved of as she'd never approved of anyone before.

"Well, for one thing," he said, the joyfulness draining out of him, "there's my daughter. In a different way, I may love her even more than Nimalka. But it's so bloody tricky. I love Jennifer like mad, but it's Nimalka that I think my first thought about in the morning, and Nimalka who's most of the air in my lungs. It's Nimalka who makes me a man, rather than just human, if you see what I mean.

"And Gemma! First girl I ever loved, and she's always stuck by me. She stuck by me through the years that I drank, and she stuck by me in the years that I gambled, and the years when I was in a pop band earning fuck-all, and putting every penny I did earn up my nose.

"You didn't know I was in a band? Big time. I was the singer." He took out his wallet and lovingly extricated a fragile newspaper cutting. It had been refolded so many times over the years that half the text was illegible, but you could tell it was Duncan pouting in the middle of the photo, in a preposterous ornate hairdo, lots of make-up, and a waist-length jacket with big padded shoulders. "Bistro d'Espair we were called. Sort of New Romantics, you'd probably say. We played broody songs with dance beats about lost love. I nicked all my parts intact off Chic records. We were really crap, but of course so were Spandau Ballet. We played the Rose Of Lee in Lewisham, just like Kate and her brother's band. Mammy was well chuffed. We tried to find the place in Putney where they'd played, but nobody could remember where it was." He shook his head and sighed. I couldn't imagine the cutting surviving three more refoldings.

"As much as I want to run off with Nimalka, I also want to keep from hurting Gems. If I weren't sure the agony of hurting Gems wouldn't be as great as the ecstasy of having Nim full time, I'd do it in a heartbeat."

★ ★ ★

Neither Radio One nor very many critics wound up liking Kate's often fervently bizarre 1982 album *The Dreaming*, which many believed could be used to bolster a plea of temporary insanity if Kate were accused of a crime, and which she would later describe as a howl of pain. Said the *Melody Maker*'s man of the title track, about the Aborigines' showdown with extinction, "It's the weirdest damn record I've ever heard." Heard by some, because of its spine-chillingly eerie vocals and guest appearance by Rolf Harris on digeridu, as an attempt to ensure there would never again be 100-yard-long queues waiting for her outside record stores, the album nonetheless reached number three. And Kate discovered that she had avid fans in unexpected places, as, for instance, the communist newspaper *The Morning Star* could hardly think of enough superlatives to heap on it. She appeared on *Looking Good, Feeling Fit* to talk about dancing and fitness.

Entirely on her own in the production cockpit now, free to indulge herself without inhibition, Kate let much, much weirdness into *The Dreaming*. 'Houdini' and the title song, the latter full of animal noises and sound effects, the sort of disjointed musical gibberish one heard so much of after the release of *Sgt. Pepper's Lonely Hearts Club Band*, when there were so very few pop singers around, and so many Artists. 'Get Out Of The House', full of reverb-drenched shrieking, ends with the chanting of an Eeyore impersonator, and may well be the single most unlistenable track of Kate's career, which is saying a great deal. (If you hadn't read that it was inspired by Stanley Kubrick's *The Shining*, what prayer would you have had of making sense of it?) The poundingly percussive 'Sat In Your Lap' was more mental patient cabaret, and the munchkins of the previous album's 'Blow Away' were back in force, to the song's limitless detriment, in the polka-derived 'Suspended In Gaffa'. Kate encouraged her bass players to play entirely too many *glissandi*. 'Twas though she ordered the necks of their instruments buttered as they entered the studio.

All that said, moments of significant pleasure abounded. 'All The Love', in part homage to Laurie Anderson, was disjointed, and, as usual, lyrically impenetrable, but genuinely affecting in places, touchingly plaintive. She managed to be harrowing in a moving, rather than off-putting way, for the first time in the tortured refrain of 'Pull Out The Pin'. And the highly theatrical 'Night Of The Swallow', apparently a dialogue between the singer and the would-be smuggler she's trying to save from himself, achieved a sort of cinematicness, using Celtic instrumentation to marvellous effect.

Melody Maker's Colin Irwin gasped, "Initially it is bewildering and not a little preposterous . . . 'Get Out Of My House' has her roaring and ranting like a caged lion, 'Leave It Open' has her yelling like a demented mynah bird. She's taken the riskiest, most uncommercial route . . ." In America, *Record*'s Nick Burton asserted, "Bush has the dramatic edge, quirkiness and delicacy of Bowie in his *Hunk Dory* period; the eclectic, almost Baroque curiosity of a Peter Gabriel; a simply amazing voice that allows her to be alternately childlike and sensuously forceful . . . The cornerstone of the album is 'Night Of The Swallow,' which . . . moves gracefully through many changing moods and patterns; it's a work of both beauty and anguish, poignancy and eeriness." Charles Faris won the cogency award, calling the album "a season in hell".

★ ★ ★

I knew all too well how Duncan felt. The problem with having grown up feeling an embarrassment was that I could never get enough affirmation from women. Even when I was living with the universal object of desire, I was forever sneaking out to prove to myself that lots of other women wanted me too, a fact of which I've come to be hugely ashamed.

The universal object of desire either didn't know or simply refused to talk to me about it. But not so her successor, the one with the best hair in Los Angeles, a breathtaking gigantic honey-coloured Afro, or perhaps Norgefro, as her parents were Minnesota Norwegians. Halfway through my two years with her, and just before I became the face of Marcel Flynn, we went to a concert at which I apparently caught the eye of George Harrison's former Hollywood mistress, who sent me a letter suggesting that we meet, and then another, more emphatic one, pretty nearly demanding it. She enclosed a photograph that suggested that she might be the last woman in Los Angeles to repudiate the *Valley Of The Dolls* look, which suited me right down to the ground, as I found outlined lips, big hair, and deep cleavage very appealing. It was all moot anyway, of course. I was going to turn down a former Beatle's former (and apparently not that long ago!) lover? No, I hardly thought so.

I took to telling my Minnesota Norwegian every Saturday morning that I was off to play basketball, would play long enough to get sweaty, would phone George Harrison's former mistress to ask if she wanted to lick the sweat off my gorgeous hairless chest, would be assured that she certainly did, and would hurry over to her place, where she'd greet me at the door dressed as though to model for *Penthouse*, with music she knew me to approve of on the stereo and neat lines of coke waiting for me on the little mirror on "my" bedside table.

Everyone wound up suffering. George Harrison's former mistress revealed that she wasn't, as she originally promised, content to see me only on Saturday mornings, and began phoning me in tears at hours my Minnesota Norwegian was likely to be at home. The night she phoned to say she'd decided to kill herself if I didn't get over there immediately, I rang a pal to lie for me, to say I'd just left his house if my Minnesota Norwegian rang to confirm my story that I was going over to see him. Passive aggressive as he'd always been, he neglected to tell his own girlfriend, though, and it was she who answered when my Minnesota Norwegian, who had a good idea by this time I was up to something, phoned.

When I got home from telling George Harrison's mistress that it was now over between us because she'd revealed herself to be an emotional blackmailer, and promised her (bluffing, of course!) that I wouldn't feel even a pang of guilt or remorse if she went through with topping herself, my Minnesota Norwegian greeted me with a torrent of kicks and punches, none of which hurt nearly so much as the look in her eyes when she calmed down, just before she began to cry. And I wasn't allowed to console her. The person with whom I'd shared my life most intimately for the past two years was in horrible, audible pain in the next room, and when I went in to try to think of something to ease it, she didn't scream at me or throw more punches, but just said, very quietly, "Please leave me alone. Please."

Which isn't to make her more heroic than she actually was. A few weeks later, as we reclined on the bed together, watching a movie on television, she suddenly decided to try to extinguish her cigarette in my face. It hurt, but not as much as the look in her eyes the night she'd found out about the affair.

It's a common affliction, the no-affirmation-is-ever-enough one.

During the Monica Lewinsky hurly-burly, it was suggested that the most powerful man in the world seemed to suffer from it as well, that Bill Clinton found it no less impossible to turn down a presentable woman (or La Lewinsky) than I.

I have often asked myself over the decades why I didn't leave my Minnesota Norwegian for George Harrison's mistress. My Minnesota Norwegian was sweet and funny and devoted, but not nearly the traffic-stopper the universal object of desire had been, and not terribly clever. George Harrison's mistress wasn't exactly Susan Sontag (as I, of course, wasn't Noah Chomsky), but she seemed, with her greater cleavage, to get a lot more attention from men, and wasn't the primary purpose of my girlfriend in those years to prove to the world that I wasn't merely as good as The Boys Who Could, but in fact far superior?

Even then, though, there was something about her wanting me so fiercely, in wanting to define herself in terms of me, that made me very uncomfortable. I mean, she was going to feel good about herself because I was her lover? Had she taken a good look at me? How could she have failed to see that, beneath the superior fashion sense and saturnine Semitic good looks, there beat the heart of a boy who not only couldn't climb the pole, but had left poor Diane Geller in the middle of the sportsnite floor, dancing with no one?

It was actually right after I left the Minnesota Norwegian, while in London with a bunch of New Zealanders who'd hired me to present the pilot of a rock video show (MTV wasn't yet a tingling in its creators' loins) they were working up to try to sell in America, that I first heard Kate. One of the New Zealanders, the one whose facial hair suggested that he thought Amish chic was right around the corner, had picked me up hitchhiking to the beach. Impressed, as the creative director of Marcel Flynn's advertising agency would be two years later, by my saturnine Semitic good looks, my usually correct use of words of three syllables, and my famous slashing wit, he asked if I'd fancy an all-expenses-paid trip to the UK. I was fed up with the beach and said sure. My use of three-syllable words notwithstanding, they treated me when we convened in London like just another pretty face, a saturnine Semitic blond bimbo. I had to badger them implacably to be allowed to attend a production meeting at which they viewed tapes of emerging British artists whose managers wanted them on the show. One of the tapes was of Kate doing 'Wuthering Heights'.

It made everyone's jaw drop open, most, though, in horror. One of the New Zealanders, a longhaired pothead in leather and denim who believed Deep Purple to be the best thing the UK had ever produced, pronounced it, between belches, the biggest pile of shit he'd ever had to sit through. The one who'd hacked off most of his hair 48 hours after our arrival and dyed what was left blue thought Kate represented everything the music he preferred was trying to eradicate. If we included Kate among the many punk acts he'd personally recruited for the show, he promised, he would hurl himself in front of a train. (I thought we should include her for that reason alone.) The one who believed that white people could play classical music, but nothing else, not really, and who was pushing a bunch of reggae acts none of the rest of us could even begin to tell apart, thought the tape a wind-up.

Only the boss, the Peter Sellers lookalike who downed enough Foster's before breakfast every morning to fill a bathtub, agreed the tape was hilarious and original, audacious and exhilarating, and thus would offer a nice contrast to everything else we had. One of the first Walk-man owners, I went out and got her cassette immediately. The first night, I must have played 'Wuthering Heights' 35 times, to the exclusion of everything else. I hadn't loved anything so much since 'Anarchy In The UK' the year before. The next afternoon I got to the rest of the album, and discovered that I liked 'The Man With The Child In His Eyes' as much as 'Wuthering'. Just exquisite, that vibrato-less whole note with which she began the choruses – and splendid work by Andrew Powell on the string arrangement. And if she was a maddeningly vague lyricist, she was one of the most imaginative melodists I'd come across in ages. The chorus of 'Them Heavy People': a melody-lover's dream come true!

"So what do you reckon?" Duncan asked, reeling me back in from my reverie. I thought of telling him about the universal object of desire, and about George Harrison's mistress and my Minnesota Norwegian, but how could I reasonably expect him to believe that someone such as I had ever been of interest to women like that? I hated myself for what I'd allowed myself to become as much as for what I'd been, back in the era of my greatest allure, and told him that, as much as I wished I could give him the answer, I could not.

I wouldn't have blamed him, in his awful uncertainty and frustration, for snarling, "What would someone like you know about this sort of thing?" and storming out, but he said nothing of the sort, and in fact embraced me. It made me ashamed of myself for having so little faith in the innate goodness of people.

18

A Respite From Buttons

AT the beginning of my next session with the inaudible little Turkish psychotherapist the NHS had provided at my insistence, I pulled my chair very near to hers before she'd even murmured anything, and admitted I'd had a very hard time hearing her the week before. It either fell on deaf ears or there was something wrong with her vocal cords. I wonder if she had lots of nightmares in which she called for help but couldn't be heard by anybody. I wondered if that wondering said something about my own pathology.

Maybe my own hearing was becoming more acute. We revisited the theme of my being too harsh in my self-judgement. She said my judging myself so harshly was maladaptive. By my own admission, according to her notes, it didn't make my behaviour more palatable to me. Its only effect, in fact, was that it made it hard for me to live in my own skin. I'd never thought of it in quite that way. What she seemed to be saying made sense pragmatically. And here I'd always presumed that shrinks were encouraging me to be less ferociously self-critical on moral grounds. What a little fool I'd been.

But, but, but. (It was hardly like me to make any actual progress, not as long as there was air in my lungs for a clever rebuttal.) It felt that if I were gentler with myself, as either she or another of the countless dozens of shrinks I'd consulted over the years had put it, I'd be letting myself off the hook for my monstrousness. It seemed right that I should hold myself fully accountable.

Something about that pleased her. She began to speak. I leaned so far forward that I nearly had my ear in her mouth. Wasn't trying to hold one's self accountable, she wondered, the impulse of a highly moral person? For one exhilarating moment, I thought she might be onto something, only to conclude that her nearly incomprehensible accent and inaudibility concealed a remarkable flair for sophistry.

When I confessed that conclusion, she pretended not to know what sophistry meant.

★　★　★

Released in America, *The Dreaming* actually showed up briefly in the *Billboard* chart, but not long enough to make it distasteful to a small, burgeoning cadre of cultists. EMI, which owned its American subsidiary, Capitol, and stood to profit from her breaking through in the world's biggest record-buying market, urged Kate to accept Fleetwood Mac's invitation to tour there with them. She declined, but agreed at least to come over and trade bons mots with David Letterman on late-night TV, only for the turbines of the Queen Elizabeth II, which had seen action in the Falklands War, to pack it in before she could set sail. A Canadian farmer spent $4,000 of his own money to try to get her to come over, but succeeded only in starting *Breakthrough*, a North American counterpart of the British fanzine *Homeground*. EMI decided that the next best thing was to send her *Live At The Hammersmith Odeon* videotape, which was rather more likely to do what it was told, out on tour.

While 'Suspended In Gaffa' did well in the more discriminating duchies of Europe, EMI promoted the single 'There Goes A Tenner' in the UK with a conspicuous absence of wellie, and then had the effrontery to tell Kate it might be a fab idea if she stopped producing herself. Piqued, she had her own state-of-the-art (for a few months at least!) 24-track recording studio fitted at East Wickham. Feeling as though she had to choose between being famous and staying as close as possible to her own work, she chose the work, and was proud of herself.

★　★　★

As I've mentioned, my understanding, when I started gaining weight, was that people thought of us fat as jolly. Judging by the recent succession of the confused or distraught or sexually ambivalent into my room, though, I'd come to believe that what people really thought was that we're terrific listeners, great providers of shoulders on which to cry. Here, in other words, came Mrs. Cavanaugh herself, redder-lipped than usual, seeming to expect it to rain in my room, in a full-length mac, buttoned nearly to the neck.

It was the anniversary of her husband's suicide. She'd spent the day listening to Kate's 'You're The One' over and over. It seemed to run in the family. She was filled with sadness, but there was no one to whom she could turn for solace. Duncan seemed preoccupied with trying to decide whether he should leave Gemma for Nimalka. Cathy's new managers had her jumping through hoops from the moment she woke to the moment they finally allowed her to stagger into bed. She'd told Gilmour not to visit unless he was sober, and he was only intermittently sober. Mrs. Cavanaugh had plenty of women friends, but since Cathy's appearance on *Megastar*, none seemed to have the time to return Mrs. Cavanaugh's calls. But if I were busy or something, Mrs. Cavanaugh would certainly understand. She kept her hand on the door.

I assured her I wasn't busy at all, and then reassured her. Finally she actually came in and sat down on the edge of the bed. She declined tea. She declined biscuits. (Ashamed of how many of hers I'd taken to eating, I'd bought my own supply.) I sat down and let her talk.

Her Roger, whom she'd married a few weeks after turning 17, had been a bus driver at first, and an amateur musician. He'd enjoyed driving the bus, and had accompanied a Dusty Springfield soundalike on guitar. Duncan was born a few months after their marriage. She had a photo.

No matter how many times this happens to me, I never seem to learn. Even while assuming that the world looks at me and sees me as my vibrant, sexy, Marcel Flynn–modelling, 33-year-old self, except with a few more creases in my forehead and slightly sparser hair, I look at middle-aged and old people and imagine they were never other than what I see before me, never not grey and sagging, never not wearing bifocals on a cord round their necks so they won't forget where they put them, never not reconciled to the boredom of being alive and waiting, though they're unlikely to admit it, to getting back where they once belonged. But here was irrefutable proof that matronly, harried, profoundly nonsexual Mrs. Cavanaugh had once been quite the fox, in a macramé choker and feather haircut, big false eyelashes, platform shoes, and a skirt just barely there. And Rog! He wouldn't have looked out of place on stage with Rod Stewart, Jack the Lad in a satin suit and an artichoke coiffure.

Once having given up on rock'n'roll, Roger drove his bus and dreamed of being able to save enough to buy a little pub somewhere and play his guitar in it if he was able to hire someone reliable to look after the bar. He gambled, but hit a couple of jackpots, and by the time Duncan was 12 and Gilmour had been born, he and Mrs. Cavanaugh were only a couple of months short of realising their dream. But then a Scottish actor called Tam MacPherson, despondent because his native Glaswegian accent always broke through on stage when he drank, and because he couldn't keep himself from drinking, stepped in front of Roger's No. 82 bus between Finchley and Golders Green one humid September afternoon and died before the ambulance could arrive.

Roger swore that Tam had intended the accident, and got a couple of passengers to corroborate his impression, but in the two months he was suspended before London Transport announced they believed him, Roger started drinking too.

"He rang Tam's family to tell them how sorry he was. I was there when he did it. They screamed at him, called him a heartless bastard and put the phone down on him. As far as they were concerned, they were the only ones whose lives were ruined by the accident. But it was as though Tam was trying from beyond the grave to pull my Rog into whatever corner of Hell he'd wound up in."

Roger had nightmares. He apparently forgot what it was like to get a decent night's sleep. He carried on drinking. He walloped those he loved. He was sacked for missing his shift too often. He began spending the money he and Mrs. Cavanaugh had saved for their pub. He took to walloping her until she armed herself. He hanged himself, leaving a note saying it would have been poetic justice for him to step in front of a bus, but he wouldn't wish the nightmares on another driver.

I told her I was very sorry. She held up her hand to silence me. "I've not told you the whole story yet. A month or two before the accident, I'd begun seeing someone. You know, on the sly. He was a writer, a playwright. He claimed to have a novel in the works too, but he never let me read any of it. Serge. I met him at the newsagent's where he worked part time for extra money.

"Actually, it's a bit of an exaggeration to say I was seeing him. I slept with him twice, and then he seemed to lose interest. I was in love with him, though, and kept in touch, hoping he'd have a change of heart. I'd be shocked to find out Rog knew anything about it, as it had been so brief, and we'd been discreet, but I think he could sense something wasn't right even before the accident."

I shook my head in commiseration, and wondered if it would be proper for me to hold her. "I'm not telling you the whole story. I didn't sleep with Serge only twice. There was a third time." She filled her lungs and put her shoulders back, steeling herself for what she had to say. "I was actually shagging my beautiful wild dark Russian poet the night my husband topped himself. And I will never be able to forgive myself for that."

So this was the torrent she was dressed for. But no tears came. When this woman steeled herself, she stayed steeled. She turned to me dry-eyed and repeated, "Never."

I told her there was something comparable for which I could never forgive myself. I recounted the incident involving Babooshka in her mascot costume after the Montgomery High School football game. My eyes didn't remain dry, nor my cheeks.

She touched my leg. "There's a very big difference, though, isn't there? No matter how long or severe your estrangement from your daughter, you can continue to hope some day you'll get the chance to make it up to her, and she to you. No such hope is available to me."

I felt foolish, and then angry, though I certainly didn't express it. Of the many psychotherapists I've seen, only around a quarter have said anything of real value, something that's stuck with me. I've told you about the little Turkish one's perception that my being hard on myself was wrong not on moral grounds, but on practical ones. Well, years before, one of her many predecessors, in response to my musing that it was stupid for me to feel as I did about something, gently pointed out that our feelings are neither wise nor stupid on their own. They are what they are, and the stupid thing is to try to deny them. None of us is in another's skin, so how can one person tell another whose pain is the greater? (Yes, yes, I know. All this goes out the window when, for instance, one hears a teenager who hasn't the most rudimentary conception of how good she has it whining because she hasn't been given the money to buy these designer jeans or, slightly later, that car. The rule clearly applies only to fully formed adults.)

On the one hand, my coming to confront my own cowardice after the Montgomery High School game did indeed seem pretty trivial in comparison to Mrs. Cavanaugh's husband hanging himself in part because he'd sensed her infidelity. But on the other, how was it her place to judge?

"You remind me somehow of Serge," she said. "Obviously you're much older than he was at the time, but I sense a real kinship. I know you think of yourself as grotesque, just as he did." She waited for affirmation, but I was too busy sulking about her adjudging my pain as inadequate to give it to her. "One of the most beautiful men I've ever laid eyes on, with the longest eyelashes in the world, and he thought himself so ugly that he had to quit the job at the newsagent's. He couldn't bear the thought of anyone seeing him. That's one of the reasons it was possible for us to be so discreet. And I sense a lot of that in you, Mr. Herskovits."

I wasn't sure I knew where this was going. I wasn't sure I was enjoying my uncertainty. "It's more than four years since I've been with a fellow," she said. "But I do miss it sometimes, the feel of a fellow's hands on my thighs and breasts. And I deserve it, Mr. Herskovits. I do. I work harder than any woman I know. And I'm not ancient, not by any means. Not yet 52. Younger than yourself by a bit, I suspect."

I had a pretty clear idea of where it was going now, as she winked, and boy, did I not want it to go there. She was indeed pretty well preserved, and she was indeed a few years younger than I, so it was insane but I thought of her as a mother figure. If she wasn't the last person on earth I'd want to interact with erotically, she was certainly near the very top of the list of people I knew.

She seemed to be reading my thoughts. "I suspect you've never viewed me as a prospective lover. I suspect, in fact, that you think of me as somehow maternal, since it's my house you live in. Well, I came prepared. I chose what I'm wearing under this mac to help you see me in a whole new light." She reached for her top button. She unbuttoned it. I felt as though I was in one of those nightmares involving sudden incapacitation of the voicebox. I wanted to shout, "No!" but was silent.

She unbuttoned a second button. " 'The thought of you sends me shivery,' " she said. " 'I'm dressed in lace, sailing down a black reverie.' Do you recognise that, Mr. Herskovits?"

Of course I did. From *The Kick Inside*'s 'L'Amour Looks A Lot Like You', which I suddenly realised I might not have appreciated to the full.

A third button. It was actually quite sexy how she was doing it, so very, very deliberately, and accompanied by a look on her face that seemed to dare me to stop her. A fourth button. And then a respite from buttons, a gentle pulling apart of the part of the mac she'd liberated. Black lace beneath it. A fifth button. No mere black lace brassiere, but a corset. And how gorgeous her breasts looked, bulging.

She got to her feet and began, with the utmost deliberateness, to undo the mac's belt, only to stop before she'd accomplished it. The tip of her tongue between her lips: a brief appearance. "I could stop at any second, you know," she taunted, her voice huskier than I'd ever heard it. "All you have to do is say the word." But her eyes said, "Just try to get me to stop."

I was quite beyond rational thought by this time, what with every spare molecule of blood in my immense body having rushed with police escort to the telephone pole between my legs. She stepped towards me, just out of my reach. She smelled like every fantasy of my teens and early twenties, of the time of my most rapacious virility, somehow transformed into an odour. I was a page in a book on the Large Print shelf in the library to her. I reached for her. She stepped backwards. "Just drink it in," she said. My hand came down. She stepped nearer again. I breathed in deeply through my nose, and then again. "I'm fed up with having to do all the unbuttoning," she said, not a fraction of 52 now, but a 24-year-old coquette. "Why don't you do a couple." She laughed at the trembling of my hands, her laughter the auditory equivalent of her smell. Large Print.

I got a button undone, and then a second. She was wearing suspenders. The white area between the tops of her stockings and the bottoms of her black lace knickers was the visual equivalent of her smell and the sound of her gently mocking laughter.

At my signal, unleash hell!

If you'd have asked me an hour before she came to me, I'd have said that in trying to make love in the missionary position, I'd have been putting my lover in mortal danger. Suffice it to say that the widow Cavanaugh survived, and rather happily.

19

Behold My Cravenness

I DIDN'T know quite how to act around her after that. We couldn't exchange meaningful glances because our eyes never met, and not because mine didn't want to. She'd always treated me fairly formally. If anything, she was even more formal with me now. Two hours before she let herself quietly into my room and offered herself to me, she would ask if I wanted more coffee as though we were Victorians first introduced 90 seconds before.

We didn't do much talking. I wasn't allowed to speak to her without first being spoken to, and she seemed, after having told me all about poor Roger that first night, not to have words to say. She asked when I'd first noticed that I was on my way to grotesque obesity. I told her instead about how the mere thought of my grandmother filled me with shame.

In my first year of university, when I lived in that corner of limbo reserved for university students who commute from their parents' homes, I visited my grandmother often because her place was free of distractions, and a good place to study. I was already beginning to work up a reasonably accurate impersonation of a hippie, with my wispy moustache, bare feet, multiple bead necklaces, and long (albeit too coarse for flowing) hair, but at heart I remained a dutiful Jewish son, one who was mindful that my university education was costing my parents money for which my dad theoretically worked hard. I therefore trudged along dutifully to all my classes and did all the assigned reading, much of it in the bedroom of my grandmother's apartment in which my uncle had topped himself a couple of years before.

My grandmother was always unnervingly delighted to see me, and honouring her with my presence made me feel rather less a cruel little bastard than in the rest of my life. I would sit in the bedroom in which my uncle had fed himself a lethal dose of sedatives and pore over my textbooks, highlighting especially salient passages with a fluorescent puce highlighting pen, greatly diminishing the books' resale value. On at least one occasion, I found what I was reading so boring that I spent the whole afternoon highlighting every word of the three assigned chapters, and giggled as I imagined what the book's next owners would infer. I can see now, in retrospect, that highlighting everything was very much a precursor to the crowd-pleasing trick I devised the following year, when my girlfriend and I would occasionally have dinner at a nearby coffee shop offering paper place mats that children could colour while their parents dined. On request, your server would provide a little box of four crayons. I made my girlfriend laugh until she wept by colouring the entirety of my place mat red, from edge to edge. Our fellow diners probably thought we were on hallucinogens. They were right.

My grandmother's family had come to America from Odessa around the turn of the century to escape the *pogroms*. Her father, according to who was telling the story, had been either a Talmudic scholar or a layabout with a very long beard, her mother the proprietress of a boarding house. I was never able to ascertain why they'd chosen to live in Minneapolis, which was either brutally hot or brutally cold, and populated mostly by xenophobic Swedes. My grandmother had married her second cousin at 19 and begun having his children the following year, starting with my mother. For the first dozen years of my mother's life, the family lived in abject squalor, and commonly sneaked out of rented flats in the dead of night to foil their landlords. They regularly lacked hot water. At around eight, my mother was sent home from school for smelling, a humiliation that would inform the rest of her life.

My grandfather, a brute and tyrant who my mother says rarely had a kind or encouraging word for his children, had no trade either. He and my grandmother moved to Los Angeles, back when it smelled of oranges, and opened a small diner. While it was going bust, my mother, at 10, had to care for her younger brother and sister, an imposition that would inform the rest of her life. She had to take them to the movies, and then walk them back to the diner in what she would refer to forever after as The Pitch Dark. There was no moonlight in the world my mother inhabited as a child, and no street lights.

After the diner failed, my grandfather took to drinking and brawling. My mother remembers him being brought home soaked in his own blood, spitting out his own incisors. But then, just as Prohibition was repealed, he suddenly made a fortune as a liquor wholesaler, and the family moved to the poshest part of the Twin Cities area that would take Jews. His new prosperity apparently didn't improve my grand-father's disposition. He took personal offence at the fact that, in early adolescence, my mother became a bedwetter. (I come naturally by my predisposition for rapacious self-loathing.) But even while she was wetting her bed, she was also becoming so beautiful and stylish that she actually inspired my grandfather to compliment her. A year after telling her – not proudly, apparently, or affectionately, or encouragingly, but in the same tone in which he might have acknowledged her being right-handed – that she was beautiful, he was dead at 42 from a heart attack. For the rest of her life, my grandmother plugged in a special memorial lamp every year on the anniversary of his death.

My mother hated my grandmother for not having defended her from my grandfather. Her hatred didn't keep her, dutiful Jewish daughter that she was, from visiting my grandmother regularly during my child-hood. They would sit across from one another in the uncomfortable Queen Anne chairs my grandmother had bought to furnish the big house in the poshest section of the Twin Cities that would take Jews, and bicker for hours while I drew pictures or, later, after some public education and my very high IQ had kicked in, tried to find something interesting in *Reader's Digest*. My grandmother subscribed.

I never knew my aunt Doris, my mother's younger sister, not to be bedridden. She had been even more beautiful than my mother at one point, but had, I found out decades later, got herself pregnant. My grandmother blamed her bedriddenness on her abortionist. She seemed to love me, which even when I was five years old felt not quite right. She shared my uncle's hatred of my mother, who, however excruciat-ingly neurotic she might have been, was in very much better nick than either of her siblings.

My aunt would die in mysterious circumstances when I was about 10. I think she may have been on some sort of life support by that time, and that my mother and grandmother had got my dad to pull her plugs. It was the sort of thing my dad, always trying to please, always failing, would have done without protest.

My mother addressed my grandmother as Mother and spoke to her in a voice pitched about a third higher than that with which she spoke to my dad. It was a good key for hectoring. What they talked about mostly were the character flaws of everyone they knew. They used a lot of Yiddish. I hated every minute of it.

My uncle, my grandmother's youngest child, my mother's little brother, lived with my grandmother. Everything that was wrong with my mother – the awful shyness, the misanthropy, the self-loathing –

was worse with my uncle. He came to be treated by a psychiatrist who prescribed a pre-first generation antidepressant that made my uncle unfit to drive a car. He drove anyway, and was in an accident in which his face was very slightly disfigured. He grew a Van Dyke to conceal that he'd lost a bit of his chin. He looked fine, but regarded himself as too ugly for anyone outside of family to see him. To humour him, my grandmother moved to the desert north-east of Los Angeles, where my uncle would never have to see anyone except my family when we drove up there every month or so.

He'd decided to become a writer. I'd shown precocity as a writer in my own right. He'd read a biography of his idol, Thomas Wolfe, in which it was revealed that the great man used to make his students agonise over every syllable of what they wrote for him. I was a self-loathing adolescent who wanted only praise, and our little sessions were torture. He also trounced me at chess, for which I seemed to have no aptitude whatever, while my dad stood in the back yard and smoked contentedly while my mother and grandmother discussed the woeful character deficiencies of their every common acquaintance.

I couldn't wait to be old enough not to have to come to the desert with my family anymore, but was too neurotic to stay on my own even at 15. I felt certain that someone had broken into the house and would leap out of the shadows and slash my throat if I abandoned one room for another. In every phase of life, I felt damned if I did, but no less if I didn't.

I helped kill my uncle. With my mother's tacit encouragement, I wrote him a letter vilifying him for having ruined my grandmother's life. I have every reason to believe it hurt him. Lazy, self-loathing, self-righteous adolescent twerp that I was, I was still as near as he had to a friend. I have much to answer for. Several months later, inconsolable in the face of being unable to get any of his short stories published, he typed a neat, bitter goodbye-and-fuck-off letter with his left hand (his right having been rendered useless in the car crash in which his face was disfigured), took a whole bottleful of his pills, decided he had a few more poison thunderbolts to hurl, and wrote, ever less legibly, with a ballpoint pen until he lost consciousness.

I found out about my uncle's death one afternoon when I arrived home from school. My sister, around seven at the time, opened the front door with the words, "Marty died." That, apparently, was all she'd been told. I, every inch the tough guy, demanded, "So?" But a few months later, when I read his last letter, the tough guy, feeling as though his heart were being ripped from his chest, sobbed so hard he thought he'd split open. He accused me of betraying him, as indeed I had. My age wasn't an excuse. I betray everybody in the end. My grandmother moved back from the desert and I started university and came over to her place to pretend to study.

When I finished university and started my modelling career, I continued to visit, less frequently. I found it difficult to converse with her. I got her to tell me what she could about her early life. She couldn't tell me much. I'd talk to her about current events. She held Jane Fonda in very low regard because of comments about Zionist thugs. When I pointed out that it had in fact been Vanessa Redgrave who'd decried Zionist thugs, my grandmother said, "Well, I don't think the other one is any great friend of the Jewish people either." I had no idea what she was basing this on. She knew virtually nothing of Judaism, but seemed to feel, as my mother would too, that her ethnicity entitled her to a certain amount of paranoia.

My grandmother knew little about actual Judaism, but much about Jewish cuisine. She made delicious *gefilte* fish, delicious potato *knishes*, delicious cheese *blintzes*. When I came to visit, she would always give me a dozen *knishes* or *blintzes* wrapped first in tin foil and then in a plastic bag. I could taste the love in them.

She began to fade away, to become hopelessly confused. When she ceased to be able to keep track of the medications she was meant to be taking, my mother got her admitted to a convalescent hospital. I visited her there even though I knew I'd be getting no *blintzes* to take home, no *knishes*, and even though conversation with her was more difficult than ever. She wore her empty handbag on her arm whenever she left her room, rather like the Queen. She thought she'd been incarcerated, and asked, "What did I do wrong to get put in here?" If I'd had a heart, it would have been broken. You got old, I thought, and confused.

I moved far away. My mother transferred my grandmother to a different convalescent hospital, one offering greater care in very much less pleasant surroundings. It was the hospital in which I would later allow my father to die. My grandmother lived on and on and on. Her 90th birthday came and went. She ceased to recognise my mother, who told me she'd started to smell.

I saw her one last time, when I came to visit my dad, for whom it must have been deeply heartening to have become a patient in the same halfway house in which his mother-in-law was rotting away. I saw her wandering the halls, looking utterly befuddled. Afraid that she'd smell, and confident she wouldn't recognise me anyway, I didn't interrupt her, didn't say hello, didn't thank her for the *knishes* and *blintzes*.

★ ★ ★

Mrs. Cavanaugh confessed to being an avid reader. She'd read the memoirs the month before of an Irish university lecturer who'd been kidnapped in Beirut and then held hostage by Islamic Jihad for nearly four years. It had made her grateful to be able to visit the loo whenever she needed, to be able to eat whatever she pleased off clean plates, to open a window and look out on the street when she liked. "It's a good thing to savour small mercies," she said. "And I don't think you do, Les." It was the only time she ever called me Les.

Neither of us smoked, so instead of ritually lighting cigarettes after lovemaking, we'd put one of Kate's CDs in my boombox. (We'd tried having it off to her accompaniment, but found that we kept getting caught up in the music and losing our places.) Mrs. Cavanaugh couldn't get enough of *The Ninth Wave*, the song cycle about drowning that had originally been Side 2 of *The Hounds Of Love*. She said she herself often felt as though drowning – in frustration, in boredom. It hadn't been her ambition to run a boarding house, but she'd been unable to get the sort of work she wanted. She didn't like to talk about it. I wondered if she was mindful of her own small mercies.

With considerable trepidation, I asked if she'd look through my catalogues with me and help me pick out a gift for Kate. She wondered why I was sending a gift, since it was well past Kate's birthday. I'd seen the confusion and concern in enough fellow Katefans' eyes when I told them how much I spent sending her things. I knew full well that not everyone feels as I do, and tried to change the subject. I admitted to having heretofore sent only a couple of birthday bouquets. I made no mention of the 2,000 emails.

I knew people who would have described us as dating, but outside my bedroom, we saw one another only as boarding house proprietress and guest, and in a way that suited me perfectly. However much I loved our erotic relationship, the part of me that insisted, in spite of my grotesqueness, that I allow myself to be seen only with women Boys Who Could would envy wasn't so sure the widow Cavanaugh looked right on my arm. She was over 50, and it was no consolation at all that she was less far over it than I. I thought of how, when 45-year-old Hugh M. Hefner first began courting one of his succession of huge-breasted young brunettes, she, aghast, informed him that she'd never been out with anyone older than 24. "Me neither," he is said to have replied. The part of me that needed other, better men to envy me would never be older than 14.

★ ★ ★

After *The Dreaming,* Kate wasn't seen for a long while, and the *Daily Mail* asked its readers to believe that months of being stuck in the recording studio gobbling chocolate and junk food had caused her to balloon up to 18 stone. She moved into the country, or at least to Eltham, south-east of London, next door to bigger brother Jay and his family, and situated her piano so she could watch the clouds rolling up through the valley towards her as she composed. She resumed dancing, coming back into town to help launch Sky, the UK's first satellite TV channel. By the dawn of 1984, the new studio was ready, and she began work on what nearly everyone but me (I prefer *The Red Shoes*) and Mr. Halibut downstairs agrees was her best album, *The Hounds Of Love,* with engineer Haydn Bendall, imported from Abbey Road.

Working at home suited her a treat. If she wanted to discuss something, she could do it around the kitchen table. If she wanted to get away from it all, she could walk her dogs Bonnie and Clyde in the garden. Bendall would later describe her remarkable transformation between control room and vocal booth. In the one, she'd be small and thoughtful. Then she'd step into the other and unleash a big, powerful voice you wouldn't have dreamed three minutes earlier could come out of her.

Not having to keep her eye on the clock, no longer charged by the hour, she was free to be as obsessive as she liked about implementing her vision, whatever her vision might come to be. Bendall was surprised by how open she was to the ideas of others. Three years and more after *The Dreaming,* Kate's fifth album, *Hounds Of Love,* was finally ready.

After convincing her that there would be lots of resistance at radio stations to the title 'Deal With God', EMI persuaded her to rename the album's opening track 'Running Up That Hill'. God only knows what she'd have been without them. She appeared on *Top Of The Pops* for the first time in seven years with much percussive accompaniment, and 'Running' got to number three, her biggest success since 'Wuthering Heights'. At long, long last, she betrayed a wee trace of the diva, bringing her own make-up person, Teena Earnshaw (Catherine's niece, later to win an Oscar for her work on *Titanic,* and just joking about Catherine's niece), rather than using the BBC's. *Kate Bush Diva Shock Horror!*

At the gigantic launch party for the album, at the London Laserium, the Paul Newman-eyed Del was unmistakably Kate's date, this after their having been a romantic pair for seven years. Naturally, the

183

tabloids found a way to make them suffer for their new candour, inducing another bassist who'd played on the album to slag Del, or at least pretending that he'd done so.

The first thing that struck me listening to the famous opening track, 'Running Up That Hill (A Deal With God)' was that Kate had finally stopped shooting herself in the foot insofar as arrangements were concerned – the loping rhythm that established itself immediately never relented, setting a wonderful precedent for the rest of the songs on what at the time was thought of as Side 1. It was also glorious to hear her singing in a proper adult register, though I, for one, could easily have done without the silly decorative background singing. (I have always believed that the singer wanted God to swap her circumstances with those of the antagonist to whom she was singing, but a major, major music magazine has gone on record as believing that she actually hoped to trade places with God. Behold the annoying ambiguousness of English pronouns! Behold that Kate's lyrics were nearly as confusing as ever.)

The title track, which evoked the first album's 'Oh To Be In Love' in its wariness of romance, was no less propulsive than 'Running', and hugely enjoyable. There were those who imagined the bombastic 'The Big Sky', in which she unleashed a couple of wonderful screams of the sort David Lee Roth would spend his career aspiring to in vain, to be an expression of her disdain for EMI's discomfort with *The Dreaming*. If so, leave it to Kate to bewail someone's failure to understand her in a song that defies comprehension. If not, forget I said that.

That she remained as . . . uncompromising as any pop recording artist extant was made clear by the opening line of 'Cloudbusting': "I still dream of Orgonon". How could anyone who didn't recognise that as the name of Wilhelm Reich's laboratory and research centre have been anything but confused? I puzzled then and continue to puzzle to this day at the line "Your son's coming out" at the end. If she hadn't been trying for a pun regarding Peter Reich's sexuality, why not "*The* sun's coming out?" In any event, I liked the insistent cellos.

The Ninth Wave suite of songs, about drowning, or a dream of drowning, or something, had moments of remarkable beauty. After 'I Dream Of Sheep', half again as gorgeous as even 'The Man With The Child In His Eyes', though, it was mostly dauntingly confusing. I have tried many times over the decades to surrender myself to it, and my confusion always slightly exceeds my pleasure. The failure may well be my own, rather than Kate's.

★　★　★

I went to another Overeaters meeting. It looked in the early stages as though it wouldn't be worth the time. Dahlia wasn't there, and Jez was moaning about his girlfriend moaning that they couldn't afford to go anywhere very interesting on holiday since his record company had fired him. He didn't fit in an ordinary coach seat. The only flights on which he could afford two adjoining seats were to places his girlfriend was fed up with. "She says she'd sooner stay home than go to Malaga again," he said. "Well, I'm bloody sorry, but I happen to like Malaga." Even Boopsie, normally fascinated by anything anyone said, was yawning.

"What do we think of the Maddox diet?" Crinolyn wondered. Nobody knew what she was talking about. It was apparently the latest fad diet to be embraced by Hollywood stars. It was like the Atkins diet, except it didn't eliminate just carbohydrates from the diet, but protein as well. You could eat all the fat you liked. Crinolyn understood Geri Halliwell to have lost half a stone in two weeks.

"Just think," Boopsie said dreamily, "getting to eat as much ice cream or cheese as you like, and washing it down with cream."

"I think you've hit the nail on the head," Graham the moderator laughed. "I think the idea is that after a couple of days you'd get thoroughly fed up with ice cream, and stop eating it. Which, if that's all you're allowed, means that you'd pretty much stop eating, full stop. Of course, how many of us could stick to that for more than a few hours?"

"If Geri bleedin' Halliwell can do it," Crinolyn demanded, "why can't we?"

"Geri Halliwell can do it because she's a glamorous celebrity," Graham theorised. "She's always got something going. It's easy not to eat when you're rushing from photo shoot to magazine interview to party to ship christening."

"What ship has Geri ever christened?" Crinolyn demanded. "You're just talking rubbish now. You're just making it up as you go along."

Then Dahlia turned up, looking this week as though on her way to work as an investment banker, that smart, that conservative. As usual, all else was shoved aside while she told us about her week, during which her weight had remained stable and she'd gone out with a Renault dealer from Surbiton who'd confessed he hadn't dated a woman weighing less than 15 stone in his entire adulthood. Dahlia wasn't so sure that anything would come of it. She'd told him she'd see him again on Wednesday night, but was seriously considering cancelling. He was fit enough, she supposed, but not very funny. She was one of those who considered a sparkling sense of humour not less indispensable than a taut little bum.

All of which had Crinolyn, who was probably grateful if she saw her husband sober two days in seven, rolling her eyes in disgust.

But she wasn't the only one not enjoying listening to Dahlia. Neither was her still-nameless sidekick, whose folded arms and glower suggested a level of disgruntlement far beyond Crinolyn's. Dahlia might have been a self-infatuated boor, but not entirely oblivious to what was going on around her. She interrupted her description of what she and the Renault dealer had ordered at dinner to ask her sidekick what was the matter.

I felt her pain. From the age of 15 until the time the girl who'd become my first girlfriend agreed to go out with me, I was myself a sidekick. Daring to imagine that one of their admirers might notice me, I insinuated myself into the entourages of a succession of good-looking, athletic, confident classmates – hating both myself for having done so and them for having things I hadn't, and perhaps never would have. But I didn't come to be perceived as attractive by association. The most that ever happened was that a girl would ask me, almost invariably without addressing me by name, to convey some important message to my more desirable friend. In junior high school, this was nearly enough, as being spoken to extracurricularly by a pretty girl in any circumstances was profoundly thrilling. *So this*, I used to marvel, *is how it feels to be normal!*

I wasn't much of a sycophant in my heart. Watching those on the periphery of whose entourages I clung playing football on Friday nights, I wished fervently they'd commit some horrific catastrophic blunder, or, alternatively, be injured. Of course, the one without the other wouldn't have been of much use. Girls seemed to find boys who'd suffered painful injuries while fighting for the glory of the school fantastically sexy.

Justice may be blind, but poetic justice is a myth. At my 20th year class reunion, I should have found that the better-looking classmates whose favour I once grovelled to curry were fat and bald and divorced and alcoholic, stuck in jobs they hated, unable to understand their children, who hated them, while I was slim and successful, with a Michelle Pfeiffer lookalike on my arm. Poetic justice is a myth perpetrated by the same people, I suspect, who brought us religion, and used for the same purpose – to keep the have-nots from lynching the haves, or at least torching their Lexuses. The boys whose favour I'd curried all seemed reasonably content, and had lost none of their winning confidence, while I have hardly known a month's contentment in this life, and am grotesquely obese.

Looking through my yearbooks after the event, it occurred to me that I was in most cases actually better-looking than they were at the time, and in all cases substantially cleverer, funnier, and more creative. It's all about confidence, innit?

Behold my cravenness. I feel nearly as ashamed of insinuating myself into the entourages of better-looking classmates as I do for having failed to greet my grandmother the last time I saw her.

20

Ordinary Little Me

"THE matter?" Dahlia's sidekick pretended to wonder. "You want to know what's the matter? Nothing at all. Not a thing. Just because I thought I could count on you, and found out otherwise this week, well, that doesn't mean anything's the matter. Just because I was a bloody fool to imagine we were really mates, a big – very big! – starlike you and ordinary little me from Neasden."

To her small credit, Dahlia looked mortified. "Oh, I was meant to ring this week, wasn't I? Oh, I'm so, so, so sorry. It was just a mad week. I hardly had a moment to . . ."

"Sod your mad week," her sidekick snarled resonantly. "That's bollocks. I know how long it takes to make a bloody phone call. Forty-five bloody seconds."

Graham mused, "I wonder if the two of you might be willing to save this conversation until after . . ."

"Shut it," Crinolyn advised him, in a way that invited no debate. "I want to hear what she's got to say."

It was as though Dahlia's sidekick was only now realising that the rest of the group was there. She flushed briefly with embarrassment, but then seemed to decide that she liked the idea of witnesses. "Two meetings ago," she told us, glaring at Dahlia, "she told me she had a bloke for me, a make-up artist from one of the shows she's been in. Well fit, she said, and not even gay. I've had too many mates set me up with blokes who took one look at me and suddenly remember urgent business at home to get my hopes up, but she was sure he'd fancy me. She said she'd described me, and that he'd seemed well keen.

"A week went by. At the end of the last meeting, I mentioned it to her. I made it sound like I'd just happened to remember, when in fact I'd been thinking about little else all week. She said oh, yes, and that she'd definitely give the bloke my mobile number this week. But she was too bloody busy."

I knew it was going to happen, and it did. The anger under which she was trying to hide her pain got dissipated, and she burst into tears. "It's always the likes of her, the pretty ones, the ones all the blokes fancy, who can't quite find the time. And the ones like me, the ones nobody notices, the ones blokes leave standing out there alone on the middle of the bloody dance floor, who spend the week waiting for the bloody phone to ring. And it never bloody fucking does." As she convulsed with sobs, Crinolyn, making clucking sounds of compassion, put her huge thick white arms around her.

"I made him up," Dahlia, unable to bear not being the centre of attention, announced. And it worked, as everyone turned back to her.

"The reason nobody rang is because there wasn't anybody to begin with. All the make-up artists I've ever worked with have been gay. And if they hadn't been gay, they probably wouldn't have fancied anybody our size."

"Why, you absolute bitch," Boopsie marvelled.

"Spare me, you cow," Dahlia told her. "I did what I did with generous intentions, to shine a bit of light on a mate's blackness. None of you gave her a lift home after these meetings. None of you has any idea of how hopeless she is. Well, I do have an idea, and I tried in the only way I could think of to throw her a lifeline."

Her sidekick howled in embarrassment and pain, and I thought I knew why. Until this point, she'd been able to imagine that, after she'd scolded Dahlia and Dahlia had worn her hair shirt and they'd embraced and made up, the whole scenario she'd envisaged might finally pan out. But now all that was out of the question.

"Oh, I had a feeling you lot would turn on me at your first opportunity," Dahlia said. "Don't think I didn't. As long as I can bring a bit of glamour and excitement to these bloody meetings, I'm everybody's fair-haired girl. But let one little thing happen, and you all desert me in a heartbeat, don't you?"

"I'm not deserting you," Graham blurted.

"Nor am I," Jez protested as well, even though he had a girlfriend, but Dahlia seemed to notice neither.

"Maybe you've noticed that I'm always the centre of attention," she said. "Does that give you any bloody clues as to the state of my self-esteem? Does someone who feels OK about herself need to hog the spotlight all the time? Of course she doesn't. Does someone who feels OK about herself discard and replace her whole bloody wardrobe every week? Not likely!

"And you probably suppose that because I'm reasonably well

known, I have my choice of blokes. I haven't! It used to be that all I met were gold-diggers, blokes who wanted to spend their lives at the pub while I supported the both of us. And now it's even worse – gold-digger chubby chasers."

"Oh, shut it, will you?" Crinolyn said. "Do you not know how grateful most of us would be for any attention at all, from anybody?"

This was getting exciting now. The question wasn't whether they'd come to blows, but who'd throw the first punch. For the first time in years and years, I remembered a fight I'd witnessed in junior high school involving two Mexican girls with huge Ronettes hair and eye-liner circling one another, hissing and snarling, calling one another *puta*, until one of them dived at the other. Each was able to grab a handful of the other's hair, stiff with hairspray though it may have been, and to pull her head backwards. There was no evidence of the razor blades such girls were said to conceal in their hair. A pair of panting teachers intervened before an actual punch could be thrown. I'd have eagerly signed on to be either girl's sex slave through age 25. Both clearly had enough testosterone for two. Exactly the kind of girl I needed!

I wasn't sure whom I favoured here. The only thing about Crinolyn I liked was that she seemed to have a pretty good idea of who she was. She may have revelled in it to an extent I found unseemly, but at least she was in touch with her own obnoxiousness. The only thing I'd ever liked about Dahlia was her make-up on Goth day. If I were going to be unable to forgive myself for leaving poor Diane Geller alone in the middle of the dance floor at my junior high school sportsnite, how was I going to not mind Dahlia's having made her poor sidekick feel just as lonely and hopeless?

The point was moot. Here, 22 minutes after the meeting was meant to have started, came Nicola, in such a way as to inflict instant amnesia on all who saw her. Sidekick's beef with Dahlia? No one, I suspect, could remember a thing about it, not in the face of Nicola looking lovelier than anyone would have dared imagine she might.

She must have lost half of herself. She was still no sylph, but at the same time she might have been hard pressed to find work as a BBW. Her glorious cornsilk hair gleamed as never before. Her skin was even more lustrous. Was it possible that her eyes were even more beautiful? We all gasped at the sight of her. No reaction other than gasping was possible. She smirked shyly, not yet used to affecting anyone as she'd affected us. Mexican gang girls with testosterone enough for two? *What* Mexican gang girls?

Everyone got up, even the women. No other reaction was possible. That brought colour to her cheeks. Graham spoke for all of us when he said, "Blimey."

The floodgate thus opened, everyone showered her with questions. Exactly how much weight had she lost? How long had it taken? Which diet was responsible? Did she fancy a drink after the meeting? Did she fancy dinner later in the week? Would she be Graham's bride?

Oh, the glance she shot me, the glance. Are you noticing this, it asked? Was I drawing breath?

There was some talk of her not being allowed to stay at the meeting. In the view of some, she was too slim now. Someone else pointed out that it hardly made sense to evict Nicola while allowing me to remain. I didn't pretend to understand that. Graham suggested that Nicola be allowed to stay as living proof of what any of us could accomplish if we were sufficiently single-minded, sufficiently determined. "Sod that," Crinolyn snorted. "I'm not going to put myself under that sort of pressure."

Graham finally declared the meeting finished. Dahlia, apparently hoping not to have to confront her sidekick one-on-one, was out of the room like a shot. Several people swarmed around Nicola. She told them she'd meet them downstairs. I was rearranging the contents of my shoulder bag in hopes of being alone with her, but her sidekick apparently seemed intent on ensuring that Dahlia's car was no longer in the car park before she ventured downstairs, and stood at the window forever. "Bitch," she said as Dahlia pulled out into the high street. And then Nicola and I were finally alone.

I treated myself to a long look at her. "Do you see something you like?" she said. The old Nicola wouldn't have had a tenth the confidence necessary to ask that. I found it inexpressibly sexy.

She said her new look was all for me. I thought she was taking the piss, but there was no sign of that. It was I who finally looked away. It occurred to me that it might not even be Nicola. Nicola could never have returned anyone's gaze so steadily. My mouth was dry and my palms damp. I could barely swallow.

"I understand you went to Ibiza right after we went out," she said. "I was absolutely gutted that you didn't ring me again."

I could hardly believe my ears. I told her I hadn't rung because she'd seemed very much more interested in Tarquin from the pub than in me. She said she was only pretending to be interested to try to make me feel competitive. Her biological father had once told her that men stay interested only in women they have to fight for. In fact, she couldn't

191

have been less interested in Tarquin at the pub, who'd been a rotten conversationalist, without lovely manners. "If you'd asked him what a person does in a conversation," she said, "I'm almost sure he'd have said speak and wait to speak again." And he was too young for her. She'd always pictured herself with an older bloke.

It's a good thing I didn't have to stand up quickly. I'd have had to worry that she'd notice the enormous bulge in my trousers. It occurred to me that she'd be the most beautiful woman I'd been seen with since the Seventies. Which wasn't to deny she still needed to lose a few pounds. She stood up. "Everyone's waiting for me downstairs," she said.

"I just have to rearrange the contents of my shoulder bag," I said, sounding a complete twat even to myself. She arched an eyebrow at me. I think she'd had them tweezed, and by someone who knew what she was doing.

"You must have some very complicated stuff in there," she said, laughing lightly. "You've been rearranging it since the meeting finished." Her teasing only made the problem worse. I told her not to wait for me, and promised I'd call.

I sat there at some length while the blood resumed flowing to other parts of my body as well, and thought what a shame it was that one couldn't have a sort of savings account in which to store his unrequited tumescence for future use. But of course since the introduction of Viagra, why would anyone bother?

★ ★ ★

"There's something uncomfortably archaic," noted the estimable Ira Robbins, writing about *Hounds Of Love*, "about a pop album that seems so anxious to be thought of as Art. Bush possesses undeniable talent, craft and intelligence, and is capable of occasional excellence, but it's sometimes hard to take her as seriously as she takes herself." In *Sounds*, Richard Cook admitted, "Most of her records smell of tarot cards, kitchen curtains, and lavender pillows to me. But bits of *Hounds Of Love* make something mischievous or even demonic come out of her throat, and 'The Big Sky' is a moment of real mad bravado. It starts like it's going to be one of the digital warrior dances Bush puts together when she wants to be uptempo and then a whole planet seems to be swirling around her voice. The best and most threatening thing that this bizarre talent has ever done." Mark Peel of *Stereo Review* noted that, "compared with her brilliant but difficult 1982 release, *The Dreaming*, it's positively tranquil." Tom Doyle observed, "This, musically and lyrically, is surely some of the most obtuse pop music to have graced a chart rundown."

She would later describe the *Running Up That Hill* video, choreographed by Dyane Grey-Cullert, performed with Michael Hervieu, as her goodbye to dance. There were those who saw it more as a tip of her hat to (or a rather brazen imitation of) the fervent dance sequence in John Sayles' 1983 film *Lianna*, about an unhappily married woman's realisation of her own lesbianism.

A production team headed by director Julian Doyle spent four days on Uffington's White Horse Hill making the silly video for 'Cloudbusting' – and feeling, though there was no one around, that someone was watching them. Someone pointed out the hill's proximity to Waylands Smithy, where, according to legend, a ghostly blacksmith waits to shoe travellers' horses, and the press was duly amused. In the short film, the psychoanalyst Dr. Wilhelm Reich, played by Donald Sutherland, is arrested by jealous evil bureaucrats in shiny shoes for inventing a rain-inducing machine. After the arrest, his son Peter, played by the not-remotely-boyish Kate, returns to the machine and makes it rain. A heartening triumph of the virtuous and inventive over petty bureaucratic short-sightedness! It was later shown in cinemas with *Back To The Future*.

★ ★ ★

It wasn't only the other Overeaters competing for Nicola's attention downstairs. There were normal people in the mix as well. I didn't know if she expected me to try to elbow my way through them. The expectant look she gave me suggested she might have done, but I've always been crap in crowds, and held back. She shrugged back at me and made her way toward the door like Madonna through *paparazzi*.

Tarquin was waiting for her. She'd only been winding me up about picturing herself with an older bloke! She turned back to me, gave me the same mischievous smile I'd seen upstairs, and exited the pub, while Tarquin gave me a look that said, "In your fucking dreams, mate." I gave them plenty of time to get in his car and drive off, and then (and only then) got angry enough to beat him like a rug.

I considered returning to Ibiza, but settled for phoning Nicola when I got home. She didn't answer her mobile, and I wasn't about to leave a message that she could ignore. I phoned her landline. Cyril answered, dreamily. He explained that he was in the midst of a vicious browbeating from the mountain of flesh, and asked if he could ring back. "Put that phone down this instant and get over here!" I heard the mountain of flesh bellow at him from across the room. He moaned with pleasure.

193

I didn't want him to leave a message for Nicola, and let him think I'd been phoning him. I said he could indeed phone back, though of course I hoped he wouldn't.

At dinner, Mrs. Cavanaugh was even colder to me than normal, but unusually solicitous with Mr. Chumaraswamy. Did he find the gravy too salty? She'd started with a different brand of chicken stock this time. How about the potatoes? Was he sure he had enough? Was there anything he especially fancied for later in the week? If so, he should tell her, and she'd make a point of making it. He had to admit he'd had a craving for lamb *biryani*. She laughed and said it had never occurred to her to attempt it before, but she'd have a go. But if she were trying to make me jealous, it wasn't working. I could think only of Nicola.

Thank God for *Fab Lab*, which I could count on to divert me for an hour. I'd come, over the previous few weeks, to feel great fondness for Huw, the big Welsh lummox. While most of the other contestants had been grooming themselves for careers as musicians or pop stars from their mid-teens, Huw, a guileless-seeming plumber from Swansea, had been singing only since the night a few months before when some mates had persuaded him to enter a karaoke contest at their local. He sang the Welsh national anthem, Tom Jones's 'Delilah'. At the end, he was said to have been gobsmacked when, instead of jeering him as they'd jeered one another, his mates had jumped to their feet, along with everyone else in the pub, to applaud. He then entered a succession of talent shows, apparently expecting to be exposed at every one as talentless, but had won every one. He was one of seven (from over 60) who auditioned in Cardiff for *Fab Lab* to be invited to the second round of competition, in London. Now he wasn't just the only Welsh contestant left, but one of only five from anywhere.

It hadn't been easy for him. At the start, seeming to expect no more than he'd expected in the original karaoke competition, he'd simply gone out and bellowed. The celebrity judges had reacted approximately as they might have to the discovery that Joseph Stalin had been reincarnated and brought before them. They'd told him he hadn't had a prayer of making it as a pop singer if he relied solely on the power of his voice, as he was seemingly inclined to. But the public apparently adored him, and voted him through to the next round.

In which it was someone's bright idea to get him to sing Elton John's 'Candle In The Wind', the original, not the one revised decades later for Princess Diana. He sat on a stool to do so. His forehead and upper lip glistened with sweat. The judges agreed he'd made no connection with the song, and had, moreover, seemed awfully nervous. When the cruellest of the judges said he'd rather listen to stereo components being removed from Styrofoam all day, Huw actually burst into embarrassed tears. It was wonderful, wonderful television. He first told the judges that he was sorry, and then told the camera the same thing. The public loved him for it, and voted him through to the next round.

In which he sang Tina Turner's 'River Deep, Mountain High' with great forcefulness, but without gesticulating in a way the judges liked. All four of them talked about how a powerful voice wasn't nearly enough. One hoping for a career in pop had to know how to move well on stage. The public continued to like him, though, and voted him through to the next round.

In which, singing a song popularised decades before by one of the celebrity judges, he seemed preoccupied with the little dance routine the *Lab*'s resident movement expert had devised for him, and sang in a voice that was a mere shadow of the one that had got him out of Cardiff. The judges didn't think the dance routine was really Huw, and wondered what had happened to his once-mighty voice. "But last week," Huw blurted, "you ignored my singing and told me I had to concentrate on moving better." For which outburst he was rewarded with a stern lecture on not thinking, at this stage in his career, assuming he'd go on to have one, that he knew more than the judges, with their combined however-many-it-was years in The Industry. But the public seemed to appreciate his sticking up for himself, and voted him through to the next round.

In which he looked like someone who only hours before had escaped religious extremists who'd held him hostage for two years in isolation. He had bags under his eyes. Apparently he'd resumed smoking, and was up to 60 a day. Smoking so much left him little time for eating, and he reportedly weighed half a stone less than at the begin-ning of the competition. He'd broken up with his girlfriend of four years over the telephone. He was subject now to outbursts of unpro-voked weeping.

He was said to worship Robbie Williams, and had been granted per-mission to sing one of his hero's anthems of self-loathing in this round. He stood perfectly still, his hands an inverted V above the microphone. At first, he sounded as though too heavily drugged for inflection. But then, around eight bars into the song, he seemed to awake. His voice regained its early power. There could be no accusing him this time of not connecting with the material, which he sang as though he'd written it. But then, halfway through, he abruptly stopped singing, and looked around as though he had no idea where or who he was. The director called for a close-up just in time for us to see the first two tears escape his eyes. And then the dam broke. He fell to his knees sobbing, pounding the stage, then banging his forehead against it until the little Scots compere and two of the other contestants could lift him to his feet. It was fantastic television.

"Well," mused the first judge, a former one hit wonder turned vocal coach with eccentric hairdo, "I don't think anyone can say Huw didn't make an emotional connection this time. But in Our Business, half a song just doesn't get the job done."

The second judge, the cruellest, the disapproving father figure, the one who was forever accusing contestants who had hit every note of singing out of tune (years heading a big record company's sales force had apparently rendered his sense of pitch more acute than other people's) pointed out that only the strong survive in This Business. The third pointed out that the beginning of Huw's performance had seemed pretty tentative. It was exactly that acumen, I thought, that was responsible for her having got her job as PA to the managing director of one of the big record companies – that acumen and her very large breasts and long legs.

How cynical I was becoming in my old age.

The last judge, the far less good-looking of the brother-sister-and-cousin act who'd had several deeply annoying worldwide hits 25 years before, reminded us that she had liked Huw's voice from the very beginning, but agreed that there'd been something dissatisfying about his performance this time.

Around the time I repatriated to the United Kingdom, jokes having to do with David Beckham's very low native intelligence had been very popular. It had occurred to me that in comparison to this judge, Beckham was Dr. Stephen Hawking.

There was an endless commercial break during which the public's votes for their favourite contestants were tabulated. The little Scot reminded us that the programme's policy was not to reveal the actual proportion of the popular vote the various contestants had received each week. But the show's producers had authorised him to reveal that Huw had just got more votes than any other contestant ever, and the show was in its second season.

He was coaxed back on stage looking like a deer in headlights. "Well, big guy," the little Scot asked him, "how does it feel to have got more votes from the public than any other contestant ever?"

Huw's forehead was glistening again. His lip was quivering. The veins in his neck protruded. He looked around, seeming to recognise nothing, not the judges, not the set, not the other contestants. "I want to go home," he said, very quietly. "I don't want to do this anymore. I want to go home."

The director gave us quick close-ups of the other contestants. There wasn't a dry eye among them. Then we saw the judges. The disapproving father figure was rolling his eyes with contempt.

And then, as Huw put his big brickie hands around the cheeky Scot's neck and lifted the little Scot off his feet, the director cut back to them. It was like the worst, most chaotic *Jerry Springer* show you'd ever seen, times ten. Everyone was shouting. Huw and the little Scot disappeared beneath a deluge of other contestants and cameramen and stagehands and several members of one of the contestants' support group. It might have been the most exciting television I'd ever seen.

21

Their Love Will Destroy Her

ONCE *Fab Lab* was over, I hoped Mrs. Cavanaugh would visit, and that she would wear the lace corset she'd worn the first night. It got later and later, though, and there was no trace of her. I didn't phone Nicola on her mobile for fear she'd let Tarquin answer it out of spite, and didn't phone her landline for fear of having to make small talk with the mountain of flesh. I went downstairs. There was no one in the kitchen. I got myself a cold can of Budweiser and a bag of grilled lamb-flavoured miniature poppadoms and took them into the lounge, where I found Mrs. Cavanaugh watching *Megastar* with Mr. Chumaraswamy. I'd forgotten it was on. "Come in, Mr. Herskovits," Mrs. Cavanaugh bade me, not very convincingly. "Cathy's going to be on later, and all the contestants have to sing one of Kate's songs this week."

"Well," I said, "only if I'm not interrupting anything."

Mr. Chumaraswamy giggled in embarrassment at the mere thought. Mrs. Cavanaugh kept her eyes on the screen. I sat down between them and offered each a poppadom in turn. The house rule was that snacks were for anyone who fancied them, so there was no real reason for Mr. Chumaraswamy to thank me, though I suppose it was more for the thought than for the actual poppadom. "Not for me, thanks," Mrs. Cavanaugh said without looking at me. "I only like the prawn-flavoured ones." If that was some sort of code, it was a code not known to me.

The blind boy who'd been imitating Mariah Carey when I came in, never letting us forget how virtuosic he was, finished 'Rubberband Girl', a strange choice on many levels, and an enormous fat girl was led before the judges, so nervous you could see her bounteous flab quivering. She sang 'Oh England My Lionheart', as I imagined they'd all wanted to, presupposing the judges' patriotism, hoping for their gentleness. She was very good.

The former assistant to Shania Twain's make-up artist yawned, drummed on the table before him with a pencil, leaned back, and put his head in his clasped hands. "Well, Beulah," he said, "it isn't your voice that's going to hold you back. Your voice is really quite good." Beulah quaked with fear. "It's that you're monstrously, repulsively overweight. When was the last time you saw someone your size on *Top Of The Pops*? Can you remember?"

She was a brave girl, Beulah. She wasn't going to give him the satisfaction of bursting into tears of shame. But the effort to control her voice made her speech very slow. "I was encouraged to audition," she said. "The producers. They said they specifically wanted larger people this time, people with disabil . . ."

"Larger?" the former assistant to Shania Twain's make-up artist interrupted. "I think you passed 'larger' around 10 stone ago, didn't you? I think titanic might be a better word for you." The long-lapsed disco dolly, beside him, buried her face in her arms on the table before her, but not before letting the camera see the playfully censorious look she gave the former assistant to Shania Twain's make-up artist, that irrepressible scamp. The record company publicist judge chimed in. "Beulah, let's say you were booked to perform at the London Palladium, just for instance. How do you suppose they'd get you on stage? They'd have to use a crane!"

"Why are they having a go?" Mrs. Cavanaugh marvelled, as though new to the show. "I thought she was a corker."

"I did too," agreed Mr. Chumaraswamy, "but these judges are experts, Aibheann."

Mr. Chumaraswamy got to call her by her first name?

There wasn't time for further debate, for here, looking frighteningly fragile, came Cathy, singing 'You're The One' from *The Red Shoes*, and singing it to break your heart, meaning every syllable (even the many solipsistically obscure ones), every note, ending it with an agonised shriek that made the memory of Kate's on the original recording seem mildly distressed. She was only mesmerising.

It was going to be a tough one for the judges, as the former disco dolly, who knew only what she reckoned she was meant to like, had to comment first. She studied the former assistant to Shania Twain's make-up artist's body language at length, trying to divine his own reaction, before she finally blurted, "I thought it was good." Seeing that the former assistant to Shania Twain's make-up artist didn't roll his eyes, she added, "smashing, in fact."

The record company publicist judge pronounced himself impressed. Finally it was the former assistant to Shania Twain's make-up artist's turn. "I'm afraid I have to disagree," he said in that way of his, and

Cathy looked even more than usual as though she might faint. "I didn't think she was very good at all." There was wholesale gasping among the studio audience, and among the three of us on Mrs. Cavanaugh's sofa as well.

You could, as I did, think of the former assistant to Shania Twain's make-up artist as a truly woeful human being, a sadist and a charlatan, but there could be no faulting his timing, as, just before the peasants came for him with pitchforks and torches, he added, "I thought she was bloody spectacular. An obvious superstar. If she doesn't starve herself to death, she'll be the next Sinéad O'Connor. You can take that to the bank."

I couldn't tell if Cathy's tears, as she collapsed to her knees, were tears of anguish or joy. It was much easier to determine that her mother's, had she cried any, would have been the former. "We're deep in the shite now," Mrs. Cavanaugh said, "well and truly fecked."

"But how can you say such a thing, Aibheann?" Mr. Chumaraswamy marvelled. "They loved her."

"And their love will destroy her. And me. And her brothers. Do you not read the newspapers, Seetharaman? Do you not watch the news? Some animals eat their young. The Brits eat their celebrities, devour 'em. Have you not noticed Kate living in virtual seclusion the past decade? Did you not see the mobs of gossip maggots out in the road the other night? Oh, sweet Jesus in the manger. We're fecked, I tell you."

"Think of the money, though," Mr. Chumaraswamy protested. "She'll be able to afford the care of top specialists."

"If, as that judge says, she doesn't starve herself to death before she even gets to the finals. Do you know what her managers told her? That she's too fat to be a pop star at the moment. Do you know the effect that has on a girl like my Cathy? They'll kill her, those two."

"Fecked, I tell you. Well and truly fecked."

"They won't kill her if I have anything to say about it," I heard myself declare. If I hadn't known the speaker, I might have believed it, as Mr. Chumaraswamy seemed to do. "Oh, bless your heart, Mr. Herskovits," he said. "That's so kind of you!" The intensely dubious look Mrs. Cavanaugh gave me was more what I deserved. But the look I returned said only that I'd be waiting for her upstairs.

She kept me waiting for the better (or, actually, worse) part of an hour, and wasn't wearing her corset for me, as I'd hoped. In fact, she hadn't changed since I'd left her in the lounge. She seemed pre-occupied.

I told her I'd despaired of her coming up at all. She said she hadn't wanted to be rude to Mr. Chumaraswamy, who might not have shown it, but had a broken heart of his own. His IT consultancy seemed to be on its last legs. People seemed to want to consult only glamorous Sri Lankan women about IT matters lately. He'd discovered that his wife had been involved for months in an arranged affair. "In his culture," Mrs. Cavanaugh said in response to the look on my face, "there's apparently such a thing as an arranged affair for people who get fed up with their arranged marriages. I hadn't known that either."

I could feel my inner four-year-old clawing his way to the top in spite of the fact that even at that age I was ravaging my own fingernails. I pointed out that she seemed to have a lot of sympathy for Mr. Chumaraswamy. I wondered if it had occurred to her that I might have needed some. I wondered also if she knew how disappointed I was to see her in the same clothes she'd worn to sympathise with Mr. Chumaraswamy.

It took her a long time to answer. "I'd have thought," she finally said, "that you'd be quite pleased to see me in anything I chose to wear, and quite possibly even grateful."

My inner four-year-old had hold of the steering wheel. Anyone with any sense would have pulled to the side of the road, set the handbrake, and run for cover. "Because I'm fat?" I demanded. "Because I'm fat I'm supposed to feel grateful for the attention of a 52-year-old Irish boarding house keeper? Well, I'm not that fat."

"You're not fat at all, in fact, except in your mind. You're actually very attractive, but not nearly so attractive to warrant an attitude like that. If I'm a 52-year-old Irish boarding house keeper, what are you, a 54-year-old Yank expat nutter with body dysmorphia and no visible means of support?"

"Get out!" the four-year-old screamed, or at least croaked.

"I won't," she said, "not until I've spoken my piece. And don't forget who owns the bloody house, you.

"Do you honestly imagine it's me who's getting the long end of the stick here? Well, think again. I know you used to be in adverts, and that you were fantastically pretty. As I said, you're still very attractive, and not just for a man your age – for any man, full stop. But who do I look like to you? Do you think the boys weren't after me from the age of 14? Do you know that when I was 23 both *Mayfair* and *Penthouse* wanted me to pose for them? And *Mayfair* wasn't rubbish then like it is now. It was upmarket in those days, a gentleman's magazine, rather than a lad's."

There'd been a time when Kate was thought to have posed for *Penthouse* – Kate who, in the early years of her fame, had always seemed deeply discomfited to be described as sexy. It had actually been another dark-haired Kate, Kate Simmons, in the photos, but that hadn't kept a succession of lowlifes from using the *Penthouse* photos on the covers of various Kate Bush bootleg albums over the years.

"And what about after my Roger topped himself?" Mrs. Cavanaugh continued. "Do you suppose I wasn't being asked out by two pop stars you've probably heard of, though who can be sure which stuff of the Brits' you got in the States, and a footballer, a striker in the Premiership, who girls were flinging themselves at? Do you suppose that even now I can go to bloody Sainsbury's without some fine bit of stuff asking for my phone number? Open your eyes, you! Open 'em up!"

"You're 52 years old," I reminded her, even though I knew I'd already lost, even though I'd much sooner she'd savagely ripped my clothes off and ravaged me. "In our culture, a 54-year-old man's got more sexual capital than a 52-year-old woman, or a 40-year-old woman, probably. How old is Robert de Niro? Al Pacino? Stallone? Richard Gere? Or Sean fucking Connery, for that matter? And they're all still huge stars! Tell me a woman their age who's paid a quarter what they're paid. Go ahead!"

"I will not have that language in my house!" she said, jumping to her feet, even her hair on fire. "And what was the last big hit Sylvester bloody Stallone was in?"

It occurred to me that *Rambo* had been 20 years ago. How time flies when you're having fun, and when you're not! "*Rocky*," I blurted, ridiculously.

"*Rocky!*" she howled. "Duncan was still a sprog when *Rocky* was out, you arrogant, egotistical gowl!"

"Not the original!" I said. "The latest sequel. *Rocky 27*. It set box-office records. They had to have mounted policemen to control the crowds."

She glared at me scorchingly, and glared at me scorchingly, and glared at me . . . and exploded, as I did too, in laughter. Oh, we screamed, but that was only at the beginning. In a wink, we were both laughing so hard that we were silent except for occasional shrieking intakes of air. Between us, we could have floated a toy boat with our tears.

Mr. Chumaraswamy tapped in annoyance on his ceiling, my floor. "Maybe," I managed, "you ought to get down there and see if he needs some more sympathy." Which struck both of us as the funniest thing ever said in English.

There was no staying on the bed. We were both on the floor, rolling across it, pounding it. Poor Mr. Chumaraswamy tapped again, louder. We both pounded back, which got us laughing even harder. I was quite sure I was going to split open. Mr. Chumaraswamy hadn't made a fortune in IT consultancy by fighting unwinnable battles. He tapped no more.

We finally regained control of ourselves. There was no trace of sexual tension between us now. It felt as though we'd turned onto a new motorway or something. I wasn't entirely sure I was pleased.

"I haven't just been sympathising with Mr. Chumaraswamy," she said. "I think it's time you knew that." I couldn't have spoken if I'd wanted to. "I've always quite fancied Asians," she sighed. "They're remarkable lovers, as you might hope that those born into the culture that gave us the *Kama Sutra* would be. But Seetharaman isn't like the others I've had."

I didn't want to know. I passionately didn't want to know. "How *could* you?" I finally managed.

"It's always been the one thing with you, Mr. Herskovits. But nobody's all dominant or all submissive, except maybe those shaven-headed macho types you see in the contact magazines, the ones who probably think if they admitted to fancying a bit of subjugation now and again, everyone would infer they're queer. Dominance and sub-mission are two movements of the same muscle. And dominant is all I ever get to be with you. That leaves a whole half of me unfulfilled."

I could feel my own nostrils flaring. "Let me get this straight. Mr. Chumaraswamy from downstairs, Mr. Chumaraswamy, who might be the only person in the world who regards *Lionheart* as Kate's best album, dominates you." I pulled a face to express my incredulity.

"It so happens that he does, and let's hope your puss doesn't freeze like that. Dominating isn't about being tall and fit, or wearing a black leather waistcoat with nothing underneath so your tattoos show. It's about understanding how exactly those things that are most repugnant to a woman in an everyday setting can be fantastically exciting in an erotic one."

I didn't know what she meant. "Being ordered about," she said. "Being treated like an accessory, a plaything. If somebody tried to do that in the real world, I'd bloody his nose for him. But in the bedroom, there's something exhilarating about having no control. As I'd hope you, of all people, would understand."

"You and Mr. Chumaraswamy. You and . . . Seetharaman."

"It's unbecoming for you to be so petulant, Mr. Herskovits. I don't remember either of us promising the other exclusivity."

I was doing the sums in my head. How could I take any pride at all in having as a lover the same woman Seetharaman bloody Chumaraswamy downstairs had? The longer I thought about it, the more mortified I became. And while I was becoming mortified, here came my inner four-year-old again, screaming for vengeance.

"We didn't," I agreed. "I've been seeing someone else too, you know."

"Bollocks," she said. "I'd have known. I'd have sensed it."

I shrugged. I felt pretty suave, shrugging.

"Anybody I'd know, assuming, just for the sake of conversation, that I believe you?"

"Oh, I don't think you'd know her," I said, examining my own ravaged fingernails, the very picture of nonchalance. "She's very much younger, you see. In her twenties." I was almost tempted to whistle.

"Sorry," she said. "That one won't work with me. Age is a chrono-logical accident. It makes no sense at all to envy someone because she's younger than you."

"Of course it does. Younger people are prettier, and have greater vitality."

"Younger people have less life experience, and only a very rudi-mentary sense, in most cases, of their own absurdity. Not being able to talk to them is a pretty high price to pay for their being a little more energetic and a lot less prone to complaining about the pain in their joints."

I felt ashamed of myself for never having realised how clever Mrs. Cavanaugh was, or how droll. But it wasn't the time to say that, and she didn't give me the chance anyway. "When you see some film star marry somebody 25 years younger, doesn't it make your flesh crawl? It does mine. You just know somebody like Demi Moore thinks a young actor's interest affirms her youthfulness, but all it really affirms is that he finds wealth and fame sexy. Well, *that's* front-page news, isn't it? *Wealth and fame make one attractive to the opposite sex shock horror!* And it isn't even film stars. They're just the ones you hear about. What about all the middle-aged entrepreneurs and captains of industry with their trophy wives? That's as sickening as somebody driving around sneering in a flash car, imagining that the car's seen as a manifestation of his viril-ity. As I said, it makes my flesh crawl."

"She isn't only younger," I said, retreating onto ground that felt pretty mushy underfoot. "She's fantastically pretty as well. She walks into rooms and conversations stop."

She shrugged. "A woman in her twenties being fantastically pretty doesn't impress me so much anymore. It's mostly to do with luck at that age, isn't it? Show me a woman who looks really good after 45 and I'll be impressed because she'll have looked after herself. And to a great extent, the kind of person she is will show in her face."

I thought, of course, of Kate. As much as I'd loved her music from first hearing, I'd never lusted after her. Going on the basis of the photographs of her taken at the Q Awards and at Rolf Harris's birthday party, she was actually much more attractive at 45 than at the time of her emergence, when her nipple on the front of buses caused the virtual collapse of the London public transport system. In her twenties, she'd seemed forever to be pulling faces, daring us to like her. At 45, she seemed serene, comfortable with herself. At 54, I found that extremely sexy.

"How's the lovemaking?" Mrs. Cavanaugh asked, bringing me back to the here-and-now. Her handsome face was remarkably blank, free of either hurt or insinuation.

I couldn't get traction on the mushy ground. The harder I tried to run, the deeper I sank. I thought of saying something about how soft the skin of a woman in her twenties was, or even how firm her breasts, but there are depths to which even I won't sink. "Really good," I finally said. "Fantastic, really."

"So in other words you haven't actually been lovers." I hadn't spoken of Nicola's soft skin, and Mrs. Cavanaugh wasn't smirking. Even completely unclothed while making love, I'd never felt so naked with her. I realised we were actually being quite gentle with one another. I thought of trying to scoff at her perception, but couldn't manage it. At the same time, though, I was able to keep myself from affirming her impression. I left it at a shrug.

She got up. We'd been gentle with one another, but there was no question that she was hurt. "Well," she said, "I suppose I'll see you at breakfast in the morning." She went to the door.

"Aibheann," I said. "Wait."

I'd have given anything at that moment not to have her looking at me as she was. She shook her finger at me. "No," she said. "Aibheann's not for you."

★ ★ ★

Kate had come, when interviewed about *Hounds Of Love*, to find promoting her work more and more onerous. In her studio, she worked in virtual isolation. There being no window, as in nearly all recording facilities, between studio and control room, she communicated with the faithful Del or whoever else was pressing the Record and Stop buttons as one whose children had emigrated to Tasmania would have, solely by voice. But then, after months of that virtual seclusion, when the album was finally complete, she was expected to traipse blithely into roomfuls of people, all of them gaping at her adoringly (or otherwise). A frightful shock to the system!

Little wonder she decided to stay well out of the public eye for a long while after *Hounds*, to spend quiet time at home thinking about what she wanted to say next. She dashed off a few songs, only to realise she wasn't happy with them. Thinking that her gift was depleted, that she hadn't anything interesting to say anymore, she did as Peter Gabriel had done years before after leaving the group with which he first came to fame – devoted herself to gardening.

Backed by Michael Kamen conducting the National Philharmonic Orchestra of London, she recorded a version of the title song for Terry Gilliam's film *Brazil*, singing it sufficiently gorgeously to crush the lilies in one's soul. Hearing her at such times, one wished fervently that she'd bring the same understated dignity to her own stuff.

Across the Atlantic, in Cambridge, Massachusetts, Harvard senior Alek Kershishian, years away from the ignominy of directing *Madonna: Truth Or Dare*, was spending $2,000 of his own money to produce a rock opera inspired by and entitled *Wuthering Heights*. As re-imagined by Kershishian for his senior thesis, Cathy and Heathcliff leave the moors for the big city and become . . . Madonna and Billy Idol. What many people who attended the show, staged at the American Repertory Theater, liked best about it was hearing Kate's music at a very high volume.

EMI realised it might be waiting quite a long time for her next album, and put together a compilation, *The Whole Story*, which it convinced the man on the Clapham omnibus he needed via the most expensive TV advertising campaign in EMI history to that point. Encouraged by the project's success, they hurriedly compiled Kate's video performances as well. Though she was thought initially to have been afraid that the whole thing smacked of the same sort of exploitation, she wrote a new song about a dastardly scientific misuse of music, 'Experiment IV', and shot an elaborate B-movie film to promote it in an old military hospital designed by Florence Nightingale. She gamely wore a life-size cast made for her by Image Animation to portray The Thing. There was some disgruntlement among Katefans about how little time she appeared on screen as herself.

When she ventured conspicuously out into the world, it was almost invariably on behalf of Good Causes. She sang 'Running Up That Hill' and 'Let It Be' with David Gilmour at Amnesty International's *The Secret Policeman's Third Ball*. After shooting the video (shown first with Nora Ephron's *Heartburn*) for her song 'Experiment IV', she and her family attended a party in her honour hosted by the *Homeground* fanzine, imagining she'd be able to have a nice meal before doing a bit of mingling. She was instead swamped by those who adored her. It gave a girl second thoughts about going out.

22

The Anorexic Eva Cassidy

I was pretty sure it was Nicola, and not Mrs. Cavanaugh, I needed as my girlfriend (and how very silly that word sounded applied to a 52-year-old grandmother), but absolutely positive that I wouldn't be able to bear Mrs. Cavanaugh thinking ill of me. What I clearly had to do was make good on my promise to protect Cathy from her managers Harold and Nepenthe.

Of course, it wasn't my way to try to do something important on my own, and I wracked my brain trying to think of someone to ask for help. Once every few months, I promise myself to try to make a friend, studies having shown that the isolated almost invariably die younger and in greater pain than those with social networks. But I never quite manage it. Even at this age, I am my mother's son. My mother, ever dreading rejection, got into the habit of rejecting people before they could reject her, as she was always sure they would do, given time. She discredited every act of kindness or generosity as being fundamentally about its perpetrator's need to see himself as a terrific guy. No one wasn't too deeply flawed for my mother to risk their hurting her.

Throughout my childhood, she could always be counted on to point out that Kid A was probably phoning to ask if I could play because Kid B, whom he greatly preferred, was busy. Nobody could ever genuinely like me for myself, any more than anyone had ever genuinely liked her. My dad, of course, adored her, but where was the pleasure in being adored by someone so thoroughly contemptible?

Of course, given that, from the age of around 11, I tried to attach myself to sportier, better-looking, more confident Boys Who Could in hope that I'd look better by association, it was only fitting that I should doubt that my affection was reciprocated.

On top of the cynicism my mother had taught me, I also had my famous low boredom threshold to contend with. It's occurred to me that if I were put in a room with Clement Freud, Oscar Wilde and John

Lennon, I'd probably be trying to think of an excuse to leave in 35 minutes. I scrupulously show voracious interest in others and then hate them for luxuriating in it. If they do manage to get in a word reciprocating my interest, I find a way to feel patronised. I am, and always have been, hard, hard work.

It eventually occurred to me that the only person I could call was Cyril, but the thought of his being my only friend paralysed me with depression until it was nearly too late to call.

It was actually Nicola who answered. She sounded pleased. The four-year-old in me wanted to ask, in a voice dripping sarcasm, why she wasn't out with Tarquin. But it was past my four-year-old's bedtime. I just very casually asked if she was all right, and, on hearing that she was, asked to speak to Cyril. She sounded a little disappointed, which I, of course, adored. I told her I'd try to phone in the next few days if I had time. I do some of my best work when knackered.

Cyril greeted me with unnerving enthusiasm. "Great to hear back from you, mate!" I wondered if he reciprocally regarded me as *his* only friend. I found the notion nauseous.

I got on-line after I'd spoken to him. Still smarting from what that unspeakable cow Hermione had said at the first Overeaters meeting I attended, I went to one of the countless dozens of sites that offered Kate's complete lyrics, and reread the lot. They were indeed mostly hopelessly abstruse, just as Hermione had suggested, but it was no more fair to consider her lyrics apart from her music than it would have been to consider Van Gogh's brush technique apart from his use of colour. It made me want to send Kate a bouquet of white roses with a note attached reading, "*Nil carborundum illigitium,*" Latin having been one of Cathy Bush's best subjects at St. Joseph's Convent Grammar School. So I did.

Don't let the bastards grind you down.

Megastar-on-tv.co.uk had the latest news about the competition, such as that "our" Cathy having been promoted to the next round. There was a page on which visitors to the website could write comments. One visitor, whose sex I wasn't able to ascertain from his or her screen name, had written, "I haven't been able to stop crying long enough to type until just a minute ago. My mum used to sing me the song Cathy did tonight when I was tiny. I didn't think anyone could ever sing it more beautifully. But Cathy did. That wasn't a musical performance. That was a gift. Thank you, Cathy."

The comments about the other young singers consisted almost entirely of comparisons of their relative fitness. It was heartening to see enormous fat boys lusted after, but I felt sure that as soon as they stopped appearing on the competition each week and went back to their lives, they could expect only vicious ridicule.

★ ★ ★

Kate sang to benefit the families of the victims of the Zeebrugge ferry disaster and on behalf of the rainforests. She endorsed a campaign launched by the Vegetarian Society to expose the barbarity of the meat trade. She turned 30 as a shopgirl at Blazer's boutique as part of an AIDS benefit. She managed a couple of songs for films – the propulsive, not very notable 'Be Kind To My Mistakes' for Nic Roeg's *Castaway* and the exquisite, heartbreaking 'This Woman's Work' for *She's Having A Baby*, by the antiRoeg, John Hughes. Pearls before swine! Hearing the song, there were those who thought maybe she'd confused Hughes with Andrei Tarkovsky, an in-joke certain to be enjoyed only by cineastes, if by them.

Roeg, beloved by cineastes everywhere for a while there, was rumoured to have invited her to appear in *Castaway* as well. Whether her declination was based on the notorious Oliver Reed playing the male lead isn't universally known, but the role went to Amanda Donohoe instead. She recorded duets with Peter Gabriel and Midge Ure, who years later would admit that the attraction wasn't purely musical. Praising her sublimely touching performance on his song 'Don't Give Up', Peter Gabriel gently observed that she sang very differently to the way she sang on her own stuff.

Ever interested in new sounds, Kate struck up friendships with the Irish uillean piper Davy Spillane and the violinist Nigel Kennedy, and conspired to get Trio Bulgarka, proponents of traditional Bulgarian folk music, to sing on her next album. The Kate Bush Club petulantly suspended publication of its newsletter in the face of having no clue when the album might be finished. And weren't those the days, when a four-year wait between albums defied credulity?

★ ★ ★

Cyril was a few minutes late turning up the next morning. The mountain of flesh had been giving him a savage bollocking, and he hadn't been able to bear to miss any of it. He said Nicola seemed a little discombobulated by the idea of me and Cyril seeing one another socially, but it was Tarquin I wanted to find out about as we walked to the train station.

Cyril thought he was a bender. I scoffed at the idea, but Cyril said I should trust him. "You don't know British pub culture like I do, mate.

210

My nephew, my sister Louise's boy, is cut from the same cloth. It used to be, a long time ago, decades, most of them were camp, at least in this country. They had longer fingernails than ordinary blokes, and coloured their hair with henna, and called themselves Quentin and Marcel. They wore boots with Cuban heels before The Beatles had got out of Liverpool. Then they were exactly the opposite of that, fantastically masculine, with really short hair and moustaches, and great huge muscles. Well, if I were a smarter man, I'd have been able to predict what was coming and make a fortune. What was coming – and what's come – is that they're certainly not camp anymore, but they're not the opposite of camp either.

"They're perfectly ordinary. They look just like everybody else. They go down the pub on Saturday afternoon to watch footie with each other. They're ferociously proud of the England rugby World Cup victory, and own DVDs of it. They wear the same gear as anyone else. They've got wives and kids and Vauxhalls and mortgages."

I couldn't pretend I was getting it. "Their having wives and kids would seem to suggest they're not gay at all," I said. "How does that make sense?"

"Since when has fashion ever made sense? Those gigantic droopy trousers the young fellows wear, the ones they could hide whole families of asylum seekers in? How do those make any sense? How about flares? Do you remember flares, back in the flower power days? Did they make sense? And then punk came along, and wearing flares was suddenly like painting *I'm gormless* on your forehead with nail polish.

"Or food. Do you know how bland our diet used to be in this country? There was a time when it was considered quite exotic to eat bloody spaghetti bolognese! If you'd said you fancied Siamese food, people would have thought you were mad. And now what do three-quarters of the pubs in London serve? It's easier to get a bowl of *pad thai* than a bloody sausage roll."

We arrived in the Kings Road. I got out my A-to-Z and we found the address, in a road on which were parked only cars new enough to still gleam. "They're doing all right for themselves, aren't they?" Cyril marvelled. "Blimey."

We were buzzed in. A small rotund girl who looked ready to audition to play Dahlia at her first Overeaters Anonymous meeting, with dyed black hair and rings through both of her nostrils, greeted us at the top of the stairs, if greeted is the right word, cigarette in hand, broad sneer on face. "Yes?" she demanded, as though we hadn't already

211

identified ourselves over the intercom before she buzzed us in. We told her again who we were. "And you're here for . . ."

"A confrontation with Harold and Nepenthe."

Her face fell apart. "But that isn't what you said downstairs!"

"If we'd told you the truth downstairs, you probably wouldn't have buzzed us in," Cyril said.

Oh, she was in a woeful state, desperate to hold back her tears, consumed by panic. "But that isn't fair!" she said, sounding no older than nine. "You didn't tell me the truth."

Cyril, not the most compassionate man in London, only shrugged.

"I could lose my job for this."

Cyril shrugged again and took a step towards the hall. "Could do, I suppose. Where exactly are they?"

"Please," the girl pleaded, throwing herself in his path, "please don't! They'll sack me for sure! I could never get another job as wicked as this." She turned back towards me. The tears came – oh, did they! "I've only been here today and yesterday. I don't know all the tricks yet. Please!"

Well, she had me on her side at least, but then the point became moot as Harold poked his head out of his office and demanded, "What's all that row?" It took him a second to remember who I was, and to realise he was highly unlikely to enjoy our visit, and to jump back in his office and loudly lock the door behind him.

Nepenthe popped out of her office, just across the hall from Harold's, looking quite capable of biting someone's ears off, and demanded, "Well, what do you want?" What I wanted at the moment of her asking was to run back to the tube station and board the first train that would take us away. But I couldn't very well say that. "A brief confrontation, if you can spare a moment," I said, aghast at my wimpiness. I hoped Cyril might add something threatening, but if his grin had been any broader, his face would have split open, with dire consequences for the pristine-looking carpeting. "She's a corker, isn't she?" he asked me out of the side of his mouth. Stupid me! It hadn't occurred to me that Nepenthe's imperiousness might neutralise Cyril.

Nepenthe sighed for the last row in the theatre and gestured for us to come to her. Cyril fairly skipped. "Get up off your knees, Desdemona," she called to the little Gothette. "Have a little bloody dignity, will you?"

Her office was breathtaking, all glossy deep reds and chrome, with a remarkable view out the window of London, as seen from the top of the BT Tower. I gathered, since we were a couple of hundred yards off the Kings Road, and on the second floor, that some digital hocus-pocus was involved. One wall was full of gold and platinum discs, another of very arty, beautifully framed photographs of a naked Cathy looking, in her emaciation, rather like a praying mantis. I averted my eyes in embarrassment. "Blimey," observed Cyril as he lowered himself into one of the red leather chairs facing her desk, and Nepenthe's lip curled in satisfied disdain.

"You've obviously been at this longer than Mr. Herskovits here told me," Cyril said. "Whose gold discs?"

"They're decorative," she explained impatiently. "Intended solely to mislead visitors. The music business is all about creating illusions. Tell me what you want." She turned towards the view, which had morphed into that from the top of the Bank of America building in San Francisco. Many years before, I'd dined in the restaurant up there. The food had been crap, of course, but what a view!

"We're concerned about Cathy," Cyril said. "She looked even skinnier on TV last night than last week. We're here to see that she eats."

"And you expected she'd be here? How colossally naive of you. We have her in seclusion, accessible only to certain key journalists and tastemakers. As of this morning, she's refusing food until they replace the former assistant to Shania Twain's make-up artist with a less sadistic judge. It's the pop music story of the century so far. The journos are absolutely mad for it. We're on the front page of tomorrow's *Telegraph*."

"I imagine you're aware of the grave danger not eating poses for someone as frail as Cathy," I said, feeling that we'd already had this conversation.

"Fully aware," she agreed with infuriating blitheness.

"She isn't going to be worth much to you dead, I reckon," Cyril attempted.

"Oh, but you're mistaken, dear fellow. The first thing we did was put her into the studio, and get two albums in the can. If her debut album is posthumous, it'll almost certainly sell up to three times as many as it would if she were still alive. We're positioning her as a sort of anorexic Eva Cassidy."

"But you'll be losing a fortune not getting her in front of live concert audiences," Cyril attempted.

"We'll have to agree to disagree on that one," Nepenthe yawned, smugness oozing from every pore. "Pop music audiences today don't care if performers are actually singing. Nearly everyone mimes to pre-recorded vocal tracks. We can put a laser simulation of Cathy out on tour. In fact, she'll be able to play multiple venues at once, even multiple countries. The technology's expensive, but gets less so every day."

I wanted to raise a moral objection, but was pretty sure she'd make me feel hopelessly uncool for it. But then the question became moot as Harold came in, his nose buried in the latest edition of *Men's Health*, his mouth oblivious to Nepenthe's having company. "So where for lunch? I understand the new noodle place in Conduit Street is adorable."

By the time he looked up from the abs he was admiring, Cyril had slipped out of his chair and blocked the exit.

"Bugger," Harold remarked, not happily.

"We'll make this as simple for you as we can," Cyril said, decisive now that it appeared he might get to hurt someone. "You make sure my mate's landlady's daughter gets properly fed, or Count Dracula here loses a few teeth, and maybe gets a shoulder or two dislocated into the bargain. Any questions?"

Harold dived whimpering under Nepenthe's desk, but Nepenthe herself, rolling her eyes, then shaking her head, could hardly have been less perturbed. "I've got a couple actually. The first one is: How can anybody be so stupid?"

"No," Harold gurgled from the south. "Don't bloody antagonise them!" The view from Nepenthe's window was now from the top of the Eiffel Tower. I have always marvelled at Paris's reputation as a beautiful city, possibly because I've only ever stayed in the more squalid *arrondisements*, but from that great height it really was quite gorgeous.

"Do you honestly imagine we'd jeopardise Cathy's health?" Nepenthe yawned. "It so happens we've got her up to 900 calories a day, and that she's under the care of a very prominent physician. My dad's his barrister. He put us in touch. How can you imagine that we'd take chances with her well-being? She's going to make us rich. She's going to replace some of these platinum discs with real ones."

I wished I were nearly anywhere else. I was where I was, though, and knew it was crap of me not to help out. "But you were just telling us how Cathy would be worth more to you dead than alive!"

She rolled her eyes again. We were to know that we really were exhausting her patience. "Irony," she said. "Irony. Is there something in your drinking water or something that makes you Yanks so crap at it? She won't be worth more to us dead until she's got a substantial back catalogue. Use your head, will you?"

Cyril, sighing, shaking his head, sat back down, and began to run his hand back through his hair, only to remember too late that he hadn't hair enough left for such an undertaking. He patted frantically at his combover, looking for a reflective surface, failing to find one.

I knew I'd wind up feeling foolish for having done so, but I asked why Cathy looked so emaciated on TV. Again Nepenthe shook her head, this time while smirking patronisingly. "It's done the same way the views from my office window are done. Digitally. The software was originally developed to make overweight presenters look slimmer. You didn't read about it last summer? The *Mail* did a major front-page exposé. *Megastar* uses it on both kinds of eating disorders. It makes someone like Cathy look more emaciated, but they can also use it to make the fatties look fatter, or the fatties look slender, or the anorexics Rubenesque.

"Cathy does all her interviews via video conferencing. We can make her look as gaunt as we like for different publications. It's going to revolutionise the way celebrities and the press interact in this country."

"So are we over our little hissy fit yet?" Harold ventured accusatorily from beneath her.

"Only one way to find out, isn't there, mate?" snarled Cyril, whom humiliation had made hostile.

"How can we be sure you're not just piling irony on irony?" I asked. "We won't leave until we've seen Cathy face to face."

"She isn't here, though, darling. She's at an undisclosed private residence in Bedfordshire. And the only additional joke I made was that the software was developed by the BBC to make its presenters look slimmer. Did you not get that one? I mean, can you, just off the top of your head, think of a single BBC presenter who isn't borderline tubby? Oh, you Yanks."

It isn't like me to stand up for myself, but I'd had more than I could stand, and Nepenthe was a woman. "Do you suppose you could stop patronising us sometime soon?" I asked, beaming.

"Wow," she said. "Sarcasm. Well played. Not quite as good as irony, but within hailing distance. And why are you the only one who gets to patronise?"

I admitted I had no idea what she was talking about.

"I could see it in your eyes from the first moment we met. You never imagined we could have anything on the ball. You reckoned we were a couple of trust fund brats, and therefore incompetent. Well, that makes no more sense than imagining that all blondes with big tits are dim. It so happens that a lot of blondes with big tits are very clever indeed. It further so happens that a lot of insufferable trust fund brats

215

have really good ideas, bold new ideas, about artiste management. And I happen to be one of them."

"And I'm another," said Harold petulantly from beneath the desk.

As Cyril and I walked back to the train, I realised it might actually have been kindness that inspired her to cite stupid blondes with big tits as a misleading sterotype, when it could just as easily have been jolly fat people, or self-loathing ones. I hoped for the sake of poor Cathy, who Nepenthe promised would phone her mum, that it was indeed kindness.

★ ★ ★

I took myself for a walk along the river. The tide was out, but it was easy to see how high it had come. The line was clearly demarcated by thousands of plastic beverage bottles and a few plastic carrier bags that had washed up on shore.

I know that a big part of the problem is that there are no water coolers in my new country. If someone goes into a train station, for instance, hoping to quench his thirst at no charge, he's out of luck, unless he's happy to try to get his face under a tap in the gents. If you want something to drink, you need to buy it, and it comes in either a plastic bottle or an aluminum can, although here they say aluminium.

A solution occurred to me. Issue everyone in the country with two empty plastic beverage bottles, refillable wherever beverages are sold. Would there be some hygiene issues? Of course there would. But would any sane Briton prefer to live in a world whose rivers, parks and gutters (and ever scarcer landfills!) are full of discarded plastic bottles, or in one where it might occasionally be necessary to walk across the road to refill on Lucozade because the geezer at the Costcutter, let's say, looks the sort who might have drunk direct from the tap?

I believe further that anyone observed simply tossing an empty plastic beverage bottle into a body of water or hedge should have the offending bottle stuck up his bum. Such a sanction would do much to make London more attractive to deep-pocketed prospective tourists.

There've been moments when I've aspired to hardness as much so I could confront litterers as stand up for myself. I feel strangely moral and other-directed at those moments, and nearly proud of myself. When I see someone casually tossing the wrapper from his KitKat bar on the pavement as he ambles along Charing Cross Road, for instance, I would like to be hard enough to be able to pick it up, catch up with him, and hand it to him. "I believe you lost this." If he gave me any lip – if he told me, as the one guy I've actually confronted this way did,

those many, many years ago, to fuck off and mind my own business –
I'd bloody his nose for him. I would love to be hard enough to ask
anyone I saw flicking a cigarette butt away, "When did the world get
appointed your ashtray, pal?"

That I am not now, nor have I ever been, hard, hurts sometimes in
more ways than I have the energy to count.

23

The Vengeful Middle-Aged

BESIDES elevated levels of testosterone, God gave some Boys Who Could remarkable quickness and agility and strength. Commonly, boys who got those also got unusually small brains, but it hardly mattered. Other boys wanted to be their friends, and girls, seemingly reacting on a strictly biological level, unconsciously inferring that the sperm of a quick, agile, strong, aggressive boy would produce offspring more likely to survive than that of a boy who couldn't climb the pole, wanted to have their babies.

When I switched high schools at age 16, leaving that at which, if I had any reputation at all, it was as one who was good with words and at drawing, but not nearly good enough to make up for being a woeful little dickhead, and getting a fresh start at another, where it took me several weeks to become known as a woeful little dickhead, I became the classmate of a boy called Ricky Abbott, who was aggressive, quick, agile, and strong, and also precociously bright. It was said that he intended to apply for admission to the Air Force Academy, and that they'd probably take him, as maths and physics were two of his best subjects. Naturally, I loathed him.

But then I got to know him a little bit, and the chair was kicked out from under me. He wasn't only a star of the football team, a prolific interceptor, as a defensive back, of opposing school's passes, and a frequent Scholar of the Month, but also avidly congenial, without a trace of arrogance, as cordial to people like me as he was to his buddies on The Team. Which made it very much more difficult, but certainly not impossible, for me to hate him. Of course I hated myself more for being so grateful for his cordiality.

As I said, he was an exception, the other really sporty boys being arrogant numbskulls who took their own fabulousness as a given.

Most major athletic stars' lives seemed to follow a similar trajectory. Early on, usually before age 10, they would win the admiration of their classmates, and, slightly later, the lust of the girls. By age 20, in many cases, they'd have signed professional contracts that, unless they entrusted the money to charlatans, would ensure their never having to get up barbarically early to catch a train on which they'd have to stand with someone's unwashed hair in their noses all the way to some god-forsaken trading estate in the ugliest building in Willesden, where they'd spend eight hours in an airless office rotting of boredom and frustration surrounded by people they'd have much preferred not to be around. Instead, wide-eyedly worshipful boys would follow them wherever they went, swooning rapturously if accorded a syllable of greeting. Journalists would beg to hear them mumble platitudes. Models and pop singers would eagerly open their gorgeous long legs for them.

Then they'd write their autobiographies. Actually, they'd spend a few hours mumbling platitudes and yawning inanities at some poor moonlighting journalist, who'd then spend months making them seem rudimentarily articulate. There'd be great huge stacks of the book at W.H. Smith and Waterstone's, which would have two drastically dis-counted copies of the poor moonlighting journalist's novel. The tab-loids would pay huge amounts of money for the right to an exclusive preview, which would highlight the book's sole vaguely interesting revelation. *When I was first introduced to the wife of So-and-So, my manager at Such-and-Such, she asked if I fancied a rim job.*

While no one but their spouses cared if those trying to cure breast cancer or muscular sclerosis lived or died, athletes' every last sprain would be analysed and agonised about by tens of thousands. Then, after years of such worshipful treatment, they'd announce their immi-nent retirements, and people who would earn a fraction over the course of their working lives what these athletes earned in a season would shower them with gifts. The stars would claim they wanted to spend more time with their families, but after two weeks at home, they'd realise that spending time with their families might involve aspects of parenting other than being a distant, godlike masculine ideal, whereupon they'd devote themselves to playing golf in four-somes with three guys content to talk about nothing but the newly retired stars' brilliant exploits.

If they were able to speak four-word sentences semi-intelligibly, they'd be offered jobs encouraging those still active to mumble the same platitudes on television that they themselves had once mumbled. *Well, we're just going to go out there and give it 120 per cent and hopefully put more balls into the back of the net than the other fellows.* And everywhere

219

they turned up for the rest of their lives, people would defer to them, praise them, rush them to good tables in restaurants in which others, with reservations, had been cooling their heels for an hour.

And all because God had enabled them to perform some utterly irrelevant physical task involving a ball.

I've admitted already that as a high school boy, I used to hope that the arrogant sporty boys to whom I tried to attach myself performed dismally, or even hurt themselves. As an adult, I came to realise that professional athletes are on the whole far more likely to be racist, homophobic, or, at best, politically reactionary – nostalgic for a time when queers didn't have parades and the dark-skinned and women knew their places – and began to watch games solely in hope of seeing someone I detested being carried off on a stretcher, writhing in pain, sure that he was leaving his career back on the pitch.

It happened too infrequently for my taste, and in time I ceased to watch anything other than England away games, during which one could always hope that the host country's fans, furious about Blair's complicity with Bush, bored with Beckham to the point of belligerence, would swarm onto the field and spirit one of Our Lads away, later to sell him into white slavery. Instead, as you know already, I took to watching programmes on which smooth-faced young singers were ritually savaged by vengeful middle-aged no-talents.

In any event, when I got back from failing to intimidate Harold and Nepenthe with Cyril, the two worlds converged. Sir Ivor Praiseworthy, the legendary Charlton Athletic striker of the early Eighties, had actually produced a commercial – an infomercial, actually – in which he appealed to viewers not to vote his youngest son, Claude, out of the *Megastar* competition. He hadn't hired a couple of chimps with a camcorder and editing software for the job, but had spent some major money. The spot opened with a montage of what I assumed (I was in California when he was scoring them) were Ivor's most illustrious goals, with the exultant roar of the crowd getting a little louder with each one. Then the frame froze and dissolved to the contemporary Ivor, shaven-headed now, maybe a pound or two heavier, but still fit and handsome, looking wistfully out of a window, sitting by a fireplace, sipping tea, looking soulful. "Ever since my youngest son, Claude, was born in 1984," he confides as the camera slowly pulled in on him, unashamed of his cragginess, "I knew there was something a bit . . . off about him."

We dissolve to some home video footage of a younger Ivor kicking a football around in their enormous back garden with his three young sons and daughter, here aged around four to 11, while his breathtaking former model wife looks on worshipfully. Two of the boys seem to have got their dad's DNA. They elbow one another mercilessly as they try to get to the ball first. But poor Claude, a little more rotund, seems more interested in protecting the garden's flowers. As the frame freezes on him, Sir Ivor's voice-over confirms our impression. "While Terence and Hugo loved nothing more than kicking the ball around with me on a warm afternoon, Claude always seemed more interested in gardening and cooking. While the other boys loved the same reggae and ska and dance hall I'd grown up on, Claude seemed drawn from the age of maybe six to the music of Judy Garland, Cher, and Madonna."

Now we saw a montage of poor little Claude, dressed in his model mum's clothing, entertaining at family get-togethers. Ivor has his face in his hands. Poor Claude's two normal older brothers are at first slack-jawed with amazement, and then mortified. Only Mum and Sis seem to enjoy his performance. Over the course of the montage, poor Claude ages from around nine to maybe 16, by which point he is very rotund indeed. We see him performing in an old folks' home, a convalescent hospital. The women – at least those aware of their surroundings – adore him. The men – at least the two aware of their surroundings – are aghast. The frame freezes and then dissolves back into Sir Ivor at his fireplace, a small tear in the corner of the eye that restored England's national pride or something by detecting a few vulnerable inches of the goal in the big game against Whoever-It-Was in Whenever-It-Was.

"I've had to admit to myself, just as his mum, my first wife, and my new partner Ivanka" [here a young blonde right off the cover of *Loaded* or *Maxim* struts protuberantly into the frame, and to Sir Ivor's side, at which she kneels worshipfully] "have all had to admit to themselves that Claude's highly unlikely to follow in my famous footsteps. He's never taken the slightest interest in anything to do with school either, though, which means his only hope is in pop music."

Here Ivanka, seemingly able to restrain herself no longer, does what one suspects she's in the habit of doing when there are cameras pointed at her. She pouts, lasciviously.

Now the three of them – Sir Ivor, Ivanka and poor Claude – are seen walking through one of Sir Ivor's forests together, to the unlikely but emotionally evocative accompaniment of a wistful melody played on Irish pipes rather like those Davy Spillane played on Kate's 'The Sensual World', with lots of reverb. Sir Ivor, in voice-over, tells us, "A few months ago, the experts said a boy like Claude couldn't reasonably look forward to much of a career in pop music either. Far too tubby, they said."

Now Sir Ivor and Ivanka and poor Claude's two brothers and sister are walking barefoot (except for Ivanka, of course, who's managing it in four-inch heels) on a beach in Cornwall, and the pipes have been joined by other traditional Celtic instruments, albeit not by the Trio Bulgarka. "But then *Megastar* came along, and gave hope to Claude and others like him, others who either can't control their appetites, or can't muster one.

"As you know if you've seen the programme, the singer who gets the fewest votes of support from the public after their performance each week is sent home. I couldn't bear for that to happen to my Claude. Singing's the only thing he can do."

Here the camera pulled in so close on Sir Ivor that you could make out the irises in his eyes, which had seemed black from a greater distance. "If I gave you or anyone you know pleasure during my career, either scoring more goals for Charlton Athletic than any other player, save one, or while scoring nine times for England in international competition, I'm asking you to please, *please* pick up the phone and vote for Claude in next week's competition."

A hero of Sir Ivor Praiseworthy's stature, one who'd never known what it was like to be picked anything other than first for any team he ever deigned to play for, was appealing with glistening eyes (and, it wasn't unreasonable to infer, on bended knee), for Joe and Jo Bloggs' help? At that moment, I knew Claude would be in the final. As if Joe Bloggs, whose life Sir Ivor had made worth living with his sterling play and revealing autobiography, were about to refuse him anything!

I had to hand it to Sir Ivor. A lot of former star athletes would have tried to have a son like poor Claude kidnapped and sold into white slavery, even though Sir Ivor himself was black, the son of immigrants from Bermuda.

★   ★   ★

As the Eighties began to run out, one began to see bootleg compilations of the demos Kate, then Cathy, had recorded ages before on the family tape recorder before EMI signed her. Thought to have been taken to America by a former EMI employee turned Arizona radio personality, they made clear why nobody had signed her. Once you got past the prettiness of her voice, there wasn't a great deal to be said for a lot of the early songs

At last, with mere weeks left of the Eighties, her sixth album, *The*

Sensual World, was released. Many found it dark, but Kate herself claimed to think of it as her happiest album, to regard the very tracks other people found scary as real knee-slappers. One wondered if maybe she needed to get over to Harrod's and among ordinary people more often.

The undervalued Chris Roberts asserted that "this album marries the physical honesty and self-pride of Marvin Gaye to the querying passionate intelligence of, say, Elizabeth Smart, and gives birth to a rare mystical and aesthetic precision. Kate Bush represents both philosopher and love object. Gertrude Stein and, oh, Ava Gardner. It is, need I tell you, a triumphant combination."

David Quantick marvelled, "The music is – at one go! – seamless and incongruously bizarre. We get the latest studio technology, natch, and we get uillean pipes. We get Bush playing the most Lionel Ritchie-type piano and we get her singing like she was a rare visitor to any known Earth language." A million miles away, in southern California, Steve Hochman told his readers, "Bush's relative seclusion over the years has coincided with an expanding musical vision, much as a cloistered child might explore exotic worlds armed only with some musty tomes and an overactive imagination. . . . the throaty quavering Eastern European voices [of Trio Bulgarka] release Bush from her Victorian inhibitions into a state of expressionist frenzy . . . The first pressings of the album are on vinyl that looks like marble, for crissakes, but this is her first outing without at least one moment to make you cringe at its feyness."

David Cavanagh pronounced her "still the most inspired nonconformist in commercial music." Tom Hibbert wrote, "Kate Bush exudes Englishness . . . Croquet and gingham and scones on the dainty patio. She is our dottiest dame since Margaret Rutherford. She still sings like the slightly crazy girl on the lacrosse team alarming the opposing Vicarage XII." The *Irish Post* exulted, "*The Sensual World* remains the most successful translation of literature into pop, the culmination of a process begun a decade earlier with 'Wuthering Heights'."

I loved it from the opening bars of the title track, which featured her sexiest vocal ever. 'Reaching Out', in which exultation alternated with reflection, demonstrated that she'd figured out how to be very dynamic without resorting to the histrionics that had made much of her early work unlistenable. When she was exultant, she sounded, with her Celtic accompanists, with her huge drum sound, like Enya times ten. Where on early albums, she'd very often come across as barking mad, she came across now, on 'Deeper Understanding', as charmingly neurotic. A major breakthrough! And when she was melancholic or tender, as on 'This Woman's Work', she absolutely shattered your heart.

★   ★   ★

It turned out that I didn't have to hand Sir Ivor Praiseworthy anything at all, as the next day was slow for news or something. With no suicide bombings in the Middle East to report, no fatal attacks on American liberators or British peacekeepers in Baghdad, and no new developments in Ben Affleck's and Jennifer Lopez's storybook romance, the media were able to exorcise their fascination with Sir Ivor's commercial without guilt. The *Guardian, Times, Observer,* and *Daily Telegraph*'s articles unanimously applauded it as the latest confirmation of the great man's greatness. The *Guardian* spoke with particular eloquence of how it hoped that other, lesser men ashamed of sons who were crap at sport, or fat, or obviously homosexual, would follow Sir Ivor's example, and learn somehow to love the boys.

The fast-moving *Daily Mail* had managed to conduct a poll, in which they'd determined that 83 per cent of the British public thought even more highly of Sir Ivor as a result of his commercial, while 12 per cent thought less of him, and five per cent reported no substantial change in their feelings. The *Mirror* had on its front page an article about the boy with whom Claude had allegedly been in love during his last year in school. He speculated that if there were such a thing as gay marriage, and if he hadn't met someone he fancied rather more than Claude, whom he'd grown to find "too tubby", he might have become Sir Ivor's son-in-law. It almost made one wish for Bennifer news.

The afternoon chat shows were full of child psychologists talking about what a wonderful thing Sir Ivor had done, and effeminate, doughy-looking boys relating through their tears how their own dads, fatally ashamed, had tried to persuade them to run away from home. The BBC's *5 O'Clock News* revealed there would be a huge *Thank You, Sir Ivor* rally in Hyde Park on Saturday. Apparently a huge group of fans in Bournemouth had pooled their money to buy him a new Yardis as a token of their appreciation. Ten Downing Street was said to be interested in having him, Claude, and Ivanka over for a tea prepared by Jamie Oliver.

By early evening, a backlash had already begun picking up momentum. Sir Trevor McDonald interviewed Sir Ivor's two older sons, both playing in Division 2. Terence seemed an imbecile, but Hugo made some interesting points about his life to this point having been a lose-lose proposition. His team-mates and managers had always been sorely disappointed in him for not being nearly as good as his dad, and now they were disappointed in him for not being completely useless like Claude, whose singing he admitted wasn't his own cup of tea. His own taste ran to The Mutilators.

Sir Ivor's lone daughter, fashion model Rhiannon, who made Terence seem like the president of MENSA, thought Claude's singing was well super. She was proud not only of him, but of her other brothers as well, and of course of her dad and mum. She thought Ivanka just super too. Having realised that one couldn't remain a model forever, she was contemplating her own career as a recording artist.

24

The Fame

I WADDLED over to the newsagent's and discovered a wonderful new magazine called *Blush*, full of photographs of celebrities with their nipples or testicles inadvertently exposed, or with dark perspiration stains under their arms, crumbs at the corners of their mouths, or hideous cellulite. I signed Kate up for a gift subscription, and asked that the card included in her first issue bear the inscription *From You-know-who*, though I had no good reason to believe she would.

Cyril rang to tell me about the job for which he'd just been hired. In the wake of Ladbroke's having identified Stevie, the little lesbian with the big voice who'd bellowed Kate's 'Breathing' with remarkable aplomb on the previous show, as its favourite to win *Fab Lab*, her family had been getting harassed more and more brazenly by the gossiparasites. In hope that the others would be scared off, they'd hit on the idea of ruining the life of one such scumbag chosen at random. Cyril thought it would never work. In his view, it would be like imagining that if you squashed one cockroach in a kitchen then all the others would scurry off in terror. But if they were willing to pay, Cyril was quite happy to accept their money. He'd enjoy my company.

We took the train together down to Peckham to confer with the family. The dad, Clement, had thinning steel-coloured hair, a saucer-sized bald spot, a long, lank ponytail, earrings in both ears, a smoker's light brown teeth, and too many of them, and a thoroughly engaging manner. His eyes twinkled with delight when we shook hands.

He suspected he'd been made redundant from his job as a car mechanic because of Stevie's lesbianism. The wife of the guy who owned the garage was a Christian zealot, and thought she was doing her part thwarting Satan by getting her husband to break all associations with sexual deviants. "Cars are rubbish," he said. "They're forever breaking down. There's no reason anybody who knows how to work on them should ever be out of work."

His wife Dorothy, whose teeth were even uglier than poor Clement's (she lit one cigarette from what was left of its predecessor), but who didn't even make eye contact, feared for the well-being of the couple's two younger children. Unscrupulous journalists had in the past week offered them sweets and cigarettes and even money for embarrassing stories about Stevie on their way home from school. "One day they're offering money," she predicted ruefully. "Who knows that the next they won't be snatching them and holding them ransom?"

I hoped, since their only income now was from the singing lessons Dorothy offered when her emphysema was in remission, that Cyril would admit he thought their idea to ruin one random tormentor's life unviable, but his lips were sealed.

"I blame myself," Dorothy admitted, unbidden. "If I weren't such a good vocal coach, Stevie probably wouldn't be as good a singer, and none of this would be happening." She began to cry. It was a bit embarrassing.

"It isn't about her singing, though, love," Clement said, putting his arms around her. "It's about the way she looks at the camera, that wonderful expression of equal parts sexual arrogance and wariness and accusation. And it isn't just me saying it, Dor. It was the bloke in the *Standard*."

"You *would* diminish me, wouldn't you?" Dorothy asked her husband. You could see where the accusatory part of Stevie's look came from. Clement sighed and tugged on his long lank ponytail and said, "Blimey, love. I'm only trying to make you feel better."

"Well, you're not bloody succeeding," Dorothy said. "Of course, why should I find that surprising? Can't even hold a bloody job, this one."

"It's the fame," poor Clement told me and Cyril, actually sucking the tip of his ponytail now. "We never used to row, not before the press began hounding us, not before they began offering our youngsters money for stories about Stevie forgetting to flush and that."

"We've rowed since the day we got back from our bloody honeymoon," Dorothy snarled. "Blackpool he takes me to. Blackpool! Wanker." It looked as though poor Clement might gnaw his ponytail off.

We got down to business, Clement and Dorothy, Cyril, and I. Effective immediately, they would start referring all of the dozens of calls per day they were now getting from gossiparasites to Cyril, who'd explain he'd been hired to deal with the press for them. He would then pick one at random to torment mercilessly.

"Is this a great, great day," he asked as we headed back to the train, "or what? Thugging's good fun – don't get me wrong – but it hardly even rates comparison to malicious mischief." He literally rubbed his little hands, his fists of stone, together with glee. "This is so much more creative. And you can actually make somebody loads more miserable than by just breaking their nose."

He told me how it worked. The fundamental concept was that people were actually devastated more by things that befell innocent loved ones than themselves. Hence, we wouldn't go after the unfortunate gossiparasite Cyril picked *per se*, but after his parents, siblings, and friends. "Some of your harder core types will also target somebody's children," Cyril explained with a shudder, "but that's right out for me, right out." He treated himself to a moment's moral indignation.

"Say the poor rotter I pick has a brother who's a plumber. What we'll do is follow him round one day. We'll go back to some of the people whose leaks he's fixed and tell them we're examiners from the Office of Plumbing Standards or some such bollocks, and that we've just come to make sure their work was done properly and that they were fairly charged. Most people feel overcharged by plumbers, and will be quite happy to let us in. While you distract them for a second, I'll sabotage the work the brother's done. Ultimately, the brother's reputation will be rubbished."

I wondered how long this process generally required. He took out a pair of reading glasses and a pocket diary, from which he ascertained that the last such job he'd undertaken had, from start to finish, taken just short of five months. He scowled when I pointed out that Clement and Dorothy and their younger children might not last two more weeks, and that he ought to return their money.

Signal problems somewhere down the line required us to stop. As we sat there, I felt worse and worse about spoiling Cyril's fun. But then, reading over the shoulder of the guy beside me, I had an idea. The guy was reading an article with the headline *Another bullying-related suicide as Minister of Education holidays in Mallorca*. It suddenly occurred to me that parents of bullied children would almost certainly be happy to pay a few quid each month to prevent their kids being tormented to the point of self-destruction. What if Cyril puts his fists of stone to a noble use, the morally defensible one of intimidating bullies?

It was too wonderful! What decent parent wouldn't be ecstatic to spend a few quid each week to ensure that his child wasn't tormented to the point of abject hopelessness? Naturally, there would be those who'd object to Cyril, an adult, however tiny, beating up 14-year-olds, but where were they when the 14-year-olds' victims were hanging themselves, or jumping off the tops of buildings, or overdosing on their parents' Cipramil?

Cyril wasn't without misgivings. He had no idea of the horror of being bullied, as he'd only ever been a bully, albeit a casual one, and he was worried that other thugs would scorn him for roughing up minors. But he acknowledged that teenage suicide was a very sad thing, and that the market was probably as enormous as it was untapped.

"Why not start today?" I suggested, suddenly manic with enthusiasm. The guy to my left closed his newspaper and moved to the newly vacated seat to his own left. But I didn't care. It was so wonderful to feel purposeful. So this was how others felt!

Cyril was sceptical, though. "Today? Don't we have to get on the Internet or something first, do some research or something, make a few phone calls?"

That was the beauty of it, I explained, so enthusiastically that the newspaper man now relocated across the aisle. We needed only to find the nearest comprehensive school, hang fire until it let out, spot the school bullies, follow them, and lower the boom. Then we'd write down my email address for the parents of the kids we'd saved, and ask them to distribute it among the parents of other bullied kids.

"It's actually quite a good idea," the newspaper man surprised me by acknowledging as he returned to the seat beside me. I wasn't accustomed to strangers on trains speaking to me, although, judging from the volume at which they hollered down their mobiles, it wasn't because they didn't want me to know the most intimate details of their lives. "I was a bit of a bully myself at school," he said. "I'd have given anything I had or could nick from my parents if there'd been chaps like you two about at the time to show me the error of my ways."

I hated having an American's deficient sense of irony.

★　★　★

Kate declined to appear at record stores on behalf of *The Sensual World*, and gave rotten interviews, refusing to divulge anything about her life away from The Work, about which she waxed vague and gaseous. "I just wanted to try and find a female energy for myself [on this album]," she proclaimed. She was forever musing that she was, at last, beginning to Come To Terms With Herself.

She fell in with the company of self-styled alternative comedians known collectively as the Comic Strip, whose Dawn French had appeared in the 'Experiment IV' video, and whose Peter Richardson had directed 'The Sensual World', and returned the compliments by scoring their *GLC – The Carnage Continues*, which imagined how Hollywood might have related the history of British socialism. Kate's troublingly Madonna-esque bespoke new song 'Ken', which opened with a scream to rival Roger Daltrey's on 'Baba O'Riley', archly celebrated the controversial future mayor of London. 'The Confrontation' musically supported Ken (as played by Robbie Coltrane's version of Charles Bronson) butting heads with Margaret Thatcher (as played by Jennifer Saunders playing Brigitte Neilson). A couple of weeks later, Kate played the chocolate-addicted bride in Peter Richardson's *Les Dogs*, an ironically Fellini-esque fusion of gallows humour and pathos, and, nearly everyone agreed, played her well.

None of the album's singles received much play. It became clear that she'd grown too old for Radio 1's smooth-cheeked listeners, who were thought to want to practise the latest dance crazes to catchy songs with lyrics they had some slender prayer of making sense of. While recording a duet with Midge Ure, who seemed to have an inflated conception of his own importance, Kate confessed that she was considering quitting music. The former Ultravox heart-throb, now losing his hair, chastened her, "You can't, because if you quit, I quit, and if I quit somebody else who cares will quit." She reverted with a vengeance to gardening. "It's literally a very down-to-earth thing, isn't it?" she asked one interviewer, apparently rhetorically.

EMI released a boxed set of everything she'd recorded for them to that point, *This Woman's Work*, in a black box, suggesting that she was closing the door on the first part of her career. It wasn't the colour of the package, though, but its price tag that made many fans see red. Twelve hundred of the faithful, who'd taken to convening in Glastonbury on her birthday (Katemas!) each year, nonetheless turned up at the Hammersmith Palais for the year-ending fan convention, at which Kate answered questions for 45 minutes and then warbled a wee ode of thanks to the tune of 'My Lagan Love' at the end. The adaptation confirmed that, when she chose to, she could indeed write coherent lyrics. The highlight for most, though, was her seeming to suggest that she fancied doing a few concerts.

Indeed, everything seemed to point to her performing live again. She'd bought two additional Fairlight IIIs, apparently to take on the road. Seemingly intent on getting in fighting trim, she was doing a lot of dancing, and working once more with Lindsey Kemp. She was said to have contacted *Muppets* man Jim Henson about his working up something for her. In the USA, one major promotions firm, thinking it had the merchandising all sewn up, was already rubbing its hands in gleeful anticipation. And then, of course, nothing at all happened, unless you count her and Hannibal Records boss Joe Boyd, who'd helped put her in touch with Trio Bulgarka, accepting invitations to a formal luncheon hosted by the then-new Prime Minister John Major in honour of the president of Bulgaria. She didn't suffer food poisoning, and a week later showed up on Del's arm for the premiere of Ben Elton's play *Silly Cow*. The paparazzi harassed the couple so mercilessly that our normally placid heroine – she too gentle even for sarcasm on the St. Joseph's playground – kicked one in the bum. The gossip press take care of their own, and the next morning's *Today* featured an unflattering photo of Kate and a slanderous appraisal of her appearance.

★   ★   ★

Cyril and I had a long lunch. I was astonished by Cyril's appetite. He actually ate more than I, and washed it down with two pints to my glass of fizzy water with lemon. I asked him about having been a bully. He said the other bullies at his school hadn't wanted him in their clique. They thought they'd look funny coming down the street five abreast, four of them biggish and him a head shorter than the next smallest. He'd suggested it might work if he were in the middle, with two bigger lads to each side, as Roger Daltrey had been effectively flanked by the much taller John Entwistle on one side and Pete Townshend on the other in his favourite band, The Who. But the other bullies were fans of such prog-rock titans as Yes, Emerson, Lake & Palmer, and Genesis (originally featuring Kate's future collaborator Peter Gabriel) and told him to fuck off. One of them had gone on to own a very successful chain of hair salons.

By and by, we got a bus down to Camberwell and asked a local for directions to the nearest comprehensive, which turned out to be the Prang Hill School for Boys, a misnomer. The school had been co-educational since 1989, but had been unable to afford to have its stationery and the sign above its portal changed. "Bloody Labour's got all the money in the world to invade bloody Iraq," the caretaker who was our source of information groused, "but if a school wants to change its name, it's bloody out of luck, innit?"

I asked him when this particular one would let out. He looked at his wristwatch and said, "Any minute. It's meant to last until half-three, but the teachers reckon they're only getting paid up until a few minutes gone two, so they set the little buggers free whenever the urge strikes."

I hurried over to a North African crafts shop across the road and bought Kate a necklace I hoped she'd like even though I generally withhold my custom from shops that have signs on their front doors reading *Maximum two children allowed in at any time.* I believe it hurts children's feelings unnecessarily.

Not ten minutes later, the doors of the school flew open and Britain's troubling future burst through them whooping and dribbling and sniffling and shuffling and strutting and, in the cases of those Cyril and I had come to help, cowering.

We didn't have to wait long before a trio of very likely suspects swaggered into view, kicking a chubby Asian boy ahead of them like some huge, whimpering football, to the limitless amusement of their gum-chewing, mobile-brandishing girlfriends, with their precipitously low-slung combat trousers and blonde highlights.

"You're bloody useless, aren't you, Gajendra?" the darkest of the boys, an Asian himself, demanded.

"Yes, sir. I probably am," the kid whimpered.

"Tell us exactly how useless," the boy in the FCUK T-shirt demanded, making his girlfriend laugh.

"Oh, very useless indeed, sir," Gajendra whimpered. His hands were in constant motion, hovering an inch or two above his body, as he tried to anticipate where they would kick him next.

"Art! What a wanky thing to be good at!" the third boy, the one who seemed to have copied the coiffure of Evelyn on *Fab Lab*, proclaimed.

"Fuck off," the FCUK T-shirt one, clearly dominant, upbraided his friend. "It's marvellous that Gajendra's so good at drawing. He's going to do us a picture now, in fact. The three of us. Like on a fucking movie poster, all heroic, with the girls clinging to us." Here he knelt to speak right into poor Gajendra's face. "And if we don't fancy your drawing, mate, can you guess what we're going to do with it?"

"Make him eat it?" Cyril wondered as he stepped up to them.

They looked at one another, not sure how to respond. "No," the FCUK T-shirt one finally said, sneering, "Stick it up his jacksie."

"Bit vehement, don't you reckon?" Cyril asked, glaring up at the kid at a 30-degree angle. "Who appointed you school art critic anyway?"

The kid's Asian friend and spiky-haired friend stepped to either side of Cyril and a bit behind him, each of the boys now 120 degrees from the next. Cyril did the absolute worst thing he could have done. He looked over at me. I don't know how I'd managed it, but I'd never even considered the possibility that I'd be involved in our new venture in anything but a consulting capacity. At that moment, as the three boys turned towards me too, it seemed the stupidest mistake I'd ever made. I was paralysed. I wouldn't have been able to speak even if I'd been able to think of anything to say. I was 14 again, and there wasn't anything about it that felt good.

The boys leered at me for an eternity before the FCUK T-shirt one finally turned back to Cyril and laughed, "Looks to me like you're in this alone, mate, unless Gajendra fancies a bit of the action." Gajendra had been inching away on hands and knees since Cyril's intrusion. One of the girls snickered.

"Alone suits me right down to my toes, sonny," Cyril told him, their eyes still locked. "And you're not man enough to call me mate."

They stayed like that for a couple of millennia, no one moving, nor even blinking, the Asian and spiky-haired ones waiting for their leader's signal to pull Cyril down from behind, still no one moving, my heart trying to beat through my chest, my mouth the Gobi Desert, my palms a swamp.

"He's a nutter," the FCUK T-shirt one finally decreed. But he took a nearly imperceptibly small step backwards as he did so, and his doing so seemed to make both the Asian and spiky-haired one an inch shorter. One of the girls sighed. It was all over but the shouting.

"And a fucking meddler," the spiky-haired one said, turning his back on Cyril, turning back towards the road.

"You had your chance, sonny," Cyril, still motionless, told the FCUK T-shirt one, "and you didn't take it. One more syllable out of any of you and I'll embarrass you in front of your girlfriend and your mates."

FCUK T-shirt wasn't locking eyes now. Now he was giving Cyril the quickest, most furtive little glance. And one of the girls was whining, "God!" and then tsk-ing. I recognised it as the universal mating cry of the teenager trapped in an unfair world.

"Got much homework tonight?" Cyril asked FCUK T-shirt. FCUK T-shirt, confused, dared another glance, and then shrugged. "Well, now you've got a bit more, all three of you, you and your mates. You're going to write a letter to Govinder or whatever his name is, a letter of apology. You're going to tell him how sorry you are for having been complete wankers."

"Bloody hell!" the spiky-haired one gasped, but not at a volume that anyone would have interpreted as representing genuine resistance. It was more along the lines of the girl's whining.

The FCUK T-shirt boy looked on the verge of tears. Oh, how I would have adored to see him burst into them. But he held them back as he blurted at Cyril's knees, "Me dad's well hard."

It was Cyril's turn for snickering. "Is he? Well, I'm harder. We're coming back here, me and my mate, in the next few days. If Govinder tells me he hasn't got all three letters, you're going to be three very sorry boys. Your old man can be Vinnie bloody Jones for all I care."

The boys shuffled off with their heads down. The girls let them go. When they were around 20 feet up the road, FCUK T-shirt looked back at us. I knew he wanted to show Cyril his middle finger, or shout something, but in the end he realised it would only make him look more of a twat.

25

Hard Geezers Like You

I HAD never loved a man as I loved Cyril on the train home from Camberwell. Naturally, as soon as the danger was past, I got terribly brave, but managed not to say something I'd have hated myself for, managed not to claim that if the Asian or spiky-haired boy had tried anything, I'd have leapt right into the fray. Cyril made no reference to my having let him down. He referred to what *we* had done, to how *we*'d made a bloody good start on our business. I wanted to put my arms around him. I wanted him to have been my dad.

He dozed off before we got to Clapham Junction. I thought at first he was remarkably relaxed, but then realised how much energy it must have taken just to stand there unflinching under FCUK's chin.

When he woke up, he confirmed my impression. "There's no way on earth I could have handled them on my own," he said, the fact of his having had to calculate those odds shaming me back to the womb. "If one of yours [here it felt as though he realised how he'd hurt me, and was trying to restore me to wholeness] had walloped me from behind, it would have been over, wouldn't it? But it isn't to do with anything real, like strength. It's all to do with front.

"When it first started, everybody's bloody adrenal gland was in overdrive. But there's almost always somebody giving too much thought to the consequences, and when you do that – when you start trying to think how much it could cost you if you get a tooth loosened or a contact lens knocked out – your brain sends a signal to your adrenal gland saying, 'Maybe this isn't a good idea.' The second that happens, your adrenal shuts off. You saw it! You saw that at a certain point I could have said anything to them. It was all over by that point. A human being can't fight without a certain level of adrenaline in his bloodstream.

"What we call courage is in fact the ability to make your mind go blank when it wants to start calculating the seriousness of the danger you're in."

I felt giddy. It was as though the key to the door that kept all my self-loathing in was in reach. My voice trembled as I asked what the trick was.

"Well," he said, "blank probably isn't the best word. Minds don't actually go blank. The trick is getting it busy with something other than the danger. What I did today with those little shitewallets was see if I could remember all the thanks and special thanks on Kate's *The Dreaming* album. And I did."

I found that hard to believe, and it showed. He smirked at me confidently and intoned, "Many thanks to: Graham Middleton, Jim Jones, Mike King, Steve Payne, Step Lang, Duncan McKay, Kay Hunter, Bob Parre and Brian Tench at Mayfair Studios, Nigel Barker and David Woolley at Air Studios, Chris Gibbons at Odyssey Studios and all at Advision and Abbey Road Studios. Special thanks to: Del Palmer, Jay, Paddy, Ma & Pa, Lisa, Hil, Andrew, Paul Hardiman, David Gilmour, Bill Whelan, Alan Murphy, Haydn and Dan-Dan the sushi man, Jon Kelly and to everyone who has helped to complete and inspire this album."

"You can wipe that smirk off," I told him affectionately. "You reversed Nigel Barker and David Woolley."

"Bloody hell!" he fumed. "I did, didn't I? I *always* do that! Bugger. But the really interesting thing is that it's the one time she thanked Del before Ma and Pa."

That was absurd, of course, but I thought his pride had been hurt quite enough, and managed somehow to hold my tongue.

★　★　★

For the Elton John/Bernie Taupin tribute album *Two Rooms*, Kate wryly chose examples of Taupin at his formidable worst. Hearing the tremulous little voice in which she sang 'Rocket Man', there were those who wondered why she hadn't changed the lyrics – 'Rocket Little Girl', perhaps? – and others who found her musical invocation of the West Indies in the chorus a bit odd. 'Candle In The Wind' worked rather too hard at coming across celestial, but she sang the undeservingly ludicrous lyrics with the same tenderness she'd brought to 'Don't Give Up'.

Oh, Bernie. One would hope that a bloody astronaut would be "higher than a kite", wouldn't one? Taupin, master of metaphors! Am I alone in regarding the latter song's central aspect as inherently ludicrous (an unsheltered candle would have its little hands full in a gentle breeze, let alone a wind, innit)? Poor Marilyn Monroe, barbiturate-addled head case, known to have blithely menstruated all over her own furniture, known to have eagerly fellated all the slimiest studio bigwigs in Hollywood in her scuffling days, here celebrated for her grace and dignity. *Hello?* For me, "Your candle burned out long before your legend ever will [pick a tense, any tense!]," is like fingernails across a blackboard.

And now back to our book, in which we note that Australia adored 'Rocket Man', which proved Kate's biggest hit there in decades. Julian Doyle, of 'Cloudbusting' video fame, directed a tasteful monochrome performance video of the song, featuring Kate pretending to play the ukulele (more about ukuleles later!) and a flickering candle, shown at one point in close-up, standing in for the recently deceased Al Murphy.

Sir Elton, not yet knighted, told an interviewer that 'Don't Give Up' had helped him through the darkest days of his addiction to cocaine. The disproportionately popular English novelist Nick Hornby, who clearly hadn't heard *This Woman's Work*, pronounced Kate's music "toxic enough to be burned". A major, major British music magazine described hers as "a ditsy English convent girl voice". Having released only the two Elton covers in the previous year, she was nominated for a Brit.

★ ★ ★

I arrived home from Camberwell feeling quite buoyant about what we'd accomplished, or what Cyril had, and got on the Internet to try to determine whether we would indeed be the United Kingdom's first anti-bully vigilantes. It's part of my nature to be very stalwart where no actual danger is involved. I had long ago promised myself to stand firm against Bill Gates and Microsoft even if the rest of the world capitulated. So it was Netscape I launched, rather than Internet Explorer. Even though it loads marginally faster, according to an anti-Microsoft screed I read in a magazine while waiting to have my teeth cleaned in San Francisco once, it wasn't yet ready to browse when there was a great thumping on my door. I couldn't pretend I wasn't home, as I'd reflexively switched on the TV on walking in the door.

It was Mr. Chumaraswamy, accompanied by a blazing-eyed big fellow in a turban and very long black beard, whom he introduced as Mohammed, and who had mastered the American petty gangster's trick of turning a toothpick 360 degrees in his mouth with his tongue, and who, not encouragingly, declined to shake my proffered hand. He smelled of spices not common in the West. He was trying to hum 'Violin' from Kate's *Never For Ever* album, a song not easily hummed.

Mr. Chumaraswamy dabbed at himself frantically with his handkerchief as he came in and sat down unbidden on my bed. "We've always enjoyed a cordial relationship, have we not, Mr. Herskovits?" he asked me.

"Wonderfully cordial," I agreed.

"I've gone out of my way to be considerate, have I not? And on those occasions when you have been otherwise, have I not gone out of my way to be tolerant?"

"Cut to the fucking chase, gov," Mohammed suggested, in an accent that bore not the slightest trace of anywhere exotic.

"I have two requests – well, demands. They are quite non-negotiable, I'm afraid." I'd never seen anyone sweat so prolifically. "First," he said, squeezing his eyes shut, as though straining to move his bowels, but in fact struggling to remember the exact wording of the short speech he'd prepared, presumably with Mohammed's help, "you will keep your fucking hands off my bird, Mrs. Cavanaugh. Second, you will immediately suspend your nascent anti-bullying operation."

"Or he'll pull your fucking esophagus out through your fucking jacksie," Mohammed was delighted to finally be able to contribute, gold incisors flashing.

I could certainly understand the Mrs. Cavanaugh part, and actually found it rather charming that he would refer to her as his bird. How Swinging London! It was the second part that confused me.

"How on earth could you know anything about . . ."

Mohammed interrupted. "It don't fucking matter, does it, mush? You'll do like the gov says, or I'll hurt you."

Mr. Chumaraswamy, still dabbing feverishly, grimaced with embarrassment. "I'm sorry to have had to bring . . . my associate along," he said, "but I couldn't take a chance of your not listening.

"As for your question about how I know about your activities this morning, word travels quickly in the anti-bullying community. As luck, or your lack of it, would have it, I and my associates had intended to add Prang Hill to our list of client schools at the beginning of next month."

Mohammed, pretty sure by now that I wasn't going to offer any resistance, sat down at my computer. "Netscape?" he marvelled unhappily. "Who uses fucking Netscape anymore? Blimey." I admitted to Mr. Chumaraswamy that I didn't understand quite what was going on.

"Anti-bullying happens to be one of the fastest-growing grey market service industries in this country at the moment," he said, "its growth obviously having to do with the government's tacit encouragement. Native Brits have pretty much cornered the market in the Northeast. A Scots-Welsh cartel control Manchester and Liverpool. The Pakistanis effectively own the Midlands, just as Eastern Europeans, mostly Albanians, dominate in the Southeast outside London. London itself remains pretty much up for grabs, with different groups seeming to have got the upper hand every week."

"Blimey," Mohammed muttered. He seemed to have found himself a site specialising in women with grotesquely huge breasts. "How does she fucking stand up?"

I admitted my confusion. If anti-bullying vigilantism were proliferating to the extent Mr. Chumaraswamy suggested, why did every other day's newspaper carry accounts of another despondent young bully magnet's suicide?

"Oh, my dear, dear fellow," Mr. Chumaraswamy said sadly, as though he'd just realised he was addressing someone of severely diminished mental capacity, "surely you can understand that it's very much in our interests to encourage the press to print such accounts. Having to turn a blind eye to especially vicious persecution of an especially fragile-seeming child isn't something that any of us feels good about, I assure you. Indeed, I have personally found it difficult to get to sleep, even after a vigorous visit from Mrs. Cavanaugh, on numerous occasions over the past several months. But this is the high price we in the industry have reconciled ourselves to having to pay."

"Good riddance to bad rubbish," Mohammed said, pushing back from my table, clasping his hands behind his turban, savouring an image of an extraordinary blonde whose breasts filled my browser window. "Survival of the fittest, innit?"

"Now it could be," Mr. Chumaraswamy continued, "that your impulse to try to protect the bullied was quite spontaneous, and possibly even noble. But I simply can't – and won't – abide freelancers. There's too much at stake, fortunes to be gained or lost. My two children from my first marriage are studying computer science at universities in America. As I'm sure you've read, that's a very expensive proposition."

★　★　★

The Internet boomed, with countless hundreds of thousands more people getting on-line each month. A great many of them launched sites expressing their adoration of Kate. Some, to the later delight of biographers, attempted to compile every article ever written about her, often peppering them with editorial asides along the lines of "These music journalists are always so astoundingly preoccupied with making sure they're coming off as cynical and hip and 'cool' in their readers' eyes that they don't even have the minimal courage to consider the wonder of the natural world – as though love and Nature were only fads of the Sixties, now somehow 'out of date'! Smug, patronizsing, supercilious jerk." Not just protective, your typical Katefan, but fiercely so!

Not that Kate needed an awful lot of protection. She'd come, it was said (by no greasy tabloid, but *The Times*, whose interviewer admitted that Kate's petiteness and self-containedness made her feel rather a thug), to bring her own tape recorder to interviews to ensure that she wasn't misquoted. Not that she actually said much anymore. She would explain that she would talk about her music, but not about her life, as though the two were neatly separable, as though her life somehow didn't inform her music.

One who'd ask her a few years hence, for instance, what specifically had inspired her to observe, in 'And So Is Love', that life and love are sad, would be informed that it was in fact Joseph Campbell's observation, and not something she necessarily believed herself. She was gallingly opaque.

And it wasn't as though the prospective interviewer got to consider her new music at leisure, but rather came to Abbey Road to hear it, and then was sent home without a cassette or test pressing, or even a lyric sheet, numbered lyric sheets having been distributed at the listening session, and then vigilantly reclaimed at the end. One wondered if Kate, in her old age, might have got a bit up herself after all.

And then another long silence, one to the absurdity of which Kate admitted to the man from the *Guardian*. "It's ridiculous, isn't it? The amount of time that's gone into writing these songs is stupid really. They're just songs, not some cathedral or something.

"Three years to make a record. The worst is that the stuff is often written very quickly – in a day, a day and a half. But once you get into the studio, it starts to take on a life of its own. I wouldn't understand if I weren't involved. I'd think it was outrageous." She and the faithful Del were said no longer to be as one. Her mother died. In every life, some rain must fall, and a great deal seemed to be falling in Kate's.

* * *

The thought of sitting down to a dinner served by Mrs. Cavanaugh across from Mr. Chumaraswamy nearly spoiled my appetite, so I headed, as I'd allowed my obesity to keep me doing for months, for the pub. It was exhilarating to realise that I could walk that far. But I'd hardly started my *kanom Bueong Youn* when my mobile rang. Cyril was on top of a 12-storey block of flats in Camberwell with the boy in the

FCUK T-shirt and his parents, all of them trying to talk the boy out of plunging to his death. I was to get over there immediately.

I found the scene exactly as Cyril had described, except he'd failed to mention the presence of half a dozen police, two television news crews, poor Plaistow and a couple of other journalists, the combat-trousered girls from school, the bully magnet Gajendra and a couple I took to be his parents, a vicar, Lady Victoria Hervey – who'd presumably followed the news crews, hoping to get into some of their footage, and now in fact was being interviewed, assuring the TV news correspondent that she thought teen suicide was very, very tragic. The boy's Asian and spiky-haired partners in crime were there too.

At the sight of me, Cyril broke away from the vicar and the boy's parents and hurried over, seething. "You got me in this mess," he said. "Now you can bloody well get me out."

He grabbed me by the arm and hustled me near to where FCUK sat on the precipice staring longingly at the street below while ignoring the police negotiator, who I apprehended immediately was taking entirely the wrong approach – reminding the kid that he had his whole life ahead of him. I'd have hoped that a police negotiator would have a confident, reassuring baritone, and maybe this one had in other circumstances, but as we got within hearing distance of him, he was speaking in a high-pitched Welsh-inflected singsong that I thought a lot more likely to induce a fatal plunge than discourage it.

"Jamie," Cyril said to the kid, "look, mate. Look who's here."

Jamie glanced over at me, but didn't find me interesting. "Who's he?"

It was certainly heartening to know what an extremely delible impression I'd made. "My mate," Cyril reminded him. "It was actually his idea to sort you out this afternoon."

"I don't remember anybody else being there," Jamie said. "And I'm getting well fed up now. If somebody's going to change my mind about this, they'd better fucking speak up."

Gajendra, tenderhearted Gajendra, ran through the police. "Sir," he implored Jamie, "please don't do this. *Please!* I'm not angry. I'm not angry at all. Listen, I've been bullied mercilessly since my first day of infants school, my teacher at which advised my parents she'd never seen anybody bring out the tyrant in other children as I did.

"And you're the best of everyone who's ever tormented me – the best! You've forgotten more about petty sadism than the others will have learned by the time they leave school without so much as an O-level between them. *Please!*"

Jamie turned towards him. "I appreciate your kindness, mate. I do, honestly. But you were a contemptible little wankbag this afternoon, and your opinion doesn't mean anything more to me now. Piss off back to Mummy and Daddy, or whatever you lot call them. Let me do what I must."

I assume the vicar had tried before. Now he tried again. He invoked Jesus's infinite compassion and forgiveness, and reminded Jamie that, since life was God's alone to take, he'd forfeit his chance to go to Heaven by leaping. "I have to admit I don't follow that," Jamie told the vicar. "If Jesus is so forgiving, why can't I be forgiven for jumping?" His two sidekicks' snickering made him smile, but not for very long. He turned once more to the abyss.

I had an idea. I breathlessly related it to Cyril. "How am I going to remember all that?" he protested when I finished, but we both knew there was no time to lose. Needs must.

"Before you jump, mate," he told Jamie, "I just want you to know that the whole time we were glaring at each other this afternoon, I was fucking terrified, pissing myself, in fact. It was only the catheter kept you from seeing. If you'd actually raised a hand to me, I'd have fainted."

He had the boy's attention. "How did I keep from bursting into tears and running away? Well, I was cheating, wasn't I? See, when I was in the Territorial Army, they taught us a special technique for raising our own testosterone levels. But I couldn't have kept it up there for five more seconds, mate. And then it would have been clear to all that you were the better man, the far better one.

"Do you fancy hip hop, mate? I'm going to guess that you do. So you'll know what I mean when I say: *You da man*."

Jamie looked at him as he'd not looked at anyone else. You could tell he wanted it to be true. Cyril looked at me. I hoped he could see the encouragement in my eyes. I didn't dare be more overt than that.

"Why was I so terrified?" Cyril continued, making this part up for himself. "Because anybody can see you're nuff hard. Being a wankbag at Prang Hill School must be about the worst idea a kid could have with hard geezers like you on the pitch."

"It is!" Gajendra affirmed frantically from behind us. "Every day I kick myself for being so stupid!"

"Everybody admires you, mate," Cyril said. "Everybody. Other boys. All the girls. The teachers. The lot. How could they not admire somebody as hard as you?"

"If we was to have a punch-up, you and me," Jamie ventured, "you'd probably wind up in the fucking hospital." And at that moment I knew his life was saved, although his mum nearly threw a spanner in the works, bleating, "I will not have that language in my home, James, and I won't have it up here either!"

Jamie's Asian mate got the idea. "It's an honour being the right-hand man of somebody as hard as you, James."

"I'm his right-hand man, you wanker," the spiky one protested. "You're his left."

But it didn't matter in the slightest. It was only a matter of time now before Jamie swung his legs back over the wall.

"Jamie's hard!" it occurred to me to begin to chant. "Jamie's hard!" I could have wound up feeling a perfect prat, but soon everyone was chanting along with me, even Lady Victoria Hervey. And here came Jamie's legs. And here a couple of coppers to pull him far clear of the precipice and handcuff him. "What are you bloody doing?" he whimpered.

"Public endangerment, innit," the cop in charge informed him. "What if you'd slipped off the wall and fallen on somebody?"

For about a millisecond, it looked as though Asian and Spiky might try to overwhelm the cops. But it fell to me, Jamie's new benefactor, to put the best face on the situation. "How many of the other hard boys at Prang Hill will be able to say they've been nicked by the Old Bill?"

"Wicked!" exulted Asian.

"Jamie's hard," Spiky reminded him, shaking his head admiringly as the cops led their leader towards the stairs.

I expected Cyril to bite my ears off, but he was gentle with me. "Next time you have a brilliant idea," he said, putting his hand avuncularly on my shoulder even though he was probably ten years my junior, "why not take it to one of your other mates?" He had no way of knowing, of course, that I hadn't any other mates, unless I counted Plaistow, which would have been rather a stretch.

And now here came Jamie's parents, his mum crying softly into a facial tissue, his dad glowering. "'Ere," the latter said, "it isn't that we don't understand what you lot were trying to do, and it isn't that we don't agree it's a good thing."

"We've tried in every way we know to stop his being a sadistic little monster," his mum sniffled. "We got him a PlayStation. We bought him an electric guitar. We bought him the Harry Potter books after hearing that even kids who don't fancy other books love them."

"He read one paragraph of the first one," his dad said. "couldn't be arsed. Told us he found it more fun tormenting his passive classmates, didn't he, Lois?"

"He did," his mum agreed. "And don't think that wasn't like a knife in our hearts. We don't have a cruel household. We haven't even eaten red meat since the whole mad cow palaver. The occasional chicken, but only if it's free range. And fish, of course."

"But you can't just snatch it away from him, the sadism," his dad said, "not any more than you could snatch Jesus away from the vicar."

"It's how he defines himself, being monstrous," his mum said, becoming more irate with each new syllable. "It's what makes him feel OK about himself, isn't it? Does it ever occur to meddlers like you lot that a bully might be as fragile deep down as any other teenager?"

I introduced Cyril to Plaistow. It seemed silly that my two best friends didn't know one another. It turned out they both supported Fulham and hated Arsenal. For the millionth time in my life, I felt insufficiently masculine in the face of such revelations. Plaistow hadn't actually boxed, but had enjoyed the *Rocky* series of films, at least through *III*. He believed Sylvester Stallone had at least one more great film in him.

His work hadn't been going brilliantly. As he saw it, there were now too many people trying to unearth too little celebrity filth. The problem with *Fab Lab* and *Megastar* was that the contestants were in most cases too young to have very many skeletons in their closets. The exception was Vijay, recently voted out of *Fab Lab*, who'd been revealed to be 33, and to look 19 only as a result of extensive cosmetic surgery. The scoop, alas, had been someone else's.

Plaistow had been poking around on the edges of the anti-bully vigilantism movement for several weeks, but didn't dare delve deeper for fear of getting on the wrong side of the Albanians. They were said to kidnap one bully at random from every school they came to control, and to ship him blindfolded and gagged back to the old country, from which they would compel him to write ever more plaintive letters to his family and friends back in the Southeast outside London. Bullying in the areas they controlled had virtually disappeared. It wasn't uncommon in Albanian-controlled areas to see former bullies polishing the shoes of those they'd once tormented with the sleeves of their own Tommy Hilfiger and other hooded sweatshirts.

Plaistow admitted he wished Jamie had jumped, as he'd been able to conduct interviews with both his parents, his Asian mate, and his girl-friend while the police and vicar tried to talk him off the precipice. "His girlfriend said he's actually quite soft-hearted when you get to know him. Fancies animals and that. Is lovely to her mum. Gives her a lot of the jewellery he makes his victims nick from their own mums."

26

Sorry Not Fr Us

FINALLY, in 1993, there was another album, *The Red Shoes*, which, according to the faithful Del, she'd originally intended to record quickly and then take out on the road! At the same time as she was having someone rig up a remote control device that would enable her to work in complete seclusion, without even the faithful Del, she was also successfully inviting the contributions of Jeff Beck, Eric Clapton, Prince, the comedian Lenny Henry, and three Bulgarian woman folk singers in their sixties, the Trio Bulgarka. 'Rubberband Girl', the unnervingly Madonna-esque opening track, led one to think she'd made a party album. But then it was back to business as usual, to melancholy ruminations on the trauma of being alive, and we loved her for it. And if the stalwart Del noticed Kate and the guitarist Danny McIntosh glancing at one another during the recording of his bits in a way suggesting that Danny would one day supplant Del as Kate's leading man, he didn't let on to any of the tabloids.

'Rubberband Girl', with its weird background voices and Kate's rubberband imitation at the end, must have made a lot of people think there'd been a frightful mistake at EMI's manufacturing facility. But it wasn't nearly as much a bucketful of ice water in the face as 'Why Should I Love You', on which Kate sounded as though making a cameo on a Prince album. I loved it, especially Prince's little organ riff. 'Big Stripey Lie', on which she played distortorama guitar just like ringin' a bell, seemed no less an homage to David Byrne's work with Brian Eno than the infectiously exultant, utterly incomprehensible 'Eat The Music' was to the music of Madagascar. I hadn't a clue what she was on about, and didn't care in the slightest. The energisingly manic title track made me chuckle. (All anyone who wanted to stop dancing needed to do was put on one of Kate's albums before *Hounds Of Love*.) 'Constellation Of The Heart', which took the remarkable step of explicitly repudiating the hopelessness of other songs, featured wonderful funky guitar work from future lover Danny McIntosh and a hilarious dialogue with the back-ground singers.

Rather more than Eric Clapton's predictable B.B. King-isms, it was Gary Brooker's brooding Hammond organ that drove 'And So Is Love' – that and Kate's vocal, which, where it suddenly changed mood and soared desperately into a higher register, made the hairs on the back of my neck stand on end again. I revelled in her unprece-dented forthrightness, as I did too in the heartbreaking Brooker-driven closing track, 'You're The One'. Not since Lorraine Ellison's like-themed 'Stay With Me' had I heard anything quite like the screech of anguish that Kate, heretofore trying so hard, and success-fully, to keep her dignity in the face of her lover's defection, unleashed in the fade-out. This was Kate Bush just below the pinnacle of her remarkable powers.

The pinnacle being the devastating, monumental 'Moments Of Pleasure', in which she laments the loss of several loved ones. Forget the solipsism of a lot of the lyrics – I honestly can't imagine anyone not being brought to the verge of tears by how she sang the bit about her recently deceased mum. And if the line about the pain of just being alive didn't send tingles down your spine, you wanted to see a neurolo-gist, quick.

There were those, expert in pagan invocations, who bristled when, in 'Lily', Kate confused Gabriel and Raphael, putting the one meant to be in front of her behind. Some of her fans seemed to need to get out more. In the even less comprehensible 'Song Of Solomon', the naughty Andy Gill noted, "Bush says, 'Don't want your bullshit/ Just want your sexuality', though she seems to have an apparently boundless appetite for the former."

She sang on a track called 'My Computer' by the Artist Formerly Known as Prince, to the accompaniment of whose music she described herself as liking to dance. They'd apparently met, and agreed to work on something together, after she attended one of the London shows of his 1990 *Nude* tour. By and by, she sent him a multitrack copy of 'Why Should I Love You'. According to Michael Koppelman, an engineer and musician who collaborated briefly with the Artist in the early Nineties, Kate's original was incalculably better than the "lame disco" version the Artist came up with for *The Red Shoes*.

She came once more to New York, to Tower Records in lower Manhattan, where 2,000 people had queued for hours in freezing weather just to tell her with tears in their eyes how much her music meant to them – and, in one case, that of a girl who'd flown all the way from San Francisco, the width of the continent away, to offer an arm to be autographed, and then the autograph made permanent by tattooing. Who but another as famous as Kate herself would have even the most crudest understanding of how terrifying and exhausting adoration of that intensity could be?

In an attempt to prevent queue jumping, Tower handed out numbered wristbands. A CNN crew showed up to film the faithful, many of whom, in hopes of improving their chances of glimpsing Kate's arrival, had commandeered garbage cans to stand on. Finally, nearly ten hours after the first fan had turned up, her limousine dispensed her, and fans were at last admitted, in groups of 10, everyone to receive a sole autograph, to the store.

They gave her three and a half big American shopping bagfuls of gifts. She wouldn't sign the San Francisco girl's arm (for fear the girl might wish in a couple of years she'd saved it for Tori Amos, for instance), but did, though she wouldn't see a penny in royalties, graciously sign a dizzying variety of heretofore-unseen bootleg albums, even one whose cover, depicting her in a halter top, visibly displeased her.

Four days later, she was in Toronto, where a mob of well-mannered (Canadian, after all) fans gathered outside CFNY's studio to gape at her through the studio's glass front. At the insistence of EMI's local dignitaries, brown wrapping paper was taped to the glass to preclude poor Kate's coming to feel like a newly imported panda in a North American zoo. When she learned that the faithful outside had got 40 signatures on their ad hoc petition asking that their gawking not be thwarted, Kate herself got up and removed the paper from the window.

How do you get 20 Canadian Kate Bush fans out of a swimming pool? You say, "All Canadian Kate Bush fans out of the pool now, please."

With regard to video, she'd been slightly ahead of the curve with the entirely plot-driven 'Cloudbusting', and seemed to want to get ahead of it again. No mere individual clips would suffice. This time, nothing less than a short film, featuring six songs from the album, would do, and she herself, the shy megalomaniac (as many in the press had come to enjoy calling her) would both star in and direct. Inspired by Michael Powell's 1948 film *The Red Shoes*, co-starring Lindsey Kemp and the estimable Miranda Richardson, and featuring a lot of dancing for one presumed to have turned her back on dance, the film depicted Kate practising to record her video of 'Rubberband Girl', only to be interrupted by a loss of electrical power. After being left alone in the studio, she's confronted by a strange woman (Richardson) who comes to her through the mirror, and offers Kate beautiful red ballet shoes in exchange for help getting home. Kate comes to regret having accepted the deal when she finds herself unable to stop dancing, as she does, frenziedly, through squishy fruit, in 'Eat The Music'.

If largely devoid of plot and poorly edited, the film was at least extremely colourful, perhaps in homage to Powell's, which was made at the dawn of the Technicolor Age. Much expense had manifestly been spared elsewhere, though, and Kate revealed herself, as an actress, to be a terrific singer. (What, one wondered, had happened to her since Comic Strip's *Les Dogs?*) Her more devout fans would nonetheless manage to find it endearingly quirky 'n' campy. At the end of its premiere screening at the Odeon West End, its London Film Festival audience rose as one, almost as though imitating that at the Liverpool Empire the first official night of the *Tour Of Life* 14 years before, and applauded until their hands ached.

The reviews weren't terrific, though. Derek Elley thought it "not so much a movie as the sort of linked sequence of promo vids pop stars are wont to hang themselves with, given a feature-length rope . . . The effect suggests a peculiarly daft corner of the Seventies." *Homeground* reader Ahmir Hassib Mirza of Newcastle wrote countless thousands of words trying to vent his displeasure. Not far from Leicester Square, audiences were rather less exultant – and very, very much sparser – than the Film Festival one. In north London, for instance, it was lucky to attract audiences of more than half a dozen. Years later, Kate would apologise for having wasted La Richardson's and others' time, and claim to be pleased with only four minutes of the film. "I had the opportunity to do something really interesting," she would sigh, "and completely blew it."

★   ★   ★

Mrs. Cavanaugh was crying. I feared the worst. The first thing that went through my mind was that maybe Cathy had died, or that Kate had announced that she'd given up on trying to make another album, or that Gilmour's mouth had got him beaten into a coma. But her tears were for herself. It appeared that she and Mr. Chumaraswamy were on the rocks. He'd been ever more distant the past couple of weeks. At first she thought he was preoccupied with a new business venture, about which he would tell her nothing, but now she'd discovered it was much more than that.

"He's been seeing someone else. The whole time we've been, well, seeing each other, he's been seeing someone else. And the worst part is that it's a bloke."

Blinking frantically, holding the tears back, she turned her face to the ceiling. "A bloke," she repeated. "This is a first for me. A feckin' bloke." Adversity seemed to have reminded her of her ethnicity.

"And not a bloke I can compete with either. A feckin' whirling dervish or something, this one. A bloody Muslim warrior."

"With a turban?" I asked. "And a very long beard?"

"Oh, perfect," she said bitterly. "So I was the last one to know."

"If we're talking about Mohammed," I said, "and we're probably not, since his interest seems to be in women with grotesquely enormous breasts, all I know is that he's Mr. Chumaraswamy's intimidator."

"And all I know is that I really can't bear much more. Which is why I've written this." She removed a couple of pages folded in quarters from the back pocket of her jeans and held them out to me. I was far too knackered for reading, but the look in her eyes made clear that I couldn't refuse. I briefly thought of trying to pretend not to be able to find my reading glasses, but they were right there atop the keyboard of my iMac. I sighed, but she wasn't interested. She stepped over to and looked out of the window while I began to read.

"No," she said. "Aloud. I want to hear it read out."

It was entitled *Aibheann Cavanaugh's Resignation from the Human Race.*

" 'At 52, after a lifetime's trying, I must, with regret, conclude that I don't belong in the human race. Because, as I write this, I am wracked by levels of frustration, boredom, despair, and self-loathing from which not even the exquisite music of Kate Bush can provide adequate relief anymore, this will constitute my farewell.

" 'Since relocating to London (to which my sons Duncan and Gilmour had moved in 1993) with my daughter Catherine in 1997, I have tried with implacable determination to establish myself as either a writer or website designer. I believe myself to be unusually good at both jobs, and am not alone in this belief. In my twenties and early thirties, the theatre criticism I wrote for *The Irish Times* was praised as far afield as New York. I have won awards for my poetry and short fiction.

" 'On relocating to London, I very much fancied the idea of starting up where I'd left off, and added journalism to criticism on my palette, writing about trends in theatre, about actors, and directors, and playwrights, and so on. My pedigree aside, though, I couldn't get anyone to pay any attention at all. Quite typically, I would spend a whole morning researching a particular subject on-line, and then spend an hour writing and rewriting what I dared imagine was a well-informed, even provocative query, which is what you call an article proposal you send an editor. If I got any response at all – and around 90 per cent of the time I didn't – it would be one hurriedly typed line, free of punctuation and capitalisation, full of typing mistakes, often saying no more than *sorry not fr us*. If I were to have a headstone, I would want *sorry not fr us* to be my epitaph.

" 'These people are probably very busy, friends have told me repeatedly over the years, as my frustration has given way to hopelessness, as I have reconciled myself to the realisation that I will never be given another chance to do what I do uncommonly, even extraordinarily, well. Bugger that. I know what it's like to be busy. At the height of my career as a critic, I wasn't just writing my reviews (and poems and short stories). I was also looking after a husband and infant son, Duncan, and doing a bloody good job of it too. And yet when a young writer took the time to write to me, I wouldn't have dreamed of being so cavalier with them.

" 'Don't imagine I'm not taking into account that it's a lot easier and faster to send an email than a letter, and that for that reason modern editors are probably receiving appeals from a great many prospective writers every day. But I know how long it takes to write an email that conveys some tiny modicum of respect for the recipient, rather than *sorry not fr us*.

" 'I design as well. I had a flair for it from early on. When it became possible to do it on computers, I was beside myself with glee. It seemed more fun than I'd ever imagined possible. And I was very good at it. When the Internet came along in the mid-Nineties, I started designing websites for friends. What a joy to make your work accessible for the whole world to see minutes after doing it, without having to wait for printers! And I was good at that as well. When the big multinational consulting firm of Lanigan & O'Keeffe opened an e-business unit in its Dublin office in 1998, I was one of the first two web designers they hired. But since I came over to London, I've had a grand total of two bloody interviews for design jobs, and one of those for a three-week contract with a client looking for someone to lay out a catalogue in bloody Quark Xpress using a template they provided. And what a naff template it was!

" 'I've been making ends meet by running a boarding house. I fell into it quite by happenstance, but don't seem to be able to fall back out! I'm good at writing, and at design. I'm bloody awful at running a boarding house.'

"But that isn't the case at all," I interrupted myself to protest. "It seems to me that you do a marvellous . . ."

That was as far as I got. It would have taken a far braver man than I to go on in the face of the look she'd turned from the window to give me, her cheeks streaked with tears that she'd cried without a sound. "Just feckin' read, you," she said, "without editorialising."

" 'And that's just my professional life,' " I continued. " 'My personal life's a nightmare all its own. Thank God for my elder son, Duncan. He's never been a moment's trouble. But the other two! Duncan's younger brother Gilmour seems intent on getting killed in a drunken brawl, and his sister Catherine on starving her poor self to death, and this after five months of living rough and not even letting me hear the sound of her sweet voice. And as God is my witness, I wasn't less kind to either of them. I love them no less than Duncan, not a bit. I adore all three. And I go to bed each night thinking that it might be the last night I'll have all three of them.

" 'The men I'm mad about don't want to know. In my day, I was gorgeous. I know this to be true. I've got bloody photographic documentation! But every month I look in the mirror and am horrified to see my own mum seeping out through the pores of my epidermis. I see my own reflection in a shop window and think, *Christ, I haven't looked like that all day, have I?* And I know I have, and that I'm never likely to look better than I do today, not being one for having her face cut up to spite the years.

" 'In the past several months, I've had relationships, one sexual, the other platonic, with two gentlemen, each wonderful in his own way, but I can tell I'm driving both of them away as I always do. There's no one strong enough in this world to deal with my despair. And there's no one I hate enough to make them have to.' "

I wondered whom, beside Mr. Chumaraswamy, she might be referring to, and was flabbergasted to realise it must be me. Her use of the word *wonderful* had put me off the scent.

It occurred to me that making me read this was her way of getting to see how desperately she needed me. If there's one thing in the world nobody wants, it's to be desperately needed.

She seemed to read my mind. "Don't worry, love," she said. "I'm past hoping we might have some sort of future together. Have been for ages." There was no hopefulness in her eyes, no ambivalence in her tone. I loved her for their absence. I hoped Mr. Chumaraswamy would cherish her as she deserved. "Keep reading," she said.

" 'I have mentioned my love of Kate Bush's music. Perhaps it's

251

greedy of me, but I have waited many years for the incomparable pleasure of a new album, and now must concede that I haven't the patience to wait any longer, having already waited over a decade. It pains me beyond my meagre ability to express to say that I have come to regard Kate as spoiled and self-indulgent, denying so many of us such intense pleasure.

" 'I wish I could say I'm bored senseless. Senseless would be an improvement. I'm bored to the point of every breath I take hurting, every bloody thought I think.

" 'I could go on and on. Don't think it hasn't occurred to me that I ought to append a list of the email addresses of all those editors whose combined staunch indifference is what brought me to this state. In fact, I even wrote the letter that I hoped someone would be willing to send them on my behalf.

" 'You won't be hearing from Aibheann Cavanaugh anymore. You may recall that she has proposed numerous articles to you over the past several months, but you were too busy to take any notice – or too lazy and complacent to investigate the work of anyone not already a member of your old boys' network. In the face of her inability to get persons such as yourself to take five minutes of their precious time to confirm that she might indeed have made a substantive contribution to your section, in the face of her boredom and mounting financial desperation, she has taken her own life. At least a few drops of her blood are on your hands.

" 'But I'm pretty sure that most of them would simply ignore the email, or, at most, write back *sorry not fr us*. And I can't bear the thought of the bastards ignoring me in death just as they ignored me in life. All I can say is I hope they all get inoperable cancers, and that no amount of morphine relieves the pain.' "

I had to stop again, as I couldn't believe my eyes. She glared at me wordlessly. "You can't let the bastards beat you, Aibheann," I finally blurted. "You just can't. *Nil illegitimus carborundum!* If you kill yourself, the people who hurt you most probably won't even notice. And those who love you will be unnecessarily devastated."

"And would that include you, Mr. Herskovits?"

She had me over a barrel. I'd sworn to myself after breaking up with my wife never to tell another woman I loved her, but what if my refusal left Cathy without a mum? "Of course it does," I said.

It looked almost as though she was contemplating smiling. "I'm not going to top myself," she said. "There are entirely too many wonderful books I've not had time to read and too many restaurants where

I've not yet dined, and more being opened every week. And I love you too."

When was the last time I'd felt nearly so foolish? Could I even think back that far? "Then why," I demanded, burning with anger, "did you write all that, for Christ's sake?"

"It's therapeutic," she said. "My psychotherapist at the NHS suggested it. She said I should write the angriest letter I could possibly write, and then not post it, or even let anyone read it. She said it's a good way to deal with anger. And she was right.

"You don't really imagine I'd wish cancer on anybody, do you? I mean, in moments of peak despair, I might, in the same way that sometimes even the most loving parents will try to imagine what deliberately hurting their children might be like."

"It isn't the same thing at all!" I snapped, literally trembling with rage now. "Not fucking at all! In the one case, you've got people who've hurt you with their indifference. On the other, you've got a complete innocent. How is that fucking anything *like* the same?" Poor Mr. Chumaraswamy, the soul of tolerance, pounded on his ceiling, my floor.

"I've never seen you so furious," Mrs. Cavanaugh said with a smile that contradicted her observation.

"I dare say you'd be furious too if I made you read . . ."

That was as far as I got, as she stood up and took off her jumper, revealing herself to be wearing her black lace corset under it.

"You're joking!" I thundered, prompting more tapping from poor Mr. Chumaraswamy. But there was at least one part of me that got the joke in a big way.

"I've always wondered," she said, managing coquettishness at 52 again, "what shagging you would be like if you were traditionally masculine for a change, instead of passive."

A part of me wanted to evict her from my room to spite her, but it was the other part that won, the action film part, the part that wanted to make her whimper for surrender, whimper with delight.

I remembered how much fun virility could be.

27

500 Quid Not Earned

A N Australian newspaper – not the one that suggested that she owed it to her fans to pose proudly with the baby son Bertie she'd had with Danny McIntosh in either *Hello* or *OK!* (the choice was entirely her own!) – estimated that the £55 million she'd earned over the course of her career made Kate the second richest British pop chanteuse, after only Annie Lennox. Her wealth clearly hadn't gone to her head. On meeting her, Don Black, who wrote the book and lyrics for the West End production of *Sunset Boulevard*, was gobsmacked to learn that she'd only ever attended one West End musical, *Godspell*, decades before. Accustomed to yawning megastars who'd been to absolutely everything, and got pretty jaded in the process, he was delighted in her childlike delight in the show.

She, Danny, and Bertie were said to divide their time between a six-acre mansion on a small river island in Berkshire, a vast Victorian mansion in Greenwich on a main road, but surrounded on three sides by impenetrable woodland, and a riverside penthouse in Battersea, with the loyal Paddy and his collection of musical exotica next door. Bertie was said by his proud mum to do a remarkable Elvis imitation. A good Elvis impersonator is rarely out of work.

The Belfast singer/songwriter Brian Kennedy ratified Black's impression of Kate as down-to-earth and generous. As a kid, he'd been transported by 'The Man With The Child In His Eyes', and sworn, if he ever got to make a record of his own, that he'd send her a copy, with a note of appreciation. On receiving his *The Great War Of Words*, she wrote back to express her great pleasure and even invited him to dinner. She not only answered the door barefoot, but also, when he and she and Del and Stuart Elliot went out for a Chinese, introduced him to crispy seaweed.

Good old Bob Mercer, who'd signed her to her original sponsorship deal with EMI, asserted that there were only two kinds of people –

those who loved her, and those who hadn't met her. Sweet as everyone agreed she was, though, she seemed very much to be treading water creatively. With George Martin producing, she recorded a version of 'The Man I Love' for the *Glory Of Gershwin* album, with the gout-afflicted harmonica virtuoso Larry Adler, whom she treated with great tenderness. She was said, over and over again, to be about to contribute a song to a Nick Drake tribute album that never materialised. She leapt out of a cake in a flesh-coloured body stocking at Rolf Harris's 70th birthday party. I'm only joking. But she did attend it, and was photographed smiling at the birthday boy in a way that we would all like to be smiled at.

She was thought to have been observed in Harrod's with Enya, of all people, shopping for Joanna Lumley's OBE party. On another occasion, she was seen looking at Art Deco-style furniture with great interest. She was said to be producing two tracks for the master Celtic harpist Alan Stivell, for whom big brother Jay was writing lyrics. 'Twas said that she could teach the British intelligence, uh, community a thing or two about keeping a secret. She declined to produce Erasure.

The irrepressible Fred Vermorel presented a lecture at London's Royal College of Art entitled *What I Did To Kate Bush* in which he revealed that he'd been inspired by Woody Allen's *Stardust Memories* to go to her house without her knowing it and climb her drainpipe. Exactly the sort of thing a woman considering children wants to contemplate!

The local council asked her to open the restored Brontë Bridge (the first having been washed away by floods in March 1990) spanning the narrow stream in Haworth Moor. When she declined, they got Tori Amos instead.

I'm joking, and the truest things are said in jest. There were those who believed that La Amos wasn't only the beneficiary of an unprecedentedly clever niche marketing campaign, but that the campaign had been suggested by market researchers' analysis of Kate, to the American cover of whose *Kick Inside* the cover of Amos's *Little Earthquakes* bore an unignorable resemblance. Would you like it if Kate toured more often, they'd been asked. *Oh, yes!* How about the lyrics being a little less confusing? *Oh, yes, please!* Well, meet Tori Amos.

At whose first gigs in the UK, *Vox* asked members of the audience what they thought. What they thought, by and large, was that, because Kate showed no inclination to tour ever again, Tori would have to do.

The Brontë Society, which had been ungracious to the point of hostility in the decade following the success of 'Wuthering Heights', changed its tune, and in its journal devoted a whole article to the song, which it acknowledged "captured the imperious Cathy . . . and her sense of abandonment and utter loneliness". Sinéad O'Connor didn't repudiate the awful things she'd said about the Pope, but did admit to feeling inadequate when Peter Gabriel invited her to sing Kate's part on 'Don't Give Up', as he'd earlier recruited Tracy Chapman, at an Amnesty International benefit in Chile. She blithely informed a major, major British music magazine, "I've got to admire her because Peter Gabriel tried to shag her and she wasn't having any. She's the only woman on Earth who ever resisted him, including me."

★   ★   ★

Nicola phoned, furious at me for not calling, and at herself for having called to tell me that my not calling made her furious. I told her I'd been intending to call, but had been very busy. She said bollocks. She said she knew I was just trying to get her to want me. What really infuriated her was that it was working. I might be interested to know she'd lost another nine pounds and was looking sensational. Lechers pretending to be photographers had started slipping her business cards as she waited for buses – or telling her that no one as attractive as she should have to ride the bus. If I knew what was good for me, I'd take her to dinner.

I reflected on how much less discomfited I was by great beauty than I'd been as a younger man, when I'd hardly been able to sit still in the same room at first with my universal object of desire. By my forties, though, all this had finished. I decided that it wasn't because of diminished sex drive, but because I'd got some perspective, had come to realise that the gorgeous were living on borrowed time, that they were walking time bombs. Deep inside their every cell, their DNA was conspiring to pull them back down with the rest of us.

If anything, Nicola had understated the case. She was now officially ravishing, now officially the most jaw-droppingly gorgeous woman I'd ever have been seen with. When we entered the chic trattoria in Sidcup where she'd suggested we dine, it was as though the world lost its audio feed for a second. No one was even able to inhale. But I was surprised to find myself embarrassed, rather than exhilarated.

Nicola wasn't enjoying it so much herself. "Bloody hell," she said, hiding first behind her menu and then the wine list. "I can't get used to this," she said. "I feel as though everybody's mistaking me for somebody else. I feel as though someone at any minute is going to expose me as an impostor. Or maybe somebody who remembers me from school will leap up and say, 'What's all the palaver? It's just Nic the Stick.'" I was shocked to learn that until mid-adolescence, she'd been skinny.

She told me about her new workout regimen. I told her about persuading Jamie in the FCUK T-shirt not to jump off the top of the block of flats. She told me about having attempted suicide herself when she was 16. She said she hadn't really wanted to die, but was just calling out for help in the most dramatic way she could think of. I told her that sort of thing was common among adolescents. She was a lot more beautiful than Mrs. Cavanaugh, but not nearly as much fun to talk to. We left the subject of Tarquin unaddressed until after our starters were delivered.

I asked if she was still seeing him. Instead of answering, she told me how fiercely jealous he was. He'd apparently gone mad with jealousy only the previous week just watching her walk past a trio of bricklayers who paused from their labours to watch her admiringly, and had taken all three on at once. They'd broken his right arm in two places, and he was right-handed. They'd also broken his jaw.

And here he was now, having butted the waiter aside, looming over us, glowering. "Maybe," he told Nicola through clenched teeth, "you'd like to tell me what you're doing with . . . him." At first he seemed to be doing a bad Clint Eastwood impression, but then I realised his jaw was probably wired shut. Various friends had covered the cast that enclosed his arm with clever notations about his injuries making it difficult for him to masturbate.

Nicola looked at me helplessly. The restaurant was silent again. It occurred to me to use one of the knives on the table in front of me on him, but none of them looked nearly sharp enough for the job. It occurred to me to pretend to need to visit the gents', but that was too craven even for me. I couldn't pretend I didn't know I had to say something.

"Do you suppose maybe the two of you could discuss the situation later?" I finally managed, in a voice so small I doubted the waiter could hear me. I'd have liked to have addressed him in that sarcastic way the Brits have when they're getting in one another's faces, as mate, but it was beyond me.

"What's wrong with right now?" he demanded. The waiter hurried away, I hoped he'd gone for a huge saucepan with which to whack Tarquin over the head.

"Well," I stammered, "we're just about to . . . out of consideration for our fellow diners . . . this is neither the time nor the . . ." I couldn't complete a thought.

257

"Neither the time nor the bloody place, mate? Well, you're probably right. Why don't the two of us step outside?"

"Sort him out," someone said encouragingly from behind. I was afraid they were talking to me. I was nearly sure of it. I wanted to burst into tears. I wanted to evaporate. "I don't think so," I finally said, even more quietly than before, desperate to be heard by as few people as possible. "My starter will get cold."

"It's a bloody green salad, mate!"

Nicola's eyes welled with tears. She looked away. Forget evaporating. I wanted to die. I didn't deserve to live.

I dared make eye contact with Tarquin, and was surprised by the look on his face. It didn't look so much like anger as pity. He shook his head. He left us.

Even in that uniquely excruciating moment, my sense of humour didn't fail me. It occurred to me to ask Nicola, referring to her scallops, "So how's yours?" But I dashed for the gents' instead.

He was in there, sitting on the toilet with his face in his hands. His arm wasn't really broken. Nor, I realised as he addressed me, was his jaw really wired shut. "Blimey, mate," he said, more disappointedly than belligerently, "what does it bloody take to get you to stand up and be bloody counted?"

I just gaped at him.

"A geezer with a broken arm and a wired-together jaw comes over and challenges you in front of your bird and you don't take him outside and beat him senseless? A broken bloody arm, mate! Jesus. What sort of fight is somebody with a broken arm going to put up?"

I kept gaping, terrified of what he might say next.

"It was a done deal, mate. I was trying to make it easy for you. How much easier could I have made it than to have one arm in a cast? Her mum and stepdad hired me. The idea was to help you with your self-esteem. You'd have flattened me, mate. You'd have flattened me after the Overeaters' meeting at the pub that time. I was going to bloody let you!"

He leaned on the basin and shook his head in disgust. "Well that's 500 quid not earned, isn't it? If I go to her stepdad not black and blue, he won't pay me a penny."

He looked at me hopefully. "Do it now, mate. Here. A good one in the chin. Or the eye's good as well. Give me a real shiner. Or break my nose." He lifted his chin at me and closed his eyes. "Come on, mate. Do your worst. I need the dosh. It'll be bloody Christmas before we turn around."

I bolted. I got out of the gents' and headed for the street without even looking back at my and Nicola's table. And there she was, as I burst out of the place, just about to get into a cab, her cheeks streaked with tears.

28

The Daughter Geezer

BABOOSHKA was coming to London. It was in the *Telegraph*, in an article about how the producers of *Fab Lab*, having noted *Megastar*'s great, great success there, was trying to break their own show in America. They'd broadcast an episode and invited viewers aged 16–21 to write a 200-word essay about which of the singers was their favourite, the prize being a trip to London to meet their favourite before the climactic show of the series. My daughter, who, to her considerable credit, had written about the anarchic, atonal Evelyn, was one of the four winners, and the only Californian. In the face of the British viewing public having got fed up with Evelyn and voted him off *Fab Lab* the week before, Bab had switched her allegiance to . . . Cathy!

I phoned the production company and asked where the American contest winners would be put up. The girl on the phone said she wasn't allowed to say. I phoned the *Telegraph* writer who'd written the story about the contest. I left two phone messages and sent an email with no response. I tried the phone again and got her. "That's yesterday's news," she pointed out annoyedly, "and how would I know which bloody hotel?" She put the phone down on me without saying goodbye. I phoned the production company back and asked how I could get tickets to be part of the studio audience for the show my daughter would have been flown over to witness. The girl insisted there were no tickets.

I had another idea. I did some research on the Internet and determined that it was the notorious Niraj Ganapathy, normally in the business of brokering the sale of bimbos' stories of their nights of sin with married MPs and BBC news readers, who handled Sir Ivor Praiseworthy's public relations. I phoned Ganapathy's office and asked to speak to one of his lieutenants, which I neglected to pronounce Britishly. The girl who answered the phone demanded, "Lieutenants? What are you on about?" She *did* pronounce it the British way, as though the first syllable ends in an f. I told her the whole story of my estrangement from my daughter, and how I hoped we might be reunited at the set of *Fab Lab*, which I would need Sir Ivor's help to attend. She passed me without comment up the food chain. I recited my whole tale of woe a second time for a guy, Sandeep, with the eager phone manner of an estate agent. He interrupted me to put me on hold so often that I despaired of his understanding what I was asking for. And he didn't. When I finally finished, he asked, "So what is it that you hope NGPR to do for you?" Niraj Ganapathy Public Relations, I surmised.

"Convey to Sir Ivor that I need tickets to the finals of *Fab Lab*." Again he put me on hold.

"Listen," I said, trying not to sigh in exasperation when he finally returned. "Think of how you could pitch this to the press. One loving dad, whose son is a contestant, helping reunite another loving dad with his daughter. Imagine how the British public will love him for this."

"They already *do* love him," he pointed out scoldingly. I acknowledged that of course he was right, and he, patronising me with all his might, said he'd run it by Niraj and get back to me. I expected he was the sort who was only pretending to be able to get Niraj's attention at will, but a secretary phoned 35 minutes later to advise me to expect a call from one of Ganapathy's top personal assistants in two hours' time.

She rang in a few minutes short of three. Once more I recited *One Loving Dad Helping Another*, which I liked to imagine had become slightly more poignant with every retelling. "I think Arohi may like that," she said. "I honestly do." I had no idea whom she was talking about, and admitted it. There was a hint of censure in her voice as she explained that Arohi was her boss, and one of Niraj's top aides. She would phone me within the hour.

She phoned me within five minutes. An assistant actually made the call to ensure that I was available to speak. Apparently Arohi hadn't a moment to squander. She came on the line sounding breathless, but with no idea who I was. I was a few sentences into my spiel when she impatiently stopped me. "Niraj may fancy that," she marvelled. I was to stay right by the phone. Niraj himself would be with me in the next five minutes.

I amused myself in the meantime by bookmarking several web pages depicting items I hoped Kate might enjoy receiving as gifts. I was almost sure she'd like the machine that generated bubbles in time to whatever music you played into it. Finally, around 82 minutes after the fact, the phone rang. Once again, an assistant made me promise that I was indeed available. I held and held and held, and then held a few minutes more. Just as I was about to conclude that Niraj had decided on the spur of the moment to go on holiday, he came on the line, sounding as though about to audition to play an East End barrow boy on the West End stage, demanding, "You're the daughter geezer, right?" I confirmed it. "So what have you got in mind, mate? I don't have all afternoon, do I?" It was a few minutes before ten at night. I gave him the spiel, which I had pretty well memorised by now.

"Bit corny, that, innit?" he yawned down the phone. "Might work, though. Let me mention it to Himself."

Mrs. Cavanaugh came up while I recovered from my exertions, but not to see if I were feeling virile again. Indeed, she was as distraught as I'd seen her since Cathy's non-suicide. It seemed, in the face of dwindling ratings, that the producers of *Fab Lab* and *Megastar* had decided to merge their two shows. Cathy wouldn't be competing now against only the cream of Britain's young bulimics, anorexics, harelips, clubfoots, and blind and deaf, but against the cream of *Fab Lab* too. "By what possible feckin' measure is that fair?" Mrs. Cavanaugh demanded, nibbling a cuticle in agitation. "Just when it begins to look as though she might win the race, they reposition the feckin' finish line!" I pointed out that, with the wonderful anarchic Evelyn long since voted off, the cream of *Fab Lab* hadn't a prayer against the *Lame, Halt, and Blind* kids.

★ ★ ★

While the faithful yearned in vain for a new album, Kate accepted the gigantic international advertising agency Chiat-Day's invitation to compose music for the new Fruitopia line of fruit drinks with which their client Coca-Cola hoped to muscle in on America's $2 billion a year "alternative non-carbonated beverages" market. Having commissioned expensive research suggesting that the target consumer sought refreshment not only for his body, but for his mind and spirit as well, Coke was said to be prepared to spend $30 million to try to get Americans to turn away from Snapple. Kate did 10 snippets of music that weren't heard in the UK, where the Cocteau Twins got the nod after she presumably asked for too much more of what remained of the $30 million.

Her music wasn't anything any competent composer with some small rhythmic and melodic imagination couldn't have cranked out in 48 hours. Some scurrilous curmudgeon (not Charles Shaar Murray this time) pointed out that hundreds of times as many Americans were likely to hear 'Iced Tea Inner Light' (I'm not making this up) than had heard all of her albums combined. Another noted that Fruitopia came in bottles "covered with silly pseudo-environmentalist verbiage, faux peace 'n' love bollocks, and a pretty poor imitation of Peter Max's [painting style]." Kate presumably suffered acute embarrassment all the way to the bank.

An American music critic explained that "in this country, Bush's florid vocal eccentricity – undulating gulps and shrieks of meandering melody – have consigned her to the rank of oddball, English Division." Meanwhile, a British writer referred to her as "the Pre-Raphaelite nymph with Minnie Mouse's soprano." If Kate were perturbed, she kept it quiet.

Davy Spillane, who'd played on the *Hounds Of Love*, released his album *A Place Among The Stars* in mid-1994, but without Kate's version of Marvin Gaye's 'Sexual Healing' (I'm not making this up), which he explained didn't fit the mood of the balance of the album. A decade later, it would remain possible to download via the Internet an MP3 version of the song seemingly recorded through the pickup of a cheap Korean electric guitar.

She managed to endure only a few minutes of the 1994 fan convention, but was the perfect guest at the People's Banquet, a Whitehall do to celebrate Her Majesty's having been married for 50 years to her tactless Greek husband, and sat with her old china, former PM John Major, cricketer Mike Atherton, and ballerina Darcy Bussell, with whom one imagines she found it rather easier to chat than with poor Mike. The old-fashioned American soul crooner Maxwell recorded a version of her 'This Woman's Work' in his beautiful falsetto.

In the *Irish Times*, that condescending git Mick Moroney observed of Kate's contribution to Donal Lunny's *Common Ground – Voices Of Modern Irish Music* compilation, on which she was featured alongside Elvis Costello, the Finn brothers, and a couple of U2, "The biggest chuckle is Kate Bush's Darby O'Gill-accented 'Mna na h-Eireann', histrionically dragging swatches of O'Riada orchestration along behind her, but with a whipping knife edge of emotion which makes it all worthwhile." A whipping knife edge of emotion, Mick? The Irish *Hot Press* suggested that Sinéad O'Connor's 'Raglan Road' stole the show.

★   ★   ★

Sandeep finally phoned to say that Sir Ivor was concerned about my daughter having flown over to support Cathy. But he thought my daughter switching allegiance to Sir Ivor's son Claude would probably produce the ticket for which I yearned. I pointed out that, since we weren't even in touch, I was hardly in a position to try to influence my daughter one way or the other. Whereupon, suddenly sounding bored with me, he pointed out that 150 tickets would be distributed free to ordinary punters on the day on a first-come/first-served basis, suggested I get there very early, and put the phone down on me.

And thus it came to pass that at a few minutes gone one in the morning before the day the final was to be shot, I became approximately the 50th person to queue outside Teddington Studios, the first over 50, and the first and probably last member of the obscenely obese.

The two teenagers from Surbiton in front of me, Sally and Deborah, were friendly enough for little Brits. The one who showed up a few minutes later, a Goth from Fulwell, couldn't have been more sullen. Or maybe her sullenness was part of her attire. When, at a few minutes before four, I asked if she'd save my place while I used the toilet, she looked at me as though I'd just introduced myself as the inventor of menstrual cramping. "Where are these toilets you intend to use?" Sally wondered groggily from her sleeping bag. This elicited something resembling a snicker from the little Goth, who finally spoke, to tell me there were no loos available. "You didn't really not bring plastic bags, did you?" Sally asked incredulously.

Word of my stupidity shot back and forth across the queue like an electric current. Unable to wait for dawn, teens woke their mates to advise them of my colossal ill-preparedness. Dying inside, I did my best to laugh along with them. I felt as though back in junior high school. Finally, when most of them were asleep again, I asked Sally if I could pose a stupid question. She and Deborah looked at one another and giggled. As though I were likely to pose any other kind! I asked what one did with the bag once having peed in it. "You hang onto it until they let us in, mate, and then empty it down the bog, don't you?" a skinny boy four or five people behind me offered. His chums chortled. I had no idea whether I could believe him. I hate having an American's deficient sense of irony. But I loved having my portable CD player, my earphones, and all of Kate's CDs to listen to. And I did listen to them, in order, replaying several of my favourite tracks multiple times, getting to 'Constellation Of The Heart' on *The Red Shoes*, about which I'd read an amusing story on one of the Katesites I'd surfed a few evenings before.

Apparently hoping to capture something of its melancholic liturgical atmosphere in 'You're The One', whose lyrics allude to it, Kate was said to have had an emissary seek out the musician responsible for the re-purposing of Bach in Procol Harum's 'A Whiter Shade Of Pale'.

The emissary had come back not with Matthew Fisher, who'd played the celebrated organ part on 'Pale', but with no less than lead singer and piano player Gary Brooker, who'd never been observed, not even at sound checks, not even by his closest friends, to play organ. Hearing him on that track, though (and on 'Constellation Of The Heart'), one didn't miss the grumpy, supercilious Fisher in the slightest. One wondered if Kate had ever known she'd been brought the wrong man.

When we finally got in, there was a mob scene at the entrance to the toilets, as everyone was impatient to get his or her plastic bag emptied and discarded, and then go grab a good seat. By the time I got into the studio, only crap ones remained. I took one.

About a year before our last estrangement, I made an appointment for my daughter and me to confer with a psychotherapist at the health maintenance organisation by which I was insured. As was my custom, I arrived 20 minutes early. As was my ex-wife's custom, she showed up five minutes late with my daughter, who looked at me and then pretended she didn't know me. It was one of the most painful experiences of my life to that time. The therapist invited her in first, and then summoned me after they'd spoken in private for 10 minutes. Within 60 seconds of being admitted to the office, I was howling at my daughter, telling her I was ashamed to be the father of someone capable of such cruelty. At first, she just gave me a defiant fuck-you smirk, but then burst into tears. The therapist, thinking he'd lost control (as indeed he had), was beside himself. Everyone calmed down until around 30 seconds before the session ended. My daughter suddenly resumed sobbing. I realised, as the therapist declared the session finished, and she bolted out of the office, that she wanted Mommy to see the awful pain I'd inflicted.

History repeated itself. As she and the other American contest winners were led to the ringside seats reserved for them, Bab noticed me. I wish I'd had one of those cameras that takes multiple shots in a second. In the first, you'd have seen shock in her eyes, and then delight. And then, maybe half a second after the shock, she was pretending that she hadn't seen me at all. And in that same fraction of a second, I went from elation to great, great pain.

She'd lost weight. She was no sylph yet, but probably four stone lighter than the last time I'd seen her, and moving in a way I'd never seen before. She'd waddled before. Now her walk was that of a young woman who knew her own power.

And she had a boyfriend, a bad boy, of all things, a lank-haired leerer with tattoos, the kind of boy you could count on to get your daughter pregnant and then disappear. You could tell that, 45 seconds after his last one, he was aching for a cigarette. A Boy Who Could, but couldn't be troubled to.

They sat down and he draped his arm over my daughter's shoulders, but his eyes were wandering, looking for big tits on which to alight. He'd break her heart at his earliest opportunity, and I wanted to go over there and pull his arm out of its socket. My daughter made a point of not looking in my direction. I died a little.

The little Scots compere came out and told a few deliberately awful jokes. The assembled teens howled derisively. The little Scot goaded them, and they howled more loudly. My daughter and new boyfriend didn't join in the fun. They looked bored and impatient. I looked around for Sir Ivor, but couldn't spot him anywhere. I imagined that fear of the teens' derision might have kept him away.

The competition's three finalists, all from *Megastar*, as it turned out, performed in turn. In person, Cathy really did appear to have put on a few pounds. If she managed a few more, it would actually be possible to describe her as skinny, and not emaciated. This week, the contestants could sing anything they chose. She had the audacity to sing Kate's 'All The Love', from *The Dreaming*. It made the little hairs on the back of my neck stand up. When she finished, there were two seconds of absolute stunned silence before the studio erupted in cheering. Even the cheeky little Scot was at a loss for words. Cathy stood sobbing soundlessly, overwhelmed by the realisation of her own genius. I couldn't imagine anyone in the studio ever forgetting the moment, with the exception of my daughter and her new boyfriend, who seemed to have their tongues down one another's throats.

The second of the three finalists was Philippa, a medium-functioning Down's syndrome victim from Cardiff who performed the Aretha Franklin classic 'A Natural Woman'. Her diction wasn't spectacular – that of someone whose tongue was too thick for her mouth – but there could be no disputing her soulfulness. As the waves of applause washed over her, she just stood there blinking uncomprehendingly. Your heart couldn't help but go out to her.

I don't know whose idea it was to have the little Scot try to interview her, but it served no one, as she responded to every question she understood (and the trickier ones, such as that about how she'd chosen 'A Natural Woman' to perform, only made her gape in befuddlement) with eager monosyllables. Had she enjoyed singing? *Yes!* Was she excited to be in the finals? *Yes!* Had she enjoyed Cathy's performance? *Yes!*

266

And then it was poor Claude Praiseworthy's turn. He waddled out looking as though he might hyperventilate from terror at any second. But then, to the accompaniment of just a piano (both Cathy and Philippa had had full orchestras, though Cathy's had made itself scarce until the final verse and refrain), he began to sing the ancient Southern soul classic 'When A Man Loves A Woman', and was transformed, channelling the anguish of every poor bastard who'd ever loved a woman who didn't love him back. He fell to his knees and moaned. He pounded the stage. He was blinded by his own sweat. If Percy Sledge, the lapsed gospel singer who'd recorded the magnificent original, had been watching, his jaw would surely have dropped open, for as riveting as his own performance had been, old Percy had never dreamed of how much feeling the song could accommodate.

The little hairs on the back of my neck had never had such a workout.

There'd been two seconds of stunned silence after Cathy's perform-ance. There were two more – or more – after poor Claude's. The little Scot just stood there at the side of the stage shaking his head, his micro-phone down by his hip. My daughter and her boyfriend showed no sign they'd heard a note.

The little Scot finally remembered where and who he was, and managed to ask poor Claude a few questions. Poor Claude seemed utterly befuddled, as though someone had awakened him in the middle of a confusing dream. He seemed to have no memory of his perform-ance. He looked as though he might faint. He spoke more thick-tonguedly than poor Philippa had sung. What did he think of his chances as compared to Cathy's and Philippa's? The little Scot might as well have asked who he thought would lead the London Kinder Towers basketball team in free throw shooting next season. My daugh-ter and her boyfriend paid no attention.

29

A Toast To My Memory

THERE was a break from shooting. It was time for the British public to vote by phone for its favourite. We in the studio audience were free to do whatever we liked for 50 minutes. The Thames, if we wanted to have a look at it, was just behind the car park, and there were benches and tables on and at which we could sit.

As those to either side of them rose, my daughter and her boyfriend finally removed their tongues from one another's mouths. My daughter produced a packet of fags. It broke my heart, but I'd known it was coming. Her boyfriend, not the type to be constrained by others' arbitrary rules, lit one where he stood. An employee of the studio rushed over, presumably to ask him to snuff it out. From my great distance, I couldn't tell what my daughter's boyfriend told the guy, but I do know it stopped him in his tracks and made his mouth drop open. My daughter's boyfriend leered satisfiedly as the guy retreated. I had a pretty good idea what I was up against.

We had 50 minutes before taping resumed. I wasted nearly 20 of them not being able to steel myself for the task at hand. I watched from a distance as Bab and her boyfriend seated themselves at one of the picnic tables between the car park and the river. They both chain-smoked. Then my daughter excused herself, presumably to use the loo. As soon as she was out of sight, her boyfriend got up and ambled over to a pair of pretty blonde girls. He looked over his shoulder repeatedly as they chatted. I got the impression he didn't want my daughter to see them together.

I threw caution to the wind and headed over to them. My daughter's boyfriend turned only when he realised both the blondes were looking quizzically over his shoulder at me. I was struck both by how young he looked, and how familiar. I recognised his contemptuous what-are-you-gonna-do-about-it smirk on the face of every petty sadist who'd ever intimidated me on a playground.

I told him who I was. "Wicked," he said sarcastically. "Can't you see you're interrupting something?" Deference to elders wasn't in this guy's repertoire. He looked at the little English blondes and then back at me and sighed. "Well, what is it then?"

What was it? How about: *get out of my daughter's life, you horrid little twerp, or I'll* . . . what? The veins in his biceps bulged. He had more testosterone in his little finger than I had in my whole body, than I'd had in my whole body the whole time I'd been on earth. He was the kind of kid who'd almost certainly get sent to prison, and once in prison victimise other prisoners.

"Listen, mate," he said, looking as bored as he could, "if you've got something to say to me, why don't you bloody . . ."

The dam broke. I reared back and swung at him, right-handed, with all my might. It might well have knocked him unconscious had he not seen the punch coming, and managed to get out of the way of nearly all of it. My fist skimmed the side of his face. For a thousandth of a second, his shock made him look around 12. And then I was on my back, with him atop me, with his strong hands around my neck, with my weaker hands trying to pull them off, with his awful crazed face above me, and the blondes screaming, and a bunch of other faces appearing behind him, horrified faces, aghast ones.

And then I heard my daughter's voice and saw her face close up for the first time in 26 months, as she got back from wherever she'd been and began trying to pull her boyfriend off me by his hair. He let go of my neck. "Let go of him," she screamed. "Let go of him!"

That she cared whether I lived or died was unmistakable!

I wouldn't have been surprised if, for pulling his hair, he'd lashed out at her. And what a nightmare that would have been, with me half-conscious for the oxygen I'd been deprived while he had his hands around my neck, with me clearly incapable of fazing him even with the hardest punch it was in me to throw, and when he hadn't expected it. But he was content to scream at her. And soon she was in tears.

They didn't slow him down. "What the bloody hell do you think you're doing pulling my bloody hair, you mad bitch?" he screamed into the beautiful face of the child I'd promised myself I'd find a way to protect. "Tell me! Fucking tell me!" I looked for a weapon. A rock. A brick fragment. But of course there were only empty plastic bottles. I could hardly breathe. I thought he might have ruptured my trachea or something.

I had no more need of a weapon, as he screamed, "Fuck!" at the top of his lungs into her face, spun on his heel, and stormed away, leaving my daughter sobbing in humiliation where she stood.

We looked at each other. And I'd imagined that her boyfriend's face had been awful! It was the face of serenity and gentleness compared to Babooshka's as she demanded, "Why did you come here? Why don't you fucking leave me alone? Why don't you get it through your head that I never want to fucking see you again? I hate you!"

That was bad. God knows that was bad. But it was about to get much worse. She too stormed away sobbing, but then returned, controlled now, speaking not from rage, but from the heart, speaking more quietly, but inflicting more pain than her boyfriend would have done with his hands if he'd been atop me for 10 more minutes. "It's never going to be different," she said. "You're not going to change my mind. These are wounds that time isn't going to heal. Do you understand? Well, do you?" I couldn't speak. "I will never hate you less than I do at this moment," she said. "So get back out of my life, and stay out of it this time."

When I was a much younger man, I was astonished by one of the songs on The Beatles' *Revolver* album, that in which Paul McCartney described himself as being able to detect no sign of love in the eyes of someone who was abandoning him. I was young and naive then, and imagined that, as co-king of the world, McCartney could never have been subjected to anything like that. But if he hadn't, how could he have described the feeling so perfectly in his song? And now, nearly 40 years later, the saddest song any Beatle had ever written had come true for me again. No sign of love behind tears cried for no one.

★   ★   ★

Kate told Q why she went silent after *The Red Shoes*. "There were a lot of things I wanted to look at in my life. I was exhausted on every level. There was part of me that didn't want to work. I'd got to a point where it was something I didn't feel good about. It was as if I was testing myself to see if I could write, but I didn't like what I was writing. I thought, No, if you don't want to do it, it will be rubbish. Basically, the batteries were completely run out and I needed to restimulate again."

There was much excited talk of her contributing a song to the soundtrack of the Disney animated film *Dinosaur*. Such talk was doomed to extinction, *ta da dum*! It was thought that Disney had originally invited her to provide a song that would be heard at the film's emotional turning point. Troubling data collected at test screenings suggested that audiences weren't responding to her lyrics. And, in view of the fact that the film would eventually have to be translated into a great many languages, maybe the best idea was to have no lyrics at all, but instead use her song as instrumental accompaniment. Whereupon she apparently decided to pack in the whole undertaking and get back to her gardening and mothering.

West of Germany and slightly below sea level, Dutch Katefans Mike, Anton, Justina, Arie, Jos, Angela, Ilja, Marleen, Els, Marion, Edwin, Martin, Martijn, Tony, Marcel, Barend and Kinky the Lovehound congregated to celebrate Kate's 42nd birthday (Katemas!) by watching her videos and listening to her music together. In Osaka, celebrations of her birthday seemed more about MIDI karaoke. In Brisbane, Aussies celebrated the silver anniversary of 'Wuthering Heights' reaching number one Down Under by dancing to the music of All Yours Babooshka, a Kate Bush tribute band.

Stars In Their Eyes contestant Louise Halliday brought with her to the 2001 *Homeground* convention at Glastonbury the very cloak Kate had worn in the 'Babooshka' video decades before, and later sent her as a gift. Those allowed to touch the hallowed garment later reported that they no longer suffered from astigmatism or rheumatoid arthritis. I am, with the famous Victor Mature film *The Robe* in mind, making this up. Over and over, when we stop being snide for a moment, we get a picture of our heroine as kind and thoughtful, a person you either love, or don't have the pleasure of knowing.

At her first live performance in 15 years, with Dave Gilmour at the Royal Festival Hall in mid-January, 2002, she sang ('Comfortably Numb') as evocatively as ever. She attended a special ceremony at the Royal Academy of Arts at which the Queen, as part of her Golden Jubilee celebration, handed out special prizes. Her Majesty seemed to have thought Kate and Mick Hucknall, beside whom she was standing, were a pair. (A cruel sense of humour, Her Maj's.) When Her Majesty asked what they did, Hucknall made no mention of his own rabid skirt-chasing, but said they were singers and songwriters. Not offended, gracious to the end, Kate pronounced Her Majesty both lovely and radiant.

Lauding her for having "brought her own brand of rural gothic eccentricity right to the very heart of the mainstream", the *Observer* placed her at the top of its list of Greatest Eccentrics In Music. She was thought to have given up both smoking and vegetarianism.

The Ukulele Orchestra of Great Britain, which yearned to include their version of 'Wuthering' on their debut CD, claimed that Kate had forbidden them to record the song, even if classical guitarist Richard Durant produced it, even in the face of Radio 2's purported eagerness to play it, even though George Hincliffe had wryly transformed it into the sort of jazz one might hear in the bar of a provincial hotel with delusions of sophistication, with the audience encouraged to shout, "Heathcliff!" at various points.

She became a gay icon. *The Beautiful Bend*, a programme of unrelated playlets performed at London's Central Space Theatre, ended with a Kate-inspired fashion show for which the all-male cast donned wigs and costumes based on some of her most famous ones. It came to light that Kate Devlin, a well-known American cabaret artist, had been performing a show based on Katesongs for years, and in fact had even won the purportedly prestigious Bistro Award for it in 1995. Kate declined to accept a lifetime Brit after learning she'd be expected to perform. When spotted in Harrod's babywear section with her son Bertie, the presumed beneficiary of her shopping spree, though, she was only too pleased to sign an autograph. When Midge Ure introduced Fran Healey to her at the Q Awards, the Travis lead singer was too gob-smacked to converse.

At the end of May 2003, 16-year-old Jaclyn Bell finished in third place on *Stars In Their Eyes*. Kate sent her a platinum disc from 1978 and a handwritten note, reducing her to tears. Alison Goldfrapp joined the long list of female singers (including Bjork, Jewel, Toyah, and Dido [singers known by two names seemed to prefer Joni Mitchell]) who named Kate as a prime influence, and Tricky called her the modern Billie Holiday. But then Ruby Wax, the obnoxious American comedienne, identified 'Wuthering' as her favourite song, and Nicole Kidman revealed that she'd sung Katesongs with her band Divine Madness as a 17-year-old. In every life a little rain must fall.

No new album was announced, and no new album was announced, and no new album was announced, but her music continued to be heard. 'Don't Give Up' played over the closing credits of the gory *The Bone Collector*. 'This Woman's Work' was heard in an especially poignant episode of the American teen soap *Felicity* about date rape. And there were reasons to be hopeful. Stuart Elliot related that Kate had repudiated the gated reverb sound of the mid-Eighties and was letting him play his high-hat and cymbals again on her new stuff, having opted for a more naturalistic, jazzy style, and Peter Erskine, the noted American jazz drummer, reported that she'd had him playing congas. Former Peter Gabriel accompanist African drummer Manu Katche (previously heard on the infernal Tori's *Boys For Pele)* got the call, Kate finally having a track she believed worthy of and suitable for his talents.

Her new stuff. It had a wonderful ring to it, but we'd all been disappointed too many times before.

★   ★   ★

I didn't go home to Mrs. Cavanaugh's from Teddington. I went instead to the train station, and headed up to Camberwell. I was in a kind of emotional shock, I suppose, and felt no pain. I watched my fellow travellers waiting for the train. They were neither more nor less interesting to me than usual. A middle-aged guy in a suit and loosened tie wearily massaged his own forehead as he mumbled excuses into his mobile. I supposed that he'd had something planned with his wife, but had been detained at work. Two teenage girls looked self-conscious. A guy in an untucked sport shirt picked up an *Evening Standard* left on a bench and read about sport. The train was a few minutes late, but did anyone expect anything different?

It occurred to me that I should ring Plaistow and ask if he was interested in an exclusive. I thought he might be able to interest someone on the basis of my having been the face of Marcel Flynn. But there wasn't time. I prepared to leap to my death unobserved.

When my congenital cowardice kicked in and I wound up dawdling forever on the precipice, though, someone apparently saw me from the block of flats across the road, and in a while Constables Chiang and Murray materialised, and then the kid with the digital video camera. But in the end I managed it.

It was a lot easier than I'd have guessed. This time the part of me that had always wanted to fling all of me from heights got to. One didn't see a lot of black cabs in Camberwell, but I nearly managed to land on top of one. As it was, I just hit its roof with my hand a fraction of a second before I landed, as I'd hoped I would, head first. Though the police and an ambulance were summoned, I was dead on impact.

★   ★   ★

I suspect that if people knew that, much as Jamie surmised, suicide isn't held against anyone in the big scheme of things, a lot more people would resort to it. Doctors would almost surely start advertising their services to the suicidal in the same way American lawyers began advertising their own in the early Eighties, and the physician-assisted suicide boom would quickly come to dwarf the Internet boom of the late Nineties. But I'm surely not the first resident of Heaven to wish he'd known in life what he came to realise in death.

Being omniscient, I knew just how everyone I'd left behind felt about my death. I think I was most surprised by the reaction of my daughter's mother, so distraught for a couple of days that she had to have sedatives prescribed. I was also touched by how much my departure seemed to upset Cathy. I'd have felt awful about raining on the parade of her being named one of the two co-winners of *Megastar*. After 1,200,000 viewers voted, she and poor Claude were within 100 votes of one another. There's talk at their record company of their recording together. Nepenthe and Harold believe they'll be the most successful British recording duo since Elton John and Kiki Dee.

I think I was most disappointed by the reaction of my fellow overeaters. When, at the first OA meeting after my fatal plunge, Graham announced what had become of me, there wasn't a wet eye in the house, but of course that might have had something to do with Nicola's having got too thin to bother with them. Bolshie Crinolyn wasn't even sure who I was, and neither was Jez. It's humiliating having made such a faint impression on people. "I always reckoned he was taking the piss," Boopsie admitted, and most of them seemed to concur. "And he wasn't the most outgoing chap I've ever met," Jez contributed, "especially for a Yank. Most of the Yanks I know are loads friendlier." When they congregated in the bar afterwards, it didn't occur to a single one of them to propose a toast to my memory.

Mrs. Cavanaugh took the news very hard, and I feel awful about that. She took to her bed after word reached her, and barely left it for 72 hours, though she was pretty much sleepless. She didn't tell Mr. Chumaraswamy what was wrong, and he felt useless as a result. When finally she was able to talk, she told him she'd felt that in different circumstances she could have come to adore me. Beneath the fierce self-loathing and even fiercer loathing of the rest of humanity, she said, she'd sensed real gentleness. It was almost as though she were quoting me, talking about my mother. (I'd always said that there was only one person on earth she was harder on than herself, and that was everyone else. Not strictly grammatical perhaps, but I think you see what I mean. In any event, I was duly mortified to realise I'd been even more my mother revisited than I'd imagined.)

When my sister greeted me at the front door of our family home on the afternoon of my uncle's suicide, I demanded "So?" and proceeded to feel ashamed of having done so for the next 40 years. When my daughter learned of my fatal plunge, she responded identically. What goes around comes around.

I suspect that she will come, in time, to feel as ashamed as I did. (Indeed, I hope she does, for if she doesn't, it will mean she's remained a callous little brat.) But I won't know for sure. It turns out that one remains omniscient about the affairs of the world left behind for no longer than eight weeks, and often for as few as six. It's a small price to pay for the all-pervasive euphoria I'm told one begins to feel as soon as the omniscience wears off.

Jamie, the bully in the FCUK T-shirt, is here. It turns out he leapt off the top of a block of flats about half a mile from the one on which I'd met him after it got around Prang Hill School that he and Gajendra, his whipping boy, were gay sadomasochistic lovers. They apparently got the idea from the school's geography master. And here I'd spent years ridiculing anyone who opposed hiring gay instructors.

Acknowledgements

In the course of my research, the following texts proved particularly useful:

Kate Bush: A Visual Documentary, by Kevin Cann & Sean Mayes (Omnibus Press, 1988)

The Secret History Of Kate Bush, by Fred Vermorel (Omnibus Press, 1983)

Homeground, edited Krystyna FitzGerald-Morris, Peter FitzGerald Morris, and David Cross Issues 50-53, 55-62, 64-70, 72

"Season Of The Witch", by Phil Sutcliffe (*Mojo*, February 2003)

"Dear Diary: The Secret World of Kate Bush", by David Sinclair (*Rolling Stone*, February 24, 1994)

"A Tightly Wound Conversation With The Rubberband Girl", Interview by Roger Trilling, the West Coast editor of *Details* (*Details*, March 1994)

"Two Sisters In Song . . . Of Sorts" by Peter Galvin (*New York Times*, February 6, 1994)

"Del Palmer, Kate Bush's Right Hand" by Richard Buskin (*Fachblatt Musikmagazin*, January 1994)

"A Return to Innocence" by Tom Moon (*Philadelphia Inquirer*, January, 1994)

"Kate Bush: Will She Or Won't She?" by Nick Krewen (*Spectator*, Hamilton, Ontario, December 16, 1993)

"Booze, Fags, Blokes And Me" – The New Q Interview with Kate Bush (December 1993)

"Who's That Girl?" by Colin Irwin (*Rock World*, October 1993)

"Beating About The Bush" by Chrissie Iley (*The Sunday Times*, London, September 12, 1993)

"Rubber Souls" by Marianne Jenssen (*Vox*, November 1993)

"Well red" – *Future Music* interview with Del Palmer (November, 1993)

"The Baffling, Alluring World Of Kate Bush" by Terry Atkinson (*Los Angeles Times*, January 28, 1990)

"Kate Bush's Theater Of The Senses" by John Diliberto (*Musician*, February 1990)

"In The Realm Of The Senses" by Len Brown (*New Musical Express*, October 7, 1989)

"Bushwacked by Kate" by Adam Sweeting (*Guardian*, October 12, 1989)

"Iron Maiden" by Phil Sutcliffe (*Q*, November 1989)

"The Girl With the Stars in Her Eyes" by Richard Cook (*Sounds*, June 7, 1986)

"Down At The Old Bul' And Bush" by Len Brown (*New Musical Express*, November 12, 1988)

"Kate Bush (not) In Wild Orgy Of Hotel Destruction Shock" (*Sounds*, May 10, 1979)

"Bull And Bush" (*London Observer*, November 12, 1978)

"You Don't Have To Be Beautiful . . ." by Donna McAllister (*Sounds*, March 11, 1978)

I also found a world of information on the following websites, which I urge anyone interested in Kate Bush to visit soon and often.

http://www.iq451.com/music/sites/kate-bush-web.htm
  A list of Kate Bush websites

http://gaffa.org/
  Gaffaweb

http://www.kate-bush.org/
  Kate Bush, Musical Genius

http://children.ofthenight.org/cloudbusting/
  Cloudbusting Kate Bush in Her Own Words

http://homepage.tinet.ie/~twoms/hgback.htm
  Kate Bush News and Information

http://www.shoesmith.net/mp3/mp3.html
  Kate Bush B-sides and cameos

http://www.geocities.com/thander_uk/katebush.html
  Kate Bush The Fog

Especial thanks to Andrew Marvick, perhaps the Western democracies' pre-eminent Kate scholar, and to my editor and mate Chris Charlesworth.